Integrated Skills Group

Integratedskillsgroup@gmail.com

www.integratedskillsgroup.com

Carry the Fire

by Aaron Moyer

Integrated Skills Group

Nonfiction

Integrated Skills Group

Thank you and Dedication

First and foremost, thank you, reader, for choosing *Carry the Fire*. Many times, authors tend to thank the people who support the author's efforts, while most readers go unrecognized. That is not the case here.

Second, I want to thank three people without whom this book wouldn't be possible:

My beautiful wife Vanessa, who has provided me with stability, honesty, love, and encouragement. Gino, who has had my back without fail and has supported this project, often while running ISG's day-to-day without any recognition or reward. And my mother, for an upbringing that cannot be duplicated, and who shaped me in ways I wouldn't understand for decades.

Third and finally, I want to thank the following people for their mentorship and guidance throughout the process:

Barry V. (whose work appears in this book as the resident subject matter expert on sustainable agriculture), Mark Jones, Rob McLean, Charles Schroeder (RIP), Joe Young (RIP), Nathan Wagar, Greg Ellifritz, and the Moyer Clan (my family), all of whom, knowingly or not, have imparted on me knowledge, values, and skills that would have remained vacant space.

I only hope that this book lives up to your standards.

INTEGRATED SKILLS GROUP

Be Prepared

The strange gray space we at ISG occupy means we don't easily fit into a category that people recognize. We're not preppers, mechanics, hunters, survivalists, gun guys, martial artists, or hobbyists, and you, as part of the community, might not be either. You may do those things but limiting who you are to those descriptions is not articulating that the whole is greater than the sum of its parts...there's something missing. Why?

Because our guiding principle—be prepared—is an incomplete sentence. What we are capable of isn't what we are...it's what we do with those skills.

The Other Half

ISG emphasizes readiness in every way: tactical, technical, mental, and physical. As a part of our mission, this serves two purposes:

- It generates a self-selected audience who already believes that personal development is rewarding, and;
- It brings people who are strong, capable, and motivated into the ISG community.

Plenty of other organizations do this as well, at least superficially.

What we want to emphasize is that we aren't telling you to *be prepared* so you can sulk in a bunker during some impending collapse. We spend a good amount of time discussing why those events, while worth considering, are not the most likely disruptions, and we discuss how to prioritize addressing them without fear and panic. Why do we want you to be prepared?

The other half of *be prepared* is…*to help*. Be prepared to help. That's what makes us different.

For what?

We circle many of our topics back to Understanding Emergencies because it gives us a way to truly understand threats and how we address them. This is necessary because we exist on the fringes of a society that is selling fear, not rationale.

We build on the foundation of two of our core philosophies: Understanding Emergencies and Spheres of Violence to establish the following points:

Bad things happen to good people without warning or explanation. Emergencies are not homogenous. What they means to a solider is different than for a police officer or a citizen.

We have to approach these situations as we are at our most basic: citizens who are capable of acting as first responders. This means entirely rethinking the way many of us were trained to do things…and being ready for both the actions and the consequences. We will revisit Understanding Emergencies and Spheres of Violence soon (and often), but at this point, it's only important to understand these two points.

We organized *Carry the Fire* so you can build ground-up skills that will cover the bases from the most difficult position first. If you happen to be (or decide to become) a first responder, operator, service member, or police officer, the template and framework provided within these pages will still apply, and whatever learning you do in those roles will simply add more specific competence to your overall skill base.

We emphasize mobility, medical, protection, security, and primitive skills because if you can develop them, the areas in which they overlap will make you more capable. For example, the exit protocols used when you're mobile overlap with medical protocols when you happen upon a car wreck. Not stepping into traffic or getting nervous and forgetting to park is a serious threat. Furthermore, we draw on primitive skills to recognize the priority of treatment: oxygenated blood and protection from the elements (which can cause or exacerbate shock).

What we are doing is creating a web through which problems can't pass. Within the web, we discuss skill, philosophy, mindset, and equipment only to facilitate the end goal of ISG: to create competent people who, when all else fails, can rise to the challenge and help those in need.

Be Prepared to Help

The point of being prepared isn't to simply survive. It's to retain our culture, our humanity, and our way of life. No matter what the scale of the emergency (Type I, II, or III), the ISG way is to have some solution to offer—even if it's just composure and facilitating the better qualified to do their work.

Every generation has its struggles, and eventually, those struggles will become insurmountable. Our society will fail. It may be eight years from now, it may be eight hundred, but with a living philosophy of quiet capability, the ISG culture is meant to bring small pockets of stability that can be built on...built with trust, respect, competence, and capability.

We aren't looking to simply outlast catastrophes. Our goals are threefold:

- Continually improve - develop skill, knowledge, and purpose.
- Be an asset - be ready to help your community, physically and mentally.

- Carry the fire - be a guiding light to others when there are problems.

Even when we combine these goals, the ISG philosophy falls flat without having a purpose. That purpose is being of use to our people. We can provide a cogent philosophy, and a template for skill building, but without purpose and our communities, none of it will matter.

With this in mind, go forth and complete the sentence. Be prepared… to help.

PREFACE

There are a lot of books dedicated to disasters, preparedness, and survival. There are how-to manuals, there are missives, and there are expert-driven instructions on how to perform tasks so the reader can gain knowledge. Most of these books end up being quick, interesting reads, and then they are left to collect dust or coffee stains, and the skills contained within remain theoretical.

This book is not one of those. In an age where everyone is clamoring to stand out and be different, it's difficult to demonstrate *how* you are different—especially if you intend to keep your soul, avoid selling out, and maintain a normal life. Here's why this manual stands apart from its peers:

Everything within is experiential learning. We've done it—not once or twice, but over and over again until we feel comfortable making statements about best practices.

It's written from a variety of perspectives. Our team features an incredibly diverse background of military, law enforcement, and private security experience, disaster management, field science, and of course, life experience.

We don't assume that what works for a soldier in Afghanistan will work for a citizen in Baltimore. The information we give will be useful to you no matter who you are because we've taken the time to consider how you're likely to use the information in your life.

We start from the ground up in our approach. We don't start with plans for regional vice directors of disaster coordination, as do most professional disaster management plans. We believe that:

> This mentality contributes to national-level failings in terms of swift, effective responses to disasters, and;

The individual is the first functional unit of resiliency. If the individuals are weakened or compromised, they cannot self-rescue.

We begin with you, the individual. Whether you're looking for a casual reference to deal with the unexpected, you're planning a trip to a nation or region that has little infrastructure, or you fear that serious shifts in society are coming, this book is a tool to diagnose your deficiencies and determine how the reaper acts on those deficiencies. It provides you two tools for slippin' the net when death comes calling:

Understanding how to recognize and categorize emergencies. Building the knowledge and skill sets to avoid and mitigate the threat these emergencies present.

Finally, reaching these goals and becoming more resilient shouldn't be a chore. You can enjoy yourself while validating the skills we discuss. After all, how different is a family camping trip from a power outage? Get out and have fun, test your skills, and don't fall victim to the bunker mentality of "any day now."

The exercises in this book will be mentally and physically challenging. They will wear you out, make you question your motivations, and ultimately humble you when you see just how much there is to know. We are going to talk about how to live like refugees, how to take filthy water and make it drinkable, and how to turn a mess of nature into a shelter. We're going to talk about how to move, how to avoid conflict, how to think on your feet, and how to take the steps to harden yourself against hard times.

Fair warning: you'll share this process with spiders, water, cold, and looming discomfort—but you will wake up the next morning, and from your own hands, you will grant yourself each day anew the opportunity to improve your lot, even in the worst situations this world can throw at you. You'll find yourself miserable in the snow, huddled around a weak, struggling fire, and eating food you captured or scavenged. You might find yourself surrounded by people who don't speak your language, who have strange customs, and who eat things you can't identify. It could be after walking twelve miles with a pack to get out of a catastrophe while stopping to render aid to those who need it most, and you will smile, knowing that you are facing the reaper, playing his game, on his turf and terms, and you are winning. You are staying just out of his reach and helping others do the same.

Subject Matter

EVERYDAY CARRY

WEATHER

BOOK 1: TECHNICAL

UNDERSTANDING EMERGENCIES

What Is an Emergency?

During Hurricane Katrina, ambulances sat waiting for directives for three full days. During Hurricane Sandy and the 2003 New York City blackout, there was widespread looting and chaos for days before order was restored. Why? Because the allocation of resources is planned by Command and Control, but they cannot always control the use of these assets. Destroyed roads, unsecured areas, collapsed bridges, fires, and flooding all dramatically impact the ability to deliver aid. While this is a headache for mission coordinators, it translates to more time in the fire at the ground level of an emergency…and being stranded, alone, and cut off from aid means that your chances for survival diminish.

When an emergency hits near you, the cause becomes secondary to the impact; you care less about the possibility of a chemical spill at Home Depot than you do about a fire in your neighborhood or a relative who needs refrigerated insulin during a prolonged outage. So, what happens on the ground floor of a disaster? How do we plan our strategy while government agencies prepare to act? If the top-down approach to emergency management leaves you without assistance, how will you react?

Humans, and most other mammals, have an innate compensatory system—the sympathetic nervous system—that provides us with the ability to survive. As we will explore, emergencies evoke our most primal and basic impulses, and the longer they last, the more these impulses act on us. As we plan for emergencies, we will find it's important to have a frame of reference, some experience, and an understanding of how we react in life-or-death situations in addition to a cogent plan. But a plan alone won't cover every possibility. We must learn to react immediately and progressively to new situations as they unfold. This organic approach to emergency management is evident in our very nature—our ability to rationalize goes out the window during the deadliest encounters with disaster, and we become creatures of reflex and habit. We default to our experiences and often act without conscious thought. This can be both a curse and a boon; many people's natural inclination is to help. These are the people to look out for, assist, and work with. But not everyone operates this way, and because of the others, you'll need to consider the darker side of human nature—those apex predator inclinations that make disasters even harder to navigate.

Because emergencies are never consistent, it is almost unnatural to think we can sit and discuss, with any accuracy, the way future events may unfold. Yet, this is often the first step among emergency planners—a step that, when relied upon, becomes a weak foundation that delays and prevents action when it is needed most. If we *expect* something and an entirely different situation unfolds, we must orient ourselves anew. Often, exercises held to prepare responders leave out important details, which make field problems far more difficult. Because of this, we see planning that caters to involving organizations such as HAZMAT, law enforcement, and emergency medical support (EMS) to increase joint response flexibility. It gives everyone some game time to test their ability to respond, even if it means less realistic event scenarios.

This focus on agency involvement is a top-down or managerial model of disaster preparedness. What is proposed in this book is a bottom-up plan for individuals, families, and communities. It is a method of planning in which the individual is as ready and as flexible as possible and can recognize and react to emergencies quickly while larger relief efforts are still being planned.

A strong bottom-up approach starts with an understanding of what an emergency is. We can generally state that an emergency occurs when vital resources or infrastructure are compromised. This broadly defines everything from a local snowstorm to global pandemics.

In any emergency, we're concerned with the breakdown of infrastructure and shortages. EMS, police, food and water, energy, and transportation were compromised during Hurricane Katrina, Typhoon Haiyan, the attacks in Nairobi and Mumbai, and in the many active shooter crises, and emergencies ensued. In other words, an emergency can be defined as a lack of anything necessary to survive.

Duration, Intensity, Probability and Proximity

Over the years, many emergencies have shown that the duration and the intensity of an event impact survival. In planning, we can assess the probability and associated risk and then look at associated impacts based on our proximity to the disaster.

In any case of shortage, be it breathable air or the ability to shelter yourself from the elements, a critical factor is always present and can be expressed as a balance between four distinct, uniform concepts:

Duration – How long is the event likely to last?
Intensity – How severe are the consequences of the event?
Probability – How likely is it that the event will happen?
Proximity – How close to the event are you likely to be?

Even a very survivable situation can be deadly when coupled with a protracted duration. The longer the duration, the more we see an emergence of secondary and tertiary emergencies that result from a lack of resources. What are these? The likes of dehydration, disease, starvation, blood loss, thermal injury, violence accompanying shortage, and so forth. These incidents, in and of themselves, are negative and become more severe the longer they go unresolved. In short, the intensity compounds over duration.

While we don't think anyone would argue that being shot at is a *good* situation, it is a *survivable* situation. However, the longer you take fire, the lower your odds of survival. Because of this, our immediate emphasis is always on preventing the situation from becoming more out of hand. The way we achieve this is by managing emergencies to the best of our ability and as quickly as possible. The longer we are in an emergency situation, the greater the likelihood that we will face other threats created by that emergency. This requires mobility—both mentally and physically. It is important to be able to categorize the likely impact of an emergency from the ground up.

Defining Types of Emergencies

If you live in the Pacific Northwest, it will be unlikely that you're going to need storm shutters or stilts on your home to mitigate a stray hurricane bearing down on your spot of the coast. Inversely, Floridians don't need to spend much time assessing the effects of an earthquake, so we can also include where you live in our impetus when we assess emergencies. First, let's look at our definitions:

The TYPE I Emergency

Situation of High Intensity, Short Duration

These events occur very quickly, in most cases on a timeline of seconds to minutes, and they are marked by being a direct threat to you or to loved ones in your immediate vicinity. The Type I emergency requires you take immediate action to preserve life or reduce threats. These emergencies occur on timelines of seconds to minutes and rarely exceed one day due to the brief and immediate nature of the threat.

Because of the nature of the Type I emergency, our first and most immediate goal is to do one of two things: escape or stop the threat. To do so, we must assess the emergencies we're likely to face, understand how they restrict our access to critical resources, and know what we need to have and do to escape them.

Common Type I emergencies include robberies or assaults, active shooter situations, car wrecks, or medical emergencies (choking, anaphylaxis, bleeding, et cetera).

Conceptual Checkpoint:

Identify three Type I emergencies you've been in or heard of during the course of your life. How did your reaction alter the outcome of the situation? Alternately, if you've not experienced the emergency but have heard of one, consider how your reaction would alter the outcome of the situation. Think of ways you could have improved your performance in those situations, and consider things you did that you'd like to maintain if ever faced with a similar situation again.

Before going on, consider something: If your house caught on fire right now, what would you do?

If your answer didn't include a fire extinguisher and/or relying on an authority, then you're not ready for that emergency. Granted, it's great to have professionals to help us, but there is a subtle and critical point here: We have to learn to rely on ourselves as much as possible. It's the only way to really move toward personal/family resilience.

The TYPE II Emergency

Disaster of Moderate Intensity, Moderate Duration

While the high intensity Type I emergency stresses the body physically and physiologically, the moderate intensity Type II emergency taxes the victim mentally. This is where problem solving becomes paramount and where issues such as water purification, sustenance, physical security, and sanitation start seeping into position to compromise your health. Moderate intensity situations are those that carry a very real threat of violence or injury, but injury is either unintended or would be incidental; in other words, you're not the target, but you could become a victim of circumstance.

The defining characteristic of the Type II emergency is that while you're not actively being targeted, you may be pressed into defending or providing for yourself. While the short duration, Type I emergency timeline is one second to twenty-four hours, Type II emergencies generally affect their victims for more "moderate" durations—these could last from two days up to several weeks. It's important to note that while these situations may *seem* very intense, they differ from immediate, high-intensity emergencies in that you're not being actively targeted or directly affected by the emergency. In other words, food may become scarce, but it's not because someone is taking it from you.

Incidences of Type II emergencies include:

- Riots
- Rolling blackouts
- Large-scale infrastructural damage, such as that which accompanies hurricanes or earthquakes
- Temporary weather emergencies, such as significant winter weather events, tornadoes, or flooding
- Breakdown of law/looting
- An event that leaves you stranded for a short duration (approximately 2 weeks or so)

Another way to identify a Type II emergency is to consider this real-life scenario: During Hurricane Katrina (Or Sandy, or Harvey), the initial storm surge and subsequent wind created a Type I emergency; it directly threatened lives by way of drowning, flying debris, falling limbs, and the like. Once the direct threat passed, the emergency wasn't over. What came next was the Type II emergency. This second-stage emergency cut off roads, meaning supplies couldn't get through. EMS and fire departments were cut off from the emergencies they could have otherwise handled. The toxic stew that flooded the landscape wasn't going to kill you immediately, but it definitely posed a risk to your safety and affected access to resources such as sanitation and clean water.

Perhaps the most important thing to remember about the Type II emergency is that once it sets in, the most immediate threat is gone, but it creates a scenario where increased incidences of Type I emergencies are likely.

Remember the looting that followed the last major disaster? While access to civil services was compromised for the law-abiding, it's important to remember that those services often hold the line and opportunists fill the void in their absence. Sometimes they're violent. However—and we believe this is important—these events happen with regularity, and the "survival" community drastically overestimates the number of looters and guns. The National Institute of Medicine has done a great job of debunking a lot of the claims of civil breakdown. Their work essentially cited the top ten disaster myths that came out of Hurricane Katrina. Taking from their excellent work, those myths are:

Myth #1: Foreign medical volunteers with any kind of clinical background are needed.

Fact: The local population almost always provides for its own immediate health needs. Only medical personnel with skills that are not available in the affected country may be needed.

Myth #2: Any kind of international assistance is needed immediately.

Fact: A hasty response, not based on an impartial evaluation, contributes to the chaos. Most needs are met by the victims themselves and their government and local agencies, not by foreign aid workers.

Myth #3: Epidemics and plagues are inevitable after every disaster.

Fact: Epidemics seldom occur after a disaster, and dead bodies do not lead to catastrophic outbreaks of infectious diseases. Improving sanitary conditions and educating the public on hygienic measures are the best means of preventing disease.

Myth #4: Disasters bring out the worst in people (looting, rioting etc).

Fact: While there are isolated cases of antisocial behavior which tend to be highlighted by the media, most people respond positively and generously.

Myth #5: The affected population is too shocked and helpless to take responsibility for its own survival.

Fact: Many people find new strength and resiliency during an emergency.

Myth #6: Disasters are random killers.

Fact: Disasters strike the most vulnerable groups the hardest, i.e., minorities and the poor, especially women, children, and the elderly.

Myth #7: Locating disaster victims in temporary settlements is the best solution to the housing problem.

Fact: This is the least desirable option. The preferred strategy is to purchase construction materials and rebuild.

Myth #8: Food aid is always required for the victims of natural disasters.

Fact: Massive food aid is not usually required; natural disasters only rarely cause loss of crops.

Myth #9: Clothing is always needed by disaster victims.

Fact: Clothing is almost never needed; it is usually culturally inappropriate, and although it is accepted by disaster victims, it is almost never worn.

Myth #10: Things return to normal within a few weeks.

Fact: Disasters have enduring effects and major economic consequences. International interest tends to wane just as needs and shortages become more pressing.

These Type II emergencies extend from several hours to several weeks, and in rare instances (such as Hurricane Katrina) they can last months, so we need to have a plan that goes beyond the official government 72-Hour Emergency Kit. But let's not get carried away thinking society is going to descend into anarchy in three days or whatever the trope is. History has shown us time and time again that just isn't what happens with any regularity. So, it's time to put down the survivalist magazines and think about where you'll poop if the water treatment plants aren't operational. That's the stuff that doesn't make it onto television or into apocalyptic pop culture.

A type II emergency can impact in other ways, including infrastructure damage and possibly an increased likelihood of a type I emergency occurring. During Katrina, survivors of the initial storm still had an entire city of three hundred sixty thousand people who were not prepared to live on their own in a city with no infrastructure for five weeks. The survivors weren't ready for a city without delivery trucks. New Orleans had a badly damaged fire/EMS/police response framework and damaged sanitation systems. People were unable to travel because the roads and bridges were destroyed. The result was not glamourous. People were left on their own, and many didn't have the skills, mobility, or supplies to see them through.

Embedded in the problems from the point above is the chance of becoming a victim of interpersonal violence. The likelihood can increase dramatically during a type II emergency. This is the logical outflow of resource scarcity—when there is not enough of a resource to go around, it becomes more valuable. The list of things people will do to acquire those items grows to include criminal behavior. We call this phenomenon *resource hysteria*. People who are increasingly desperate for a decreasing number of supplies quickly revert to *me first* behavior. We saw during the early stages of the COVID-19 pandemic in 2020 when stores were utterly unable to keep toilet paper in stock. Was there any indication that there would be toilet paper shortages as a result of the illness? Absolutely not. If anything, the most significant projections were looking toward pharmaceutical drugs like antibiotics (the US gets some 80 percent of their antibiotics from overseas as of the time of this writing). When panic sets in, it is often wildly irrational, and supplies of all types can be vulnerable. The lesson here is to have enough consumable provisions to last you several weeks, at a minimum, but it's also important to understand the psychology of scarcity, and as importantly, the effects of shortages on populations.

While we will discuss food and water shortly, be aware that a significant amount of people in any given country are chemically dependent on some substance or another. This might be as insane as morning coffee or as enslaving as methamphetamines but understanding how you and your family will be impacted by those shortages is important. Breaking it down to its core, we simply need to be aware of what drug use in our area looks like (part of our area study, discussed later), and we need to be aware that scarcity is likely to introduce an increase in home invasions or theft (Type I emergencies) within the larger framework of the Type II disasters and the Type III catastrophes. We don't need to hyper-focus on exactly what will happen, because the way we harden ourselves to the second-order effects caused by scarcity is pretty simple: early warning systems, good security hygiene, and some planning for home security—all discussed in their own chapters.

For further reading, Eleanor Learmonth and Jenny Tabakoff's excellent book, *No Mercy: True Stories of Disaster, Survival, and Brutality*, does a good job illustrating resource hysteria. Read it; it's worth your time, and we'll return to discuss some of their findings in our chapter on Mindset.

The two points made above occur on an indefinite timeline, but they have definable end points—usually within a month or two of onset. This is important because there is a relationship between duration and survivability: the longer the situation affects you, the more likely you are to succumb to it. While the Type II emergency may not be resolved quickly, it's important to note that the situation is always resolved. So, as dicey as these situations may be, they are temporary. With that acknowledged, if all you have is seventy-two hours' worth of supplies, where are you when you reach hour eight hundred forty, as happened in New Orleans? How do you feel when you've gone through everything and you're not even 10 percent of the way to the situation resolving? Reread that last part.

The TYPE III Emergency
Low Intensity, Protracted Duration Catastrophe

The Type III emergency has two key differences from the Type II, but it is otherwise very similar. First, it occurs on a timeline that is measured in years, such as a civil war, or comes in oscillations that last for years, such as a pandemic. Second, it fundamentally changes the way you live.

The catastrophe doesn't resolve because events that precipitate catastrophes often leave minimal or non-functioning governments in their wake. Another crucial element is that the catastrophe affects many governments, which slows response and foreign aid that might otherwise return things to normalcy more quickly.

Incidences that qualify as low intensity, protracted duration are:
- Occupation by military
- Depression or economic collapse
- Endemic or pandemic, outbreak of contagious disease
- Revolution/civil war
- Being stranded after an air accident, shipwreck, or similar
- Monetary system collapse/banking crisis

It's important to note that these don't often happen in isolation. That is to say, if you have a depression, it opens the door for disease. If you have a civil war, it opens the door to depression, and so on. The Type III is a constant swirl of large-scale bad situations. The collapse of the USSR entirely cut off Cuba and North Korea from oil imports. The lives of their citizens changed in ways that would impact generations, and the nations both dealt with the problem very differently. This wasn't a political problem as there was no way to solve it. It was a predicament; there were no solutions, only outcomes.

So, while the Type III is the most common emergency to stress over, it is the least common when it comes to occurrence. They may happen a few times a century, and they form the outer fringe of our web of preparedness—those events that aren't especially likely but have a tremendous impact when they do happen.

As of the time of this writing, our lives have been fundamentally changed for an indefinite period by the emergence of the SARSCoV2 virus. The fundamental changes that occur with a Type III emergency mean you will be required to accept being thrust into a new role. In this type of emergency—also known as a collapse—you have a low intensity, long duration predicament. For example, if you were an American professional in 1929, the next thirteen years of your life would have been fundamentally reshaped. If your profession didn't become obsolete, it's highly likely it would have been difficult to receive payment because the financial suffering of clients meant they may not have had currency to pay you. This is a fundamental shift, both in the way we think of commerce as well as the way we interact with the people in our community and the world around us. These events represent the most varied and dangerous situations because they occur along an exceptionally long timeline and they fundamentally change the nature of our lives, and much of that happens on account of how our leadership responds.

To return to Cuba and North Korea—the North Koreans' approach to losing the tailwind of Soviet support was to turn inward and isolate. Their leadership looked to ensure their own continuity first and did little to protect the commoners from starvation and crippling shortages. Cuba, on the other hand, told their citizens to find any patch of undeveloped ground and start sowing seeds. The outcome of that crisis was significantly less severe for the Cubans, regardless of what we may think about them.

Fieldcraft: Emergencies

Whereas we have Type I situations that represent physical challenges and Type II disasters that begin to challenge our problem solving, the Type III emergency challenges endurance and adaptability. Low intensity Type III catastrophes are easiest understood as the *vectors* for many of the worst-case scenarios as they typically contain more traumatic, high intensity/short duration situations and moderate intensity situation disasters.

A useful example would be the persecution of the Boers in South Africa in the early 2000s. The situation (a cultural revolution) created a general situation of local and regional resource scarcity, including a lack of functioning legal institutes. Because of this, tragic and horrible atrocities were committed against Boer farmers. When emergency and infrastructural services are tapped, the incidences of more acute problems (robbery, structure fires, et cetera) increase, and more moderate duration, moderate intensity Type II disasters arise as well (such as downed electrical grids or backup sewage treatment plants).

The Type III emergency is what we would think of as a "collapsed" society in which there is little to no law and order, there is rampant corruption and violence, and the responsibility for survival rests on the shoulders of community members who are able to work with one another for an indefinite period of time. These situations require solid footing in all the areas of development—skill set, mindset and tactics—as well as the benefits of community, and they may require rudimentary (and now, mostly forgotten) skills such as agriculture and gardening, canning, animal husbandry, curing meat, and more. These problems will require all the skills, mindset, and equipment you can muster, plus the knowledge and ability to adapt and improvise solutions.

Probability and Proximity

With the above grim prospects to consider, we should be awash in fears, and it would be almost impossible to nail down any way to provide a sound "solution" to the problems, or perhaps more importantly, know how to take the first step.

Enter probability and proximity. While we can't foresee the future, most can clearly see that the position we find our global community in is laden with economic, socio-political, and military encumbrances that cannot be reconciled. Each of us individually must scrutinize for ourselves what we believe to be the most likely situations and how our local area will be impacted. Most emergencies or conflicts begin long before the problems arise, so the first step is to evaluate how probable a situation is. Perhaps the easiest way to do this is to use the Punnet square. This model allows us to evaluate an event and the associated risks simply and decisively. A sample Punnet square is a simple box, with a "plus" shape dividing it into four columns. In this instance, we put "low impact" and high impact" at the top, and "low probability" and "high probability" along the left. Then, we use the boxes to identify threats that are both high probability and high impact, and start working from there!

Using this model, we can assess any emergency, from a house fire to a civil war, based on information we gather, and we can use that information to create an actionable template. Once we understand how likely a situation is and the degree to which it will impact us, we can begin to assess how we prepare for it.

Consistency Across Categories

As with all matters in this text, the results will be highly individual. The needs of someone in Detroit, Michigan, will be significantly different than someone living in the countryside of Belgium. However, we will apply the idea of *consistency across categories*, a concept I first heard about from martial artist Marc Denny.

Consistency across categories means we take precautions that will address the widest range of events first. We will consistently need food, water, shelter, medical, and security, no matter what problems we find ourselves confronted with. Said another way, the preparations we make should help carry us through, regardless of what specific event is occurring.

OODA

Air Force Colonel John Boyd devised a method of analyzing how we act and react under stress. His model, known as OODA, is a continually repeating process (a loop) of Observation, Orientation, Decision, and Action.

While this process in and of itself doesn't train us in a measurable way, you will notice that under stress, this is precisely how the mind works. With that in mind, in any crisis, it's important to recognize Col. Boyd's contribution as an extremely valuable tool for working through stress. Each situation is going to require that you either use the OODA loop to assess the situation, make good decisions and act upon them, or follow someone else's lead. For this reason, training, martial arts, rehearsals, and other exercises to flex your decision-making ability can greatly reduce the time it takes to make difficult decisions under pressure.

This is a topic we will continually revisit, so take a moment to memorize the acronym OODA: Observation, Orientation, Decision, Action. You don't have to fully understand it right at this second, but it is important to file it away as a future decision-making tool.

Responding to Emergencies

Emergencies test us from our calm up. The root word of emergency is *emerge*, and as such, the most logical place to start is what happens to our psychological and physiological state when a threat to our safety emerges.

The first thing that happens upon perception of a threat is that the body begins to release neurotransmitters—chemicals in the brain responsible for stimulating the body. The commonly understood neurotransmitters are cortisol and epinephrine (also referred to as adrenaline). Biologically, these prime our body for conflict, and more generally, for "fight or flight." While cortisol diverts resources from the immune system and releases chemicals to facilitate the synthesis of fats and proteins, epinephrine increases the rate of the heart and respiration and puts the liver on a temporary break.

This is all to allow your body to focus immediately on the Type I emergency, and eating, communication, and higher reasoning get put on the back burner. Whether you've got steel nerves from dealing with various tense situations or you're completely new to preparing for the unknown, there is a general template that can help you efficiently prioritize once the initial threat is gone: Think ACE: Accountability, Casualties (and damage), and Equipment.

Accountability: Find out as soon as possible if anyone is missing and get people to a point where they're out of harm's way. Pair up if at all possible. In short, get a headcount, get people to look out for each other, and move if necessary. If you don't know anyone, quickly get to know them—does anyone have medical experience? Engineering? Any prior military or law enforcement? Find out where people fit in to fixing the situation—and don't forget yourself.

Casualties/Damage: Identify anyone who has been injured or killed and determine whether there is any damage that needs to be addressed. Now is the time to take care of grievous wounds.

Equipment: Do a quick spot check to see if there is helpful equipment available. If you're dealing with a situation that requires consumable equipment (ammunition, bandages, water), have each person give a quick account of anything they may have.

This template can be summed up by the simple acronym ACE, and it's a good first step in establishing some control over the environment. Delegating tasks is a great way to occupy otherwise panicking minds, and it builds a sense of cooperation. That might sound hokey, but there's a common theme in long-term survival: a common sense of purpose and cooperation. Another thing—be willing to follow. If you can lead, all the better, but recognize that others may have strengths and experience that you don't. Learn from them.

If you're coming onto the scene of an emergency, have a plan beforehand and do not expect it to conform to your past experience, training, or anything else. These situations evolve pretty organically. If you're needed, it'll be obvious quickly. If someone with more experience is already on point, help them as you can.

Keep in mind the threats may not be gone. If the emergency is something like an auto accident, make sure there are markers to give drivers enough time to respond to the collision. In a situation like an active shooter, do not assume the scene is clear until the shooter is dead! You may or may not be able to treat the injured. Your first priority is to evade capture and injury. The Westgate Mall siege in Nairobi, Kenya, and the Taj Mahal Hotel siege in Mumbai, India, provide case studies in what you can expect. The Beslan school siege, the Bolshoi theater siege, and the Aurora and Columbine shootings all illustrate the types of attacks that typify the worst-case active shooter scenarios. As a part of mental preparation, these are worth studying.

Storytime!

During my late teens, my family lived on a very rural hairpin turn. During one span of six months, we witnessed five accidents on that turn, including a fatal motorcycle wreck. In two of the accidents, the drivers were intoxicated or on drugs and fled into the bushes. One guy had a girlfriend whose face went right through the windshield. She had glass caked in her cuts. In that particular situation, I was eighteen years old and had no idea how to treat an injury like hers, and I was surprised when they knocked on our door (sometime around 10 p.m.). It was a mess. I was not efficient, and I failed to do anything that nature wouldn't have done on its own—including removing the glass.

On another occasion, much later in life, I heard an accident, grabbed my kit, and ran to the road knowing there was an accident. When I arrived at the site, there were people with horrific cuts and blood all over their clothes, but they were up and walking around. I started looking at the injured and asking diagnostic questions, checking for signs of concussion or serious injury. One person stopped me. He said, "We just came from a MASCAL [Mass casualty] exercise! We're fine! Check on her!" indicating to a middle-aged woman in a sedan. I was far better prepared, mentally and materially, but it was still quite a challenge to my established OODA loop. The woman in the car was pretty bad off, but she made it.

In 2008, I was a part of an interdepartmental training exercise for reacting to active shooters, and we were to be trained on how to stop active shooters. After a few iterations of training, my team and I were feeling great. We'd effectively stopped the "bad guy" and quickly "rescued" the casualties. During the final iteration, I engaged a threat and then turned to find several individuals rushing me. I shot as quickly and as accurately as I could, scoring four good hits on two targets...both of whom were hospital patient role players trying to escape. It was only training, but it stuck with me. I would have killed two people who were not only innocent but also injured or ill and trying to escape a bad guy.

Sometime later, I was called to a situation in which a man was reportedly holding hostages. Our response was strong and aggressive, and we took control of the scene. The lead officer committed to an entry, and the guy inside shot himself. As it turns out, he wasn't holding hostages; he was suicidal, and a zealous chain of command mishandled the situation. Worse yet, I knew the guy. He was a good man who was desperate due to circumstances. That stuck with me, too.

Your composure and discipline will contribute to the loss or saving of life. It's a heavy burden; treat it as such. When you arrive at a scene, your first goal should be simple: don't slow the pace of fixing the problem. Take your time getting there, even if it means being *more* ready for whatever lies ahead. Like shooting, you can't miss fast enough to win. If you rush to a scene without being prepared, you won't do much good. Don't go with preconceived notions. Pay close attention and diligently account for anything that can be accounted for, audit the damage, and set out to fix it or help those who can.

Practical Preparation and Identification of Solutions

Throughout the adventure of hardening yourself to crisis, you'll find that some themes are common and others, esoteric. Some will depend on your vision of yourself. We all have predispositions, and it's wise to assess yours now. Think of your strengths and weaknesses critically and honestly. If you are honest, you'll know what to fix. If you are critical, you'll work harder to fix the problem. From there, commit yourself to being better each day.

Miyamoto Musashi, the legendary Warrior of feudal Japan, once said, "The principle of strategy is having one thing, to know ten thousand things." We have taken this to mean *the more you know, the easier it is to learn.*

This is where you should begin your preparation and identification process: with yourself. The next step is to understand that there is no chance you'll be able to do it all yourself. As humans, we require other humans. In addition to the comfort we find in numbers and with those we hold dear close by, the skills others bring to complement our own are essential to dealing with any crisis that occurs over a critical length of time.

The Rules of 3

What you need, and when.

The notion of the Rules of 3 is introduced to military personnel at SERE school (Survive, Escape, Resist, Evade). I was first introduced to it through the US Rescue and Special Operations group (US-RSOG), who published the book [1]. Throughout this writing, I will continually lean on that text and specifically the method of prioritizing our labor in an emergency; I strongly encourage you to buy and read the book. It will elaborate extensively on many of the topics in this work and will serve well as a reference guide when you're learning all about good living in the most miserable conditions this life has to offer.

The Rules of 3 state that a healthy human can survive for:

- Three minutes without oxygenated blood
- Three hours without shelter
- Three days without water
- Three weeks without food

It is also worth noting that you're going to be one hurting unit after the first third of any of those periods has lapsed. Holding your breath for three minutes is a great example of what this means. Go ahead and give it a try. How far did you get? Expect that this same feeling will apply to body temperature, thirst, and hunger, as well. Adding stress will further complicate the process. Try tying a knot underwater without resurfacing. Try tying three. These are simple exercises that can illustrate the importance of approaching problems with calm, practicing the skills needed beforehand, and being ready for life to suck.

You can imagine extreme cold or heat, lack of water and the subsequent dehydration headaches, or the pains of not eating for a week playing similar havoc with your sense of urgency. Since your body has a built-in mechanism to warn you way ahead of time, let's work with nature in saying that in any emergency, we're going to do our best to solve these problems *before* that first third has elapsed.

EVERYDAY CARRY

The day-to-day tools of self-rescue.

The concept of everyday carry is one that supposes that skill can only take us so far. While with some items, such as a tourniquet or water filter, we can improvise, others we simply cannot. For example, a flashlight. No matter how hard we might try, we will never be able to conjure light without a mechanical device of some kind.

If you're not familiar with everyday carry, it's the concept that you should be carrying certain things on a daily basis. The skills we develop should complement the tools we carry. After all, while we may be able to improvise a tourniquet, it'll never be as effective as a purpose-built item. With that in mind, here's what we want from our everyday carry (EDC):

Accessibility: It needs to be carried in such a way that it's easy to access when needed.

Carry-ability: It needs to be of a size that makes it easy to carry and dress around.

Efficacy: It needs to be an item with a track record of reliability.

These are Items of Immediate Necessity (IINs), and they're our first line of defense against rapid onset, short duration emergencies. Because of this, we don't need to get wrapped around the axle about having "nice to have" stuff on us all the time; it's great to have a thumb drive, but it won't save anyone's life. Conversely, it doesn't matter if you have a box of emergency lighters and fire logs at home—you need to have that fire starter on your person for it to make a difference. If you don't, you better have the skill to augment your lack of equipment. It does you no good to have a tourniquet at home in a drawer if you're bleeding out on the side of the road.

While understanding emergencies is integrally tied to having the proper equipment and the skill to use them, what we almost never see is a dedicated discussion of why you're carrying equipment in the first place. The loudest voices seem to focus on two extremes: *Why would you carry all that?* Or, *if you're not going to carry x-y-z, why bother carrying anything at all?* From a rational perspective, this is a waste because not everyone has the same options, but more than that, both sides are rife with the false dilemma logical fallacy. Why? Because there's no right answer.

Our intent here isn't to tell you what the right equipment is. It's to give you some ways to think about the problem so you can best answer the question for yourself. Our focus is to discuss the situations that make such precautions necessary. That's what we're interested in, because as we'll see, EDC should be the end result of a process that involves cultivating skill and mindset. It's not a solution that you can just go to the local store and buy.

Our Approach: Probability, Skill, and Lines of Equipment

We base our planning on understanding emergencies. When we get right down to it, all our fears (and thus, our preparations) are made in response to threats to our safety. One of the most common problems we see with people's efforts to choose gear is that they don't understand how emergencies happen, and therefore, they're randomly selecting things that might help them in some undefined circumstance. With the approach laid out in Understanding Emergencies, however, we have the intellectual framework to make good sense of what might happen and how we can best deal with it. Since we have already covered the types of emergencies, we can introduce a couple more concepts.

Impact and Probability

This metric is used in conjunction with our Types of Emergencies to determine if we're really at risk. Are we close to a high-crime neighborhood? Do we live on an active fault, or in a location affected by hurricanes? Or do we live in an adult family home in upstate New York? Does a guy in Kentucky have the same options as a dude living in a flat in Westminster? We've gotta start with, *what are my options?* And more importantly, *what are the threats?*

The need of citizens to possess a gun is often questioned. While we don't want to get too off the rails with justifications, let's look at some facts: Civilians shoot criminals at between 66-75 percent the rate that police officers do. The notion that all cops run around shooting it out with bad guys all day is absurd, and according to Pew Research (go ahead, laugh at the irony), the majority, 73 percent, never fire their weapon in the line of duty.[2] So really, neither police nor citizens are overly likely to have to kill someone in self-defense. But the firearm's role in protection is a little more complicated. What are your chances of firing a weapon and not taking a life? Well, about one in three hundred twenty-five...but there's more to the number, too.

Gary Kleck and Marc Gertz exhaustively studied the role of guns in civilian hands and the circumstances around them, and what they found is that of those who fired a gun to stop a crime, very few resulted in the criminal being injured or killed. They estimated that citizens simply having firearms stopped crimes up to three million times per year[3] —that's closer to a one in one hundred chance a citizen will find himself in a self-defense situation of some sort. That's substantial, and even if we look at the low estimate of approximately 989 thousand incidences of civilians using a firearm to stop crime, that's *still* about one in three hundred twenty-five. That means the chances of using a gun to defend yourself—should you choose to carry one—aren't far-fetched.

Statistics can be misleading, and many will try to make their decisions on what to carry based on averages: What is the average distance in a fight? How many attackers? And so forth. It's also important to note that 1/100 figure above isn't spread evenly across the population. Living on the upper east side of Manhattan isn't going to be the same as living in West Memphis. Whenever you read a statistic—including ours—run it through the filter of your own personal situation.

We want to cover as many possibilities as we can because, if we're being honest with ourselves, all gunfights are outliers, and all of them are extremes. We don't need to be ready for the average; we need to understand the spectrum and work on the most common problems first. Once that's done, work your way out.

If you're training in martial arts, fight the biggest guy. If you're at the range, shoot the farthest target. Learn to pack a wound. Get good at the basics and continue to challenge yourself. Use the same Punnet square—the highest risk, highest probability is close range asocial/interpersonal problems. Find a course that works on force-on-force and scenario-based training is the next step. It will help develop your communication, your grappling, and your awareness, in addition to giving you a pressure-tested taste of what conversation-range fights with guns feel like.

Skill

To deal with the knowledge that emergencies are really a function of two metrics (duration and intensity, and probability and impact) and with the admission that bad things happen to good people without explanation, it's logical to conclude that at some point in your life, you may be faced with an emergency that requires you to act. So, what does that mean for us? We have to have some skill, and this is where we really want to drive our point home. Skill makes us efficient, and efficiency buys us time.

Duration is one of the critical elements of our emergencies, so anything we can do to buy ourselves time gives us options as to how we react. A person who neglects skill, conversely, has fewer options and less time to make their decisions. We settled on the term *Integrated Skills* because of this: A person who has a gun during a fight has options, but a guy who has some skill at grappling, an edged weapon, a sidearm, and some experiences has more options.

Part of our protective skill set is knowing when and how to employ weapons in a way that doesn't set us up for failure by trying to defang the snake. It means knowing how to quickly apply a tourniquet that will work, and not just trying to jam a tampon into a bleeding wound. Skills guarantee that when it comes to action, we can be relied upon to make decent decisions under pressure. Unlike access to equipment or control over circumstance, it's the one thing we can absolutely control.

Once you've gone through the process of identifying the things that could affect you or your loved ones, you build the skill to make sure you're not caught with your pants down. After you've developed the skill, you'll have an easier time nailing down the right equipment.

Equipment

Putting this all together, if you live in an affluent area where you work from home, but you live in an area commonly threatened by natural disasters, you might not need to go around carrying a full-sized pistol, a tourniquet, a flashlight, and a multi-tool, but that doesn't mean other people in other areas wouldn't benefit from carrying more equipment for their circumstances.

Furthermore, skills give us options, but equipment streamlines how we apply skill. Can you try to make a tourniquet out of a belt, or a water filter from a used water bottle with sand and charcoal in it? Yes, you can. It's good to know how; but improvising will never be as good as a purposely built item. As such, we've identified the relevant emergencies and the likelihood that they'll affect us, and we've identified the skills necessary to address those emergencies. The last step is to determine what you want to carry. Given our skill groups, we have four items we believe help us in the pursuit of being useful:

Knife

Flashlight

Multi-tool

Lighter

Here's a sampling of our reasoning: Biology hasn't served us with an efficient cutting edge, a way to make heat or light, or a way to exert leverage. If you end up stranded on a back-country road, you can improvise anything you might need with those tools. If you're so inclined, they also allow us to fix common problems for others and ourselves, and if you travel outside the US, they should still mostly be available.

While we advocate having them on body, dress code and lifestyle might make that a no-go. That's fine, too. Once you've built the intellectual framework, you'll start to view your equipment as more than just stuff you're wearing that either cripples your style or makes you feel cool; you'll see it as useful tools that you know you can apply quickly for a desired outcome.

When you consider the types of emergencies and how your lines of equipment interface with them, what you carry and why will be more reasoned, justified, and accessible. So, when we discuss lines of equipment, it's not just random. They correspond with our ability to both identify and manage the types of emergencies.

First Line of Equipment

The first line of equipment is our on-body emergency equipment used to deal with direct threats to life, as well as to urgent situations. Very little discussion occurs regarding how and where to wear your equipment, so here is some helpful information to guide your efforts.

Layout

Let's break the body into planes, right down the middle. Most people have a dominant hand and a non-dominant hand. Dominance or handedness is largely a question of how good you are at performing precise tasks. With that in mind, most of the work of laying out our EDC on our person becomes very easy; items on our dominant side are those that require the use of fine motor skills, while those that do not work their way to our non-dominant side.

A useful concept is the "diver's triangle". The idea behind it is that your belt is the base of the triangle, and the jugular notch (throat) is the top. All items placed in this area are easily accessible, even in dark, difficult environments. For this reason, this is where we want our most urgent equipment. We can further split this into "dominant" and "non-dominant", based on our handedness.

The equipment listed in the column labeled "dominant" typically requires that the hand most capable of performing difficult tasks be used. Others, such as flashlights and cell phones, need very little input to be used effectively and can be used in the non-dominant hand. Medical items should be highly personalized —I keep a very small trauma pack with some Celox and a seatbelt cutter on my right-hand side, but I keep my tourniquet on the left. This isn't because the tourniquet is better suited to the support-side, but rather it'll likely become a two-handed affair if needed, and applying a tourniquet isn't something you should be doing while you're trying to tackle another task. You may need to apply pressure or hold the injured person firmly while applying it.

In any case, ask yourself the following:

Can I access my equipment easily with either hand?

Can I wear this comfortably (both physically and psychologically)?

Can I apply this layout to anything I happen to be wearing?

Three final considerations before we move on:

With first line equipment, we should be able to find or acquire anything else we may need from our Rules of 3.

It should blend seamlessly with our second line of equipment (discussed next).

It isn't necessary to carry all of this. What you carry will be largely dictated by circumstance, skill, routine, law, and if we're being honest, comfort.

Far too many people will try to make EDC about them, and they will tell everyone else what they should carry. Our goal is to simply discuss a full spectrum of options. If all you carry is a cell phone and keys, your options might be limited, but that doesn't make you useless. Just understand what it is you can contribute and how you can help with what you have.

Second Line of Equipment

The second line of equipment is our sustainment bag: a portable pack that has everything we need to sustain us while we plan and act in the initial phases of a Type II emergency. When done correctly, the sustainment bag will carry everything we need to move for several days while addressing the Rules of 3. Furthermore, it should be worn in such a way that you still have unrestricted access to all of your first line gear. This makes it possible to address Type I emergencies—those that require an immediate intervention to stop loss of life. All the skill groups are covered as efficiently as possible.

When people think about preparedness, it's hard to imagine a more ubiquitous item than the backpack. It has a variety of names —the Bug Out Bag, the INCH bag, the GOOD bag—all of which are designed to evoke images of some wandering, steely eyed hero with his backpack and AR-15 striding across the post-apocalyptic wasteland with cities burning behind him. One of our main goals is to get people to abandon the idea that emergencies look like that. A far more likely vision is overflowing sewage, people sick and filthy with diarrhea, and travel of no more than a couple miles from your home for scraps being handed out by the National Guard. If you're well provisioned, you won't be going out much, and if you evacuated ahead of the problem, your pack will help you while you travel and set up when you arrive at your destination.

What we want during a Type II emergency is the ability to deliberately plan and sustain ourselves around a rapidly changing situation. Said another way, we need just enough comfort to allow us to stay composed. Sustainment keeps you in the fight long enough to make good decisions. So, while the concept of bugging out and having a bug out bag can be a desperate gamble and a last resort, some careful planning can help you to sustain yourself in dire situations.

If you're traveling by foot with nothing but what you keep in your pack, you've failed, and there's a word for what you are: refugee. Your bag isn't to keep you alive, it's to sustain deliberate activity. Refugees don't exactly have it good, and no matter what you pack, if you don't have skill, mindset, and a plan, no bag will get you "bugged out."

Molon Labe is a common phrase in the gun community that stems from the Spartan's stand at Thermopylae. It means "Come and take them!" —a statement that was allegedly given by King Leonidas when Xerxes demanded the Spartans turn over their weapons. Now it's just a political statement that doesn't really mean much of anything. Hurricane Katrina taught us that a firearm seen was a firearm confiscated, and for all the Molons to be Labed, the truth is, if you end up at a police blockade with your tired children and wife, you're going to hand over your guns without a fight. This isn't legal (look up and print off 42 US Code 5207), but it is what happens.

Why a Backpack?

If you follow ISG for any length of time, you'll notice we pretty much always have backpacks. Given that we've taken such an extreme posture against the idea of the Bug Out Bag, *why* is a reasonable question.

To start, we don't think you need a closet full of separate backpacks for different occasions. If you set up your EDC in a logical way, your backpack is going to take the items you carry for immediate, high-intensity emergencies (Type I) and expand them so you can address the concerns of the protracted, moderate intensity emergency (Type II). If you live the ISG lifestyle, you're out camping, exploring, and gathering experience. This is one thing that differentiates ISG from traditional survivalists (and more recently, "preppers" —people for whom preparedness is a lifestyle). One of the fundamental lessons we've learned is that the stuff you need for emergencies is almost the exact same stuff you'll want if you're out enjoying nature or exploring. We don't encourage people to simply stock goods for emergencies or spend time worrying about exactly what situations the future may bring. That would be counterproductive and wouldn't facilitate getting out and experiencing the enjoyable aspects of life. If you stop to think about it, this drastically simplifies your life and puts your second line in terms that most people can relate to. It doesn't have to be weird to think ahead about life at home the same way you might think ahead for a long wilderness camping trip.

What we want from our second line of equipment is a way to address the Rules of 3: Shelter from the elements, clean water, calories, and items for medical and hygienic concerns. Therefore, our backpack should address shelter, clean water, calories, medical and hygienic concerns, tools of acquisition, and tools for protection. In other words: whatever you're doing, your backpack should sustain your efforts. Among preppers, this is commonly called the bug out bag, though chances are good that leaving home with just what you can carry on your back will not be a good solution. So, toss out the bug out bag, and start thinking in terms of sustainment.

Target Weight

If you're ever faced with these types of situations, you do not want a huge, bulky, heavy pack or kit that's prone to snagging. Before we even start talking about stuff to put in your backpack, we want to be super clear about something: as your weight goes up, your endurance goes down. This is a non-negotiable fact of life, even if you're fit and strong. We strongly encourage that you start with a target weight of no more than 20 percent of your bodyweight. As you start choosing items, look carefully at what they weigh.

We're big on what we call mobility training. Mobility is the ability to run, jump, climb, and fight in your equipment. Several members of ISG have lived under the rucks, both professionally and as citizens, and we've had to maneuver and fight under the loads. If you can't hop a fence, climb an eight-foot wall, run a mile, and walk at least six, your pack is too heavy for your level of fitness. Scale it back and start over.

Keep in mind that 20 percent added to your EDC can stack up fast. If you're at 8 percent of your body weight for your EDC items, you can quickly approach 30 percent of your body weight. Even if you're fit and still mobile under that load, it will stress your body, increase your chances for injury, and cost you calories.

Applying the Rules of 3

Recall from Rules of 3 that a human can last three minutes without air, three hours without shelter, three days without water, and three weeks without food. This is a useful guide, not hard and fast rules, but what we really want to impress upon the reader is this: Your backpack is your sustainment and should act as a wall between you and the Rules of 3, and it should address the added pressures of the Type II emergency—security, physical health care, and acquisition.

Objective-based Packing

The first thing your pack should be able to do is address the Rules of 3:

Shelter: You need to stay dry and isothermal (your temperature isn't going up or down much). To this end, lightweight tents, lean-to tarps, and even 55-gallon trash bags can offer some means of expedient insulation. It's worth noting that ground pads do an incredible job of insulating you from the cold ground, and they make your rest more productive. Small tents and ultra-lightweight equipment are more important than guns. You'll use this stuff every night (if you get out and train) or if the worst happens. Don't scoff at the price of an ultra-lite kit if you have a $2500 AR.

Water: You should have a way to both carry and purify water. There's been a big push toward Camelbak-type bladders in recent years. That's cool, but if you rely on *only* a bladder, you'll lack a convenient way to boil water. Nalgene bottles and military canteens can be had with metal cups, which can provide you with a way to drink that keeps your mouth off your bottles (a good way to keep bacteria from growing in your water source) and also allows you to heat water to kill bacteria.

When it comes to purifying, *get a water filter*. Water is a non-negotiable, frequent-use consumable. The Rules of 3 says three days, but if we're being honest, the splitting headache and cramps you'll get after sixteen hours or so of exertion without hydration is going to make your last two days of life miserable.

Food: The goal with food is to have a layered approach: fast calories (jerky, power bars, candy, etc.), meals (Mountain House, MRE, or similar, stripped), and a method to procure your own food (which requires skill). Fish are high in nutrients, typically more plentiful than game, and easier to trap. For killing small game, don't overlook the slingshot. Everyone talks about .22s or hunting with their battle rifles, but ammo runs out and rocks are free. Tackle and a slingshot are light and don't take up much space.

Hygiene and Medical: One of the most neglected things we see in people's bags is a way to clean their teeth, feet, and body. A pack of wet wipes isn't enough; if you end up needing your pack to survive indefinitely (again, probably as a refugee), you absolutely will need to be concerned with lice, fleas, ticks, bites, and dental hygiene. We often forget, but the black plague killed a third of Europe—spread by the ubiquitous flea. Have you thought about flea and tick repellant? Lice shampoo?

Another major concern when on the move is keeping your feet healthy. Even a reasonably short (fifteen miles or so) movement with a pack can leave them in rough shape. In inclement conditions where people become reluctant to take their feet from their boots, immersion foot can occur. Do you have talcum powder to keep your feet dry? A few changes of socks? Take care of your feet. Change and dry your socks daily, even if you only have a few pairs, and dry/clean your feet every day, too.

A bed up off the ground and decent shelter can go a long way toward helping, but keep in mind that you'll need a plan to keep disease at a minimum. In the extremely unlikely case of the Type III emergency, you can expect health and hygiene to play a major role in the die-off. As populations of scavengers and parasites increase and populations of bacteria bloom in the wake of disaster, the indefinite timeline will challenge your resources. Add in a lack of sanitation for solid waste and cleaning methods, and the chances of diseases increases dramatically. Even hand sanitizer is going to leave some bacteria alive—and heads up: The ones that survive eventually become the ones that reproduce. Sanitation and potable water are eternal concerns; make sure your pack provides you a measure of protection against disease, and a way to stay clean and hydrated. Finally, a camp shower is a lightweight piece of gear that can go a long way toward improving morale and hygiene. And, clean your teeth! A folding toothbrush and some mouthwash won't take up much weight or space.

Acquisition

Acquisition can mean a variety of things, and we won't get too deep into it here. The bottom line is that some very simple tools can aid you in acquiring things in a post-disaster environment that have been abandoned or rendered inaccessible to others. A simple coat hanger, siphon, screwdriver, pick set, spring punch, and door shim can go a long way in securing your ability to get critical resources. If you're resourceful and skilled, these tools can take up minimal space and open a lot of doors, figuratively and literally.

A good pry bar also goes a long way. Even stubborn locks can usually be persuaded by a combination of the tools above and a decent pry bar. As far as pry bars go, the "Cats Paw" really can't be beat for opening up stubborn doors. It can be had at any hardware store for under $20 and will open most doors. Multi-use tools like the Gerber Downrange Tomahawk have found a place in our team's gear. Just remember that doors that are locked are usually done so for a reason. Be intelligent about how you approach such situations and remember that making enemies is always bad for business.

Protection

If we're honest with ourselves, you scrolled past all the stuff above and honed in on protection. Don't do that. Protection is a serious discussion that needs to be had—so important that we don't advocate keeping it in your second line, for the most part. It should be on your person, and the sustainment bag should keep you in the fight. Like acquisition, this subject is touchy, so here's what we'll say on the matter: Rifles are a huge red flag. When they're out, people will view it as an aggressive posture. Don't project force that you can't back up.

Don't neglect interpersonal skills and managing unknown contacts. Rifle ammo goes a long way if you do your job, pistol ammo does not. Get some training in managing the collapsed urban environment. If possible, find a way to make money living in them. If you don't, don't expect that you'll know much about them. Pistols can be carried more places with less signature.

Don't neglect driving skills and security while on the road.

If you have rifles, you should probably have friends…with rifles.

If you're arranging your equipment in sequential lines, you should be able to increase your posture to include ammunition-carrying equipment that doesn't interfere with your other lines of equipment. This means you won't have to change where your first line is situated if you pack smart.

Don't forget non-lethal problems. Pepper Spray (oleoresin capsicum or OC spray) can be useful in dispersing crowds, where smoke can be used for masking movement, or for signaling.

If you do carry a pistol, carry spare ammunition and magazines. Stop training to drop them; if you're in a real emergency, those are the only things keeping your pistol from being a single shot. Worry less about being fast and more about finding cover and working the problem correctly. Train to retain, at least part of the time.

Remember a few things:

Our sidearm, some basic medical equipment, and some core EDC tools should be a part of our first line equipment.

The goal with protection is to head off problems, and if absolutely necessary, respond with a surprising and overwhelming amount of violence. If you're going to guns, you've failed. It's now a measure of damage control to see how little you can lose. Be smart and use awareness, interpersonal skills, and tactics to make the situation bend in your favor before it breaks over the chaos.

If we're being honest with ourselves, the chances of needing a fighting rifle to hold it down is really, really low. You should be spending 80 percent of your range time training with your pistol and keeping sharp by running some drills with that rifle out to 300 yards or so from time to time. Fighting in general is a high risk, low probability event, so consider it and get good, but be realistic and try not to let your guns and gear define your plan.

Conflict

Our policy on conflict is simple. Avoid it. However, it can be necessary to ensure greater capability if things get bad enough. During natural disasters, communities often come together for a common defense, and this might mean shouldering a pack and rifle. If so, it's a good idea to pack three or so magazines or some specific tools, such as armor. As with the others, if you intend to show up for a common defense, you'd better be competent, mature, and dependable.

Special Purpose Equipment

Apart from our main equipment, there are times when we know an objective will require us to have special equipment that we ordinarily don't need. When this occurs, give thought to how to split the equipment among your group. Oftentimes it's sufficient to keep this stuff as vehicle equipment, as well.

Communications

Communications generally don't need to be as elaborate as others would have you believe. Even in emergencies, cell towers go up pretty quickly, and if your phone has Wi-Fi, there are apps that turns it into a walkie-talkie. Even better, these apps allow you to form groups that prevent outside listeners. Given that handheld radios don't perform substantially better and they require extra logistics (batteries and charging docks), the cell phone is generally sufficient. That said, there are times when handhelds are great, for example when traveling by road in a convoy. Those options that don't require Bluetooth or cell towers should certainly be kept in reserve.

You'll often hear that a Ham radio is a necessary addition. What's not mentioned is that Ham operation is a very technical skill that requires some dedication to be used properly. They're excellent when used by a Ham Radio Operator (HRO) who knows his stuff, but if you're not committed to learning the radios, the cheap ones are not much better than a walkie-talkie. If you are committed, Ham radios are a tremendous asset and can be used to great effect during emergencies.

Power Production

Field expedient power is largely a myth. Our experience with using solar has been underwhelming, and as of the time of this writing, no great options for portable, efficient power have knocked our socks off. That said, solar can occasionally be a useful item for a small group to carry, especially if the goal is to use it for communications. While better suited for a vehicle or base station (mobile and base station radios have substantially more range and capability), handheld Ham radios can often reach pretty far with a good line of sight and a repeater network. As such, keeping a good 40W solar panel with your team could get a charge on handheld radios and get a signal out, provided you've got a good battery bank. Likewise, it can serve to charge cell phones, tablets or laptops, and GPS devices. These can be a huge asset in gathering information during a disaster, so having the option (especially at home or in the vehicle) is wise.

We have had good luck with EcoFlow batteries, such as the River and Delta/DeltaPro. While expensive, these devices act as a charge controller and inverter, and offer a ton of options for recharging. Done intelligently, you can be using the energy generated by a panel or your cars alternator to keep topping the batteries off, while using more elaborate setups for a true "base" of operations.

Power is finicky, and it's hard to say what the viability of alternative energy is, long term.

Bivouac/Overland

Our strategy for traveling out of our sustainment bag isn't comfort. It's more about being resourceful and using the environment to our advantage. Once we start considering larger problems that require evacuation, or of course going for a camping trip, a couple small tents or shelters can go a long way in terms of getting good rest—which is absolutely a part of health and hygiene.

When it comes to bivouac equipment, shelter, water, food, and security, the equipment can be spread across the group to increase the group's efficiency. This is especially useful in overland travel with a group where sanitation, waste, food prep and dishes, and cooking all become group tasks.

Rappelling

Like medicine or communications, rappelling is a technical skill that requires incredible attention to detail and experience to be done safely. That said, keeping a rope with some rappelling gear can keep your options open, should you need it. Most of the time, for short drop and emergency rappels, an EXO descender on one member, and a rigger's belt, some rappelling leg straps, and a pair of gloves will get you over the obstacle. Occasionally, for larger terrain features, it's good to have purpose-build dynamic rope.

Packing List

No talk about backpacks is complete without a list. We're hoping that now that you've got the reasoning, you'll be able to beat us to the punch.

32-ounce Nalgene bottle with stainless steel cup (titanium is light, but man will it burn you—literally! —as titanium tends to get hotter than steel more quickly)

- Katadyne Vario (or similar) water filter
- Siphon hose
- Bivouac appropriate for your climate. Extra insulation as needed.
- Tarp
- 55-Gallon contractor bags x3
- USCG signaling smoke

- Spare magazine (Pistol) x4
- Locking carabiners x2
- Non-locking carabiners x2
- Figure 8 descender (or Rescue 8)
- Wire hanger
- Pocket chainsaw
- Fishing kit (hooks, sinkers, line, and bobbers)
- Snare wire
- Allen wrenches
- Crescent wrench
- Compass
- US map (Local area as needed)
- Pocket knife
- ChemLights
- Fire starting items (Lighter, flint and steel, etc.)
- Headlamp
- Full grain leather gloves
- Spring punch
- Note pad and pens
- Coleman burner
- Paracord (50 feet)
- Food, Mountain House/MRE x4 (stripped to cardboard, which can be used for fire starting)
- Snacks
- Clean socks, shirt, and underwear x3
- Ground pad
- Folding cot
- Spare parts

Third Line of Equipment

The third line of equipment is our cache gear. We call it this because it could be extra equipment or supplies you keep in your vehicle, your home, or at another location. This equipment consists of extra food, medical supplies, power generation equipment, fuel, and tools to help you if life gets flipped turned upside down, and rather than a fresh prince, you find yourself without a job or prospects.

How to Wear Everyday Carry

First, how you wear your equipment is largely a matter of what you want out of your equipment, but we caution you to be consistent if you can. Even among our team, there's a wide range of differences in how we approach EDC. One of the realizations we try to acknowledge is that in the last ten years, a lot of new gun owners entering the world of firearms aren't "gun people." They're not going to wear 5.11 tactical pants with a rigger's belt and a G19 in an outside the waistband holster. They might carry a very small gun in an entirely unconventional holster, so our goal is to assist people in finding the best practice for them, even if we don't think the method is optimal.

Accessibility and retention are the most important things. If you can't access your tools while sitting, while on your back, or while grappling or buckled in your vehicle, then rethink how you're carrying. Likewise, you need to do everything you can to prevent your tools from coming loose or being taken from you. This is especially a problem with a lot of the belly band or elastic "holsters" marketed to women. If you can't run, jump, climb, or fight in it, don't rely on it. Lastly, we want to be able to access our first line gear under our second line. If you can do these things efficiently, you're on the right track.

So, if there's a mass shooting, and you find yourself in gym shorts with a .22 AirLite revolver, are you wrong? No. You just have different options than a guy who's carrying a full-sized pistol or who has recovered a rifle from his vehicle. If you're the guy rollin' with a rifle in your trunk, are you wrong? No. As long as you've correctly assessed the risks of leaving a weapon in your car and don't leave it unsecured. So, who is wrong? The guys who do these things without giving them thought, without building the necessary skills, and then selecting the equipment that makes them as efficient as possible.

Don't waste your time with squawking over whether you need a reload—get the skills, assess what's likely, then identify what equipment will make you as efficient as possible. When it comes to telling you what you need, everybody is wrong. Only you can define your needs. Fair warning: starting with gear just makes you wrong, too. Don't get too hung up about having tons of stuff in your EDC. It doesn't have to be an expanse of gear that looks like it's off a police officer's tool belt; it just needs to be the most efficient gear for your circumstances.

Keep It Concealed

A final thought on carrying a firearm: No one needs to see your gun. Some people in some places can get away with open carry, but unless you're in a profession that requires you to open carry, you're handing one of the most significant tactical advantages you have over to your adversaries: that element of surprise. If you want to make a political statement, there are better ways of doing it.

EVACUATION

There are two types of evacuation: preemptive and emergency. If you're trying to walk your way out of a catastrophe, you become a refugee, not a glamorous roughneck with a rifle and a devil-may-care attitude. You'll need a tremendous amount of fitness, skill, and specific equipment to improve your situation by leaving the affected area, especially by foot. Even if you *are* capable, how about those in your care?

Even as we discuss the utility of evacuating in a vehicle, we need to be aware that vehicles themselves can be damaged, destroyed, or succumb to poor maintenance. When this happens, we need to be aware of how the Rules of 3 can affect us. For example, if a bridge collapsed underneath you, what would your environment become and how would it change your access to the critical resources?

The Disaster Environment

One concept we use to better understand how to deal with emergencies is the post-disaster environment. In all cases, emergencies change something about our environment. Whether it's how we interact with other people, the number of trees and grass burning around us, or how much live ordnance we have to step around, disasters create hazards that ordinarily aren't present. Most of the time, disasters come in two main phases: immediate threats to your personal health and safety and restricting access to critical resources.

Once the show starts, you're dealing with the threats brought on by the disaster environment. These can be natural or man-made, so let's look at two that are both similar and separate. In recent protests, burning debris has been a component of stopping traffic and creating choke points. We see fire as a threat to health and mobility. In both cases, the emergency restricts your ability to move and your access to resources. You can't stop for fuel or to ask directions. There's no place to pull off and look over your map without an increased risk of a direct threat to your life. Both of these environments present some major hazards for travel: debris and smoke, thermal considerations (for both you and your vehicle), and situations in which more time equals decreased chances of a good outcome.

Consider how earthquakes, hurricanes, checkpoints, civil unrest, and other disasters affect your environment. If you got out ahead of the problem—congratulations! Your vehicle and driving skills probably don't really matter that much. If you didn't, the conditions around you might get really difficult, so it pays to check some boxes and have some experience driving in tough conditions.

Vehicles in Disasters

Life Support on the Go

With all this considered, it makes some sense that having a decently capable rig—one that you can live out of for a few weeks —is not only enriching from the perspective of adventure, but it can also do a lot for your personal resilience. Not only that, but it's excellent recreation that, when done right, builds confidence, familiarity, and good habits for traveling away from grid support. So, which vehicle is the best? The one you have.

Most vehicles can be made to be pretty serviceable, even more so if you've got a 4-wheel drive vehicle with a little ground clearance. Like most things, if you get out and use it, you'll find the areas that need to be improved upon, and experience is the best teacher. While there are all sorts of ultimate bugout vehicles circulating the internet with laughable $250,000 price tags, the truth is, you can do a lot with not all that much. For a hundredth of that price, you could have a well-equipped Jeep, Toyota, or even *gasp* Land Rover that, with a little love, can be a solid performer on the trails. Even older F-350 Econoline vans and the like are better choices when you consider the money going in for what you get in return (and with "van life" becoming a trend, it might actually make a pretty cool project!). Also, motorcycles set up for touring or dual-sport are lighter, faster, and provide a much better cruising range than bigger, heavier 4x4s at the cost of some storage space.

Most of the ISG crew rolls with Land Cruisers for their mechanical simplicity, toughness, off-road capability, and parts availability, but you'd truly be better off with a Subaru that you are intimately familiar with on road and trail than a $230,000 rig that you rely on simply for luxury around town but still have no real idea what life is like off-road. Establishing your vehicle's limits is something that can only be done through experience.

To polish this all off, "bugging out" is a refugee's move. As we've said over and over again, you need to have a plan. Just as with the second line sustainment bags, our vehicles can extend our sustainment by providing us an extra layer of protection against the Rules of 3 as we move—especially if we move smart, with other people, and with an eye on security. Be deliberate and stay a step ahead of the reaper. When it comes to getting out ahead of an emergency, a high-capability vehicle is one of the few prepper-culture topics that really isn't an outright flight of fantasy (but that doesn't mean your bugout rig *should* be).

Keep it sane, have a solid plan, and if that plan fails, look to your rig like you would your EDC: It's for solving the physical problems that we try to head off through good judgment and awareness. The vehicle is just another piece of equipment that gives us options for solving problems.

Vehicle Baseline: Where to Start

Before we really dig in, this is going to be largely centered around 4-wheeled vehicles, as most of the ISG crew have families, which makes motorcycles a little less practical. With that said, a good dual-sport motorcycle, like a properly set up KLR, could be an excellent setup that would be far more fuel efficient and could still store a good amount of supplies. For now, we'll talk mainly about passenger vehicles that a family could reasonably afford and comfortably fit even with some cargo to see them through the Type II emergency.

In this section, we'll prioritize some of the features that you should look for and discuss how important they are. You'll want to find a vehicle that has these following characteristics; while you can certainly do a lot without some of them, they are time-proven to be beneficial to any off-road travel.

A mechanically sound vehicle, and a vehicle everyday carry kit (VEDC) for it: For the most part, this is just a "check the box" investment in time and money. There's a staggering amount of people who have vehicles with reasonably low mileage that are in terrible shape because they don't perform routine maintenance. On the other hand, there are high mileage vehicles that are surprisingly clean because the owners change out parts before they break. If you're the latter, keep doing what you're doing. Learning to do your own maintenance and repairs is also a worthwhile investment in your time. If you can't do it yourself, make friends with someone who can and find a way to help them. Before we get to the list, here are a few things to keep in mind.

Keeping clean fluids and swapping out wearable parts will go a long way in making sure you don't end up with surprises when you need them the least.

 Keep your fuel tank above half, and ideally, above three-quarters of a tank. Not only does this ensure you'll have some range if you have to leave in a hurry, but most of the contaminants in your fuel settle to the bottom of the tank. Continually running it low pushes those contaminants through the fuel system and can cause clogged fuel filters and damage to fuel pumps. Top off and view the half-full line as empty. Some jerry cans or an auxiliary tank are a huge help—if you do end up in tough terrain, assume you're going to get about 33 percent lower fuel economy than you would during around-town driving. This can mean single digits for many larger 4x4s.

Here are some things to keep in your vehicle permanently:

- A tool kit that has sockets and wrenches common to your vehicle.
- A spare set of belts or serpentine belt
- Fluids, specially oil and cooland. Brake and steering fluid are also wise.
- Tire Repair Kit/Fix-a-flat
- Tow Straps
- Jumper Cables
  A good flashlight, and you'll probably want a head mounted one.
- FIPG - form in place gasket. This can be a lfiesaver.

Next, let's take a look at some of the common features we generally want in our vehicles. It's not necessary to have every single one, but given the purpose behind ISG, the following are things we have found useful.

4-wheel drive and some ground clearance: A solid 80 percent of the obstacles you face are going to be about approach (front), departure (rear), and break-over (center) angles so you don't trash your ride trying to get over them. A vehicle that's too low to the ground will feel the crunch of steep terrain more than one that's got a bit of lift but be aware that the lift can create a dangerously high center of gravity.

Tires that are in good condition and a full-size spare tire: Regardless of whether you're in a minivan or a Jeep, having decent tires that are capable of handling tough terrain is a consumable, mandatory component of your vehicle. A full-sized spare tire is essential if you're going to be in tough driving conditions for any duration. It's a simple thing that's easily overlooked until you need it.

Fire suppression*: Mount a couple fire extinguishers where they can be easily accessed, even when the vehicle is loaded down. The appropriate type of fire extinguisher for a vehicle is a Class 5 BC. It's effective on liquids and gasses (Class B) and energized electrical components (Class C). This is a simple, easy, and inexpensive addition that can really make a huge difference.

Medical kit*: For everything from dangerous trauma to upset stomachs, it's important than you have a well-stocked medical kit in your rig if you're going to be out of the rat race for a while. A good medical kit will have equipment for trauma, (tourniquets, chest seal, hemostatics, and shears) as well as more mundane needs, such as moleskin, bandages, gauze, and antibiotic ointments.

Differential lockers: In a vehicle with standard, unlocked differentials, the vehicle will automatically divert power to the wheel with the least amount of traction. This can be useful on a slippery surface such as snow or ice. However, off-road, when the wheel with the least amount of traction might be free-spinning in the air, it's a distinct handicap. Locking differentials allow you to reinforce success rather than failure, giving the wheels that have traction more power. For this reason, they are a very nice feature to have on a vehicle that will be off-road. Many vehicles come with different types of locking differentials—center, front, rear, or a combination thereof.

Good suspension: A good suspension that's well-matched to your vehicle will not only improve your ability to overcome obstacles, but it'll help ensure you don't damage your rig. Keep in mind that you should consider the weight of your loaded vehicle when you decide on suspension; this often comes at the cost of a heavier spring that's less comfortable "on road" but will help keep you from dragging your tail on the rocks off-road.

Even if you have an older vehicle that's paid off, there are probably some ways to invest a little money to have a more capable rig. Moreover, while the accessory market for off-road vehicles looks pretty much the same as it does for guns or any other "hobby" item, you really don't need much to get off the ground and out in the woods.

Real talk: If this is as far as you get, you're probably good to go. For emergencies, camping, and some adventuring, you've got 80 percent of it covered by checking off the above suggestions. If you want to push a little deeper into capability, there are some things you can add to your build that will push you past the ability to deal with Type I emergencies and into those longer term, less threatening situations where you need to sustain yourself without support for a couple weeks.

*Medical and fire suppression tools should be both accessible, and clearly marked! In the ISG store, we have stickers that you can use to mark the window where you keep these items for quick identification during emergencies. This is great if you have to direct someone else to recover them for you.

https://isg-store.myshopify.com/collections/stickers-patches

Upgrades: The First Steps in the "Build"
Bull Bar/Winch bumper: The only reason the bull bar is mentioned before the winch is that in most cases, you'll need something on which to mount the winch. A good bull bar is going to help prevent front-end damage to your vehicle, as well as provide a place to mount a winch and (once you've got lockers and other important upgrades) some extra lighting.

Winch: A winch is a tremendous asset for both helping recover stuck vehicles and moving obstacles. The rule of thumb when selecting a winch is to double your vehicle's weight. However, with a snatch block and some skill, you can greatly increase the amount of weight your winch is capable of pulling. Don't forget that when you're setting up for expeditions, your weight will be well in excess of the vehicles curb weight. The winch requires some skill and knowledge, so don't overlook some proper training.

Air compressor: The ability to use compressed air is one of those required items when traveling off-road. Not only is it reasonably inexpensive, but it's mandatory to get the most out of your tires if the traction gets tough. In addition to helping you air after airing down, it's a great thing to have if you happen to find you have a slow leak.

Decent Roof Rack: A decent mounting platform on the roof expands your carrying capacity and gives options for storing extra fuel or cargo. It is also necessary if you choose to add a rooftop tent.

Self-Containment: Self-Containment is the ability to set up a camp from which you can rest, cook, clean, and dispose of physical and biological waste. It's remarkably easy to set up and doesn't have to be elaborate. A simple Coleman stove, a wash basin with some cloth and a scrubber, and a few WaterBricks will cover you for most of your cooking and cleaning. For biological waste, options range from composting toilets to using a shovel to dig a cathole. How elaborate you want to go on this is entirely up to you—just remember, the more experience you have on the trail, the better you'll understand the risks and rewards of each approach.

Functional Upgrades

Armor: Once you've got some of the above options checked off, it's not a bad idea to start looking at skid plates and differential armor. One time, a Montero came into our partner shop after hitting a jack stand that had fallen out of another vehicle. The Montero's differential was blown apart by hit. This was a crippling injury for the vehicle, and while trail damage is likely to be a little more gradual, it's still a looming threat that you should address to keep your rig from being damaged when you need it the most.

Trail communications: Whether you're using a tricked-out Ham setup that you can use to talk to astronauts or a couple GMRS radios, communications (especially in longer convoys of vehicles) can really help to keep everyone in the loop. Not only is this good for morale if you're the trail leader, but it guarantees you're not going to be left behind if you're bringing up the rear and have a problem. It can also be useful for communicating approaching vehicles or hazards. It sucks being the only guy without a radio.

Sleeping Arrangements: This is a contentious point. The rooftop tent (RTT) has become a symbol for the urban escapist to signal to everyone that they make decent money and are ready for adventure at the drop of a hat. But more than just status, the RTT is truly an excellent, expedient way to set up a camp. There are some drawbacks, and there are other methods that work well, too, but having some place to rest is a big part of multi-day adventures, and an RTT goes a long way toward keeping you sheltered in emergencies. The fast setup comes at a cost though; if you're using a ground tent, you can leave and return to camp in your vehicle without having to tear down and set up again.

Luxury Upgrades

All of these upgrade suggestions might sound like a lot, and not every person needs everything on the list, but they are some pretty standard upgrades that turn a factory vehicle into a very capable off-road expedition rig. We've decided they're "luxury" because the role they fill can be filled by simpler, less expensive systems. These upgrades make life easier and more comfortable, and as such, aren't really necessary for everyone... especially if you're just starting out.

Dual battery system: If you're off road "bugging out," you're probably going to be sleeping in your vehicle or somewhere very near it. This means your vehicle is also likely your sole source of power. Most of us have radios and cell phones charging in the truck while moving, but if you've gotta cool it for a couple days, then it pays to have some extra power (solar or wind, if you can safely tie it in). Having a dual battery system is an excellent first step that shows that engineers have thought through off-road, aftermarket accessories.

Fridge and cooking utilities: It might sound like a luxury item, but if you're going anywhere out of the main channel for more than a couple days, your ice chest isn't likely to hold up. If we're talking bugging out, which could take weeks depending on how bad things are, then having an onboard refrigerator would show a lot of forethought. There are a wide variety of options out there these days, so a fridge doesn't have to break the bank. If done correctly, it should have a tie-down and some organizational drawers with it. Additionally, something as simple as a stable platform for cutting and preparing food and a simple propane burner is huge, as well. Not only do these items save on time, but the organizational aspect means you aren't digging around looking for everything.

Internal Storage and Organization: Even if all you can get your hands on are some Tupperware bins, they're *really* useful for helping you know where your trail gear or maintenance items are, and you don't have to dig through piles of clothing, toilet paper, squashed loaves of bread, and sleeping bags to get to what you need. A good system should also help secure some of those items in the event of a rollover so you don't have a bunch of projectiles flying around the cabin. Having a rack that sits above the cargo bay is an excellent way to keep more vulnerable items from being smashed, as well.

Extra Fuel: Most off-road vehicles aren't fuel efficient, and a 25-gallon tank might only take you three hundred miles or so, which is abysmal and a serious problem if you're in an emergency that has a fuel shortage. An auxiliary fuel tank is a great way to extend your range without having to strap jerry cans to the back of your rig, but they come at a heavy price—often costing in excess of $3000. The good news is they're much harder to detect and steal. Further, it's pretty hard to claim your vehicle is the *ultimate* anything for off-road if it's missing these elements.

Bug Out Vehicles

Of all the topics surrounding disaster preparedness, perhaps none is so far-fetched or flogged to death than "bugging out." With the possible exception of everyday carry, it's hard to find a more ubiquitous or overplayed topic. Our view on bugging out in vehicles is that yeah, it can actually make sense. Conceptually, people escape floods, wildfires, hurricanes, and the like all the time by packing up their vehicle, hitting the freeway, and getting out of the path of destruction.

Keep in mind that idling for hours burns through gas. Soggy grass can bog down a few vehicles, too. But here's the thing: If you plan ahead, you can "bug out" in a Prius. The Prius isn't the ultimate in anything except being the understated whipping post of the automotive world (and being the vehicle that no one bothers to look in for a side-folding AK) but getting out of a disaster is coming through doesn't usually mean going off-road. A bugged-out vehicle doesn't necessarily mean it can go anywhere, but it does mean beating the masses. You don't have to have the coolest stuff to do the best work.

Here's the pinch of all of this: We don't pick the emergency. Getting out ahead of the masses is fine if there is a hurricane and you've been watching it develop for a week. If there is an earthquake, what then? How about a volcanic eruption? What about a pandemic? What changes and what's the best all-around approach? If you don't plan ahead, chances are, unless you've got a lifestyle that emphasizes off-road adventure, you're going to simply find yourself in more trouble regardless of what you drive.

SHELTER

Drastically under appreciated, exposure-related injuries are both easy to mitigate and extremely damaging once inflicted. Even a moderate sunburn with no risk of long-term damage can cause incapacitation if it impacts the wrong area of the body. In this section, we will examine some common environments, the risks they offer, and methods of keeping out of the reaper's reach. Here, we're going to interrogate some concepts surrounding shelter— what it is, what it is not, and how to get yourself out of the elements. In addition, it is critically important as this process unfolds to be aware of the impacts that exposure can have on your health, so this will be discussed as well. Again, we offer two very strong recommendations:

Buy and read *Six Ways In and Twelve Ways Out* by US-RSOG

Go practice these skills! There is no substitute for experience. You could read one hundred books and they still won't give you the level of skill you gain from your first successful wet-weather fire and sleeping dry during a heavy rain in a shelter you built with your hands.

Preventing Exposure

The Rules of 3 give us around three hours of exposure before we begin to succumb to the elements, making shelter is one of our single most important considerations. This chapter is going to largely fill the mainstream ideas of what constitutes a wilderness shelter, but we believe in simple, effective techniques practiced toward perfection and mental flexibility. Once you understand the concepts, it becomes easier to improvise, but that doesn't mean you should set out without adequate gear and clothing. This is critically important here because it's difficult to consider all environments; it's incumbent on you to learn your area, know its tendencies, and have the mental flexibility to survive. Again, get out and be miserable. Go experience nature's cruelty instead of admiring her beauty from a distance.

Shelter can be loosely described as a *state* where the environment is not compromising your ability to survive. Why not a *place*? Well, I've met bums with their clothes stuffed with newspaper to create dead air space, huddled against walls. The place wasn't doing much for them, but the state they created was at least keeping them alive. Say what you will, but the homeless in the US are good at what they do and are, in some ways, the most resourceful people in society. Plenty more on them later.

It helps to think of thermal injuries as a sort of scale in which the time and the severity are working against you. So, whereas surviving in street clothes in 45-degree weather might be possible for 72 hours, at −45 degrees Fahrenheit, your timeline might be more like ten to twenty minutes. When we begin securing shelter, that's where we start: How bad is it and how long do we have?

Fieldcraft: Creating an Isothermal Environment

Fieldcraft is the skill of the pioneer; hunting, scavenging, building fire and shelter, and collecting water are all part of fieldcraft. In this first part, let's discuss the factors that are, by and large, controlled by you: your mode of dress and selection of equipment. Thermal injuries have common ground in that they are almost all environmental—that is to say some external factor is: Depleting water from the body faster than it is replaced, or The water in the body is crystallizing or expanding, causing cell membranes to rupture, or

The internal temperature of the body heats or cools too rapidly and can't reach equilibrium fast enough.

In a healthy human in a temperate area, these factors are moderated by homeostasis, so it's important to know that our main goal here is simply to assist our body in maintaining a core temperature of 98.6 degrees and staying properly hydrated. It cannot be understated that even in extremely cold environments, you need to drink a quart of water every hour. Drink before you become thirsty—not after.

Without going into the minutia, there is a three-legged stool we can use to keep our body well regulated:

- Physical conditioning
- Proper hydration and diet
- Appropriate attire

The first two speak for themselves, and the third is easy to misunderstand. Don't think because it came from a big-name store that it's appropriate. As mentioned before, a secret from the homeless: that water-resistant jacket stuffed with newspaper is more appropriate than the designer sweater you can't rely on to keep you warm all night. So, before we get into any of the elaborate skills for building field expedient shelters, let's state this plainly:

Dress Smart

There's a saying: Cotton kills. You'll hear experienced hikers and backpackers advise against it. While cotton itself, at least in the form of clothing, doesn't exactly kill, cotton soaks moisture and retains it nicely, especially in the high desert or mountains where temperatures drop drastically. Cotton tends to soak up sweat or rain and keep it close to your body. Once the temperature drops, this can induce hypothermia and become a major issue. Avoiding cotton in clothing is sort of like avoiding GMO foods; it can be done, but it's going to cost an arm and a leg, and the results might not be that different. If you have the choice, wearing materials that are well-suited to keeping you dry and warm are optimal, but don't believe for a second that you're going to die just because you're wearing jeans and a normal shirt when the unthinkable happens. The majority of any struggle for survival is mindset, so start off with the mentality that you'll make do with whatever you're handed. With that said, be mindful of how your clothes will help or hurt you, but don't resign yourself to death because they're not ideal.

Layering

For cold weather environments, your base layer of clothing should be Capiline, polypropylene, or a polyester composite that channels moisture away from your body. Mid-layer clothing made from polyester has always worked well for me as it doesn't trap moisture and it allows for the passage of heat. We can't emphasize enough the utility of high technology secondary mid-layers such as Polartec for keeping the heat in, but don't dismiss tried-and-true fabrics like wool. Wool is naturally one of the best materials available for warmth and water resistance in temperate climates. This, in conjunction with a good water-resistant windbreaker, will go a long way in providing you warmth while you're active. Throwing a mid-layer synthetic sweater between wool and your jacket can provide substantial insulation against any cold.

There are special considerations when you're in the extreme environments of the western deserts in Arizona, Nevada, California, and west Texas, or the inter-mountain regions of Alaska, Montana, Colorado, Utah and Wyoming. Extremes in these environments demand special considerations and skills for survival.

Cold Environments

Keep in mind that snow itself can be an insulator, and if you find yourself without shelter, a simple ice igloo with a vent can help keep some of the ambient chill off of you. When you envision an igloo, you're probably thinking of blocks of ice being stacked together. For survival, you don't have to build something semi-permanent that you can live in…it just has to get you through the night without dying. A small opening, a vent for fumes, and some snow packed to where it's not at risk of collapsing onto you will do. If you can do that, you'll likely be able to use a fire to keep warm. Remember that snow near the fire will melt, so it's a good idea to have a trench for the melted snow to run into.

To relate what you've learned from Understanding Emergencies and our Rules of 3 to survival tactics in cold environments, consider this: A family was recently killed in Colorado after a car accident. They went off the road (a Type I emergency) and came to rest in a snowy gulch. They survived the initial crash but found themselves trapped in the cold (a Type II emergency). They transitioned from a direct threat to their lives (the initial accident) to being subject to the environment. While it's difficult to say exactly what could have made the difference, being able to get to or create some shelter, fire, and signal for rescue may have saved the family from such a fate. It's a terrible tragedy that may have been preventable, at least to some degree, by an understanding of how the environment works against you.

Hot Environments

In hot environments, like the desert southwest, one of the most important considerations is the dehydrating severe heat in the daytime and the rapid cooling during the night. This can cause the moisture that is sweated out during the day to get cold and result in chills and hypothermia during the night hours. For this reason, having water as well as ways to collect it and ways to keep the heat off of you during the day is crucial.

The best hours for activity when trying to survive in this climate are those around dusk and dawn, though night can provide opportunities to move as well, depending on the light situation. A well-ventilated shelter with good protection from the sun is the first order of business. If you can find water or even vegetation, situating your camp near those can be of help, but be sure not to set up in an arroyo (a gully formed by floodwaters in the desert southwest) or other areas in which transition season floods could kill you.

Whenever you get into a situation, think about the risks of thermal injuries and consider what you have at hand. Are your shoes adequate for the conditions? Consider putting a plastic bag between your socks and boots to keep rain or snow out but remember to let your feet dry out periodically. Are your clothes soaked? If so—build a fire and wait! Allow them to dry. Like drinking before you're thirsty, stay warm and dry before you get cold and wet. Don't take risks that will compromise your thermal equilibrium if you absolutely don't have to. Survival usually means adjusting the pace at which you live life to nature's speed—not your own. It'll be a surprisingly slow effort or a surprisingly swift end.

Fieldcraft: Awareness

It might seem self-evident, but while you're out, ask yourself about your surroundings. Are you in a city, the suburbs, a forest, or a desert? What's your elevation? What kinds of flora and fauna are found here? What kind of supplies can you scavenge? What type of weather conditions can be expected here? Estimate the maximum and minimum temperatures and any wind chill that might affect you. This type of orientation will build in a natural sense that will help quickly establish priorities if you find yourself in trouble.

One of the most critical rules of survival is not letting anything go to waste. Knowing your surroundings can help turn a discarded beer can into a water filter. Knowing the types of wood around you can help determine their combustibility and their suitability for things like cooking—no one wants to have to eat pitch-flavored fish in a pinch. It's bad for morale.

This is where we need to start looking at things such as what materials you have on hand, site selection for your camp/fire/latrine, and begin assessing what materials you have at hand.

Conceptual Checkpoint

Go to your window and look out: write down what you see and what you know about it. Spend a few minutes observing: What's going on out there? Is it hot? Cold? Are there blocks of busy people or a herd of goats? Is there litter? Can it be used? List all the objects you see, even if they seem to have no use. Think about what's there, how you can use it, and what you could do to avoid thermal hazards.

Oftentimes, thing we're not used to using look useless. Try to develop an eye for how something can be used, and then give it a try. In temperate environments, most shelter can be made out of mostly natural materials. Branches and boughs from evergreens are good protection from rain and decent insulation from the cold ground. Lashing your materials together can be done by improvising cordage, which can be made out of anything from existing rope or shoelaces to lengths of ivy.

Improvising Rope or Cordage

To improvise rope, take a twelve-inch section of a material that can be bound together, such as vines, shoelaces, salvaged wires, whatever, and cut it into alternating lengths of six and twelve inches. This isn't a hard and fast rule, but it helps keep the weave of the cordage tighter than using much longer lengths. If you only have longer lengths, that's fine, but consider tying them off every four or so. Wrap the six-inch and twelve-inch lengths around each another and tie the loose end of the six-inch length to the next

twelve-inch length. Continue wrapping and repeat the process until you've got cordage long enough for your intended task (lengthening existing rope can be done using the double fisherman's knot). The QR code above will direct you to a video example of how to tie improvised cordage together.

Shelter building is largely an experiential task. Get out, give it a try, and sleep in your creation. As you get better at building more efficient shelters, gradually use less-sophisticated equipment (if your environment allows you to) until you know what you can get away with in terms of what you absolutely must have and what things simply make life more comfortable.

OXYGEN

The most vital resource we ignore.

Oxygen needs no introduction. You know it, you love it, and we take it perilously for granted. In some ways, oxygen should be the last topic we talk about. The situations that deprive you of it are, in general, the ones that require the quickest thinking over the shortest possible timeline. So, let's talk oxygen.

Oxygen makes up about 21 percent of the air you breathe. The rest is Nitrogen (~78%) and Argon and other trace gasses (~1%), which are not used in respiration. At any given time, your body uses about 8 percent of the oxygen you breathe in, and this is why you're able to give that other 13 percent to those in need via CPR. Oxygenation of your bloodstream causes diffusion between your cells (which themselves breathe, trading fresh oxygen for waste and carbon dioxide) and allows your body to channel nutrients into your cells and waste products out. Interruptions to this process, as you might guess, are harmful to your health.

What might cause an interruption to normal breathing? It's easiest to frame scenarios in which we might be short on oxygen into two cases, best and worst case, and then assess the median for probability. So, let's cut out the middleman and take a look at a likely culprit: The I35W bridge collapse in Minnesota. It wasn't an earthquake that caused it. It wasn't terrorists, cosmic rays, or male pattern baldness, either. It just collapsed due to wear and tear.

This could happen anywhere. The probability might be low (though increasing), but your normal routine may bring you into this disaster's direct proximity (considering most areas have some major rivers and feature bridges), and you'd never even know it.

The United States has among the worst ratings in the Western world in terms of its infrastructure, but as with most "common" emergencies, they're not sexy or exciting enough to think about, so they go largely ignored by preppers and survivalists.

So, if you're driving and a bridge collapses, you end up in the water, and your access to a critical resource, oxygenated blood, is on a ticking clock. This isn't the only threat to your oxygen supply; there are also swimming accidents, loss of cabin pressure in an airline, being choked, and carbon monoxide poisoning. But for now, let's think about what we would do in this situation because: The longer you take, the worse your chances are.

There's little or nothing you can do to mitigate this particular disaster (unlike swimming or barbecuing indoors).

This is also a really likable example for a few other reasons—it has to do with being in a car, (which is discussed in detail later), it will likely result in spatial disorientation, it's something I have a frame of reference for (having been through military rollover training and, more importantly, lived through a rollover), and there are ways to prepare that are simple.

So, your car plummets into the water…

You're jolted as it hits, and the wind is knocked out of you. You hardly notice because your brain has already decided *this is it* and started giving up. You see water pouring in from the dashboard and through the firewall, and your hands are shaking so much that you forgot how to unbuckle your seatbelt. Your hands feel like flippers, and you can't see anything other than the seat buckle as your fingers try to remember how to work it. In the back seat, your child is screaming, having not come even close to giving up and utterly lacking any ability to do anything about it, but you can't hear the cries because your senses are overloaded. The cold hits you, and with this, you snap back, realizing you've got the pedal floored and the engine sputters, then goes quiet. The water is up to the windows now, and you try to push your door open to no avail. The force being exerted is more than ten people could match. It's decision time.

Have you any idea of how you'd react? What would you do?

Most people are going to fall somewhere in the range of dying and making a terribly sad headline in the local paper to using the seat belt cutter hanging off their driver's side belt to slash through the shoulder belt and quickly take the child from his seat, pulling the glass breaker from the console as they start to assess the vehicles orientation by watching the bubbles leaving as the last of the oxygen in the tailpipe floats upwards toward the surface. Since this person knows the front end of the car is heavier, they orient themselves to swim away. Covering their faces, this person uses the glass breaker to bust out the driver's side window and positions for the inevitable 90-degree shift in the car's orientation while bracing for that feeling in the lungs as the cold water floods over. Then, diving in, child wrapped in their shirt or jacket, they tread water until they can orient themselves to the fastest route to shore.

This situation tests your determination and ability to use your OODA loop effectively, challenges your calm, puts your survival clock on a very short timeline, and requires you use tools that you may or may not have. It is, in essence, a mental exercise that highlights all the elements of skill set, mindset, and tactics that we can use to navigate disasters. While this particular example is the only one in which a detailed explanation of how to gain the resource is not offered, it is a tremendously valuable thought exercise that will begin the foundation for all the other preparations made.

Conceptual Checkpoint

Where would you fall on the spectrum of "Die" to "Awe-inspiring Escape"?

Have you thought of escaping from a submerging vehicle before? What type of emergency is this, and what others can you think of that similarly put oxygen as our "survival saw" necessity that is at stake?

At this point, oxygen is our example of worst-case scenarios that require split second thinking. Consider things like this. Mental rehearsal is a crucial component of constructing a passable plan.

FIRE

Sustained combustion and environmental modification

As discussed earlier, "survival" is neither a topic nor a way of life. It's a measure of adaptability. Casual discussions of methods of starting fires, building shelters, and procuring clean water and food are the academic equivalent of describing the process of surgery without having ever seen a scalpel. Therefore, this will not be geared toward the rugged woodsman who knows just how difficult it is to survive off the land; this chapter is written for the layman who knows little or nothing of life outside the modern first world.

As a matter of course, this primer is here to assist you in practicing these skills over time. It is not a reference to draw upon when suddenly needed. Without a practical, hands-on approach, it, like all other skills, will fail you when you need it the most. This is no different than exercise. In order to build a level of fitness, you must use your free time to condition yourself.

The first step in developing your skill is to begin building a database in your mind from which you can draw upon. So, what is survival, really? It's the maintenance of systems. It's the integration of respiration and consumption with a balance of heat energy. Remove any one of the above and it becomes very difficult to survive. The key concept here is our beloved Rules of 3.

Because this chapter is meant as a practical means for developing a skill set, we're going to focus first on the issue of creating a means of survival for the "medium term" —meaning something that needs maintenance once complete but does not require that we start completely over each time…if managed correctly. Combined with a shelter, a fire is one of the most practical survival tools in your personal toolbox.

Fieldcraft: The Art of Sustained Combustion

Throughout history, several innovations have led to humans' ability to adapt their environment to themselves rather than the other way around. The definitive moment for humankind was the mastery of fire. Plainly stated, fire is a change in state that results in the release of energy. Oxygen is used to facilitate the rapid oxidation of the material being burned, and the resulting energy is given as heat. This heat is used to minimize the impact of environmental conditions such as cold, improper or non-existent shelter, bacteria in our food and water, and so on.

The ability to build a fire from scratch using a bow drill, fireboard, or tricks like using battery current and steel wool are also valuable, but here we're going to approach this from the perspective that you have several items you should keep in your first line gear—in other words, things you (should) carry every day: A knife and a lighter, waterproof matches, or a magnesium fire-starting block. Advancing your skills in primitive fire starting is a great idea - but it is almost entirely experiential, and is best learned in a class, or with a trusted guide who can assist you.

As you develop your skills, it's prudent to adjust the level of difficulty accordingly. What we want to avoid is an overwhelming experience that leaves you with no room to improve, and with fire, moving into more advanced techniques offers greater adaptability.

So, what do we need to make fire?

- A safe area in which to build
- Fuel
- Heat

- Oxygen

The challenge is combining the fuel, heat, and oxygen in a way that creates enough heat to maintain an even, consistent burn without running out of material. With that in mind, the first objective in fire-building is site selection. When determining or assembling the area where you will build your fire, take a moment to consider the following:

- Is it easy to reflect the heat?
- Is it close enough to your temporary shelter that it will provide warmth?
- Is it far enough from your temporary shelter that it will not put you at risk?
- Is there adequate ventilation?
- Is it close enough to a fuel source/water source to make it convenient?
- Are there tactical or situational factors that make a high-visibility fire a liability?

Once you've answered these questions and selected a site, it's time to get your material together. First and foremost, the most important ingredient: patience. If you're not patient and don't pace yourself, you'll find yourself wasting time and material—two things we don't have a lot of during emergencies. Manage both wisely.

This is when observation and experience really become paramount. For example, in the Pacific Northwest, things are wet almost all the time, but this doesn't mean that all things are retaining water. Search around the trunks of trees and high up (under or on) larger branches; these can provide tinder, thin and dry sticks, and so forth.

As we look for materials to build our fire, here's a simple way of thinking about what to collect:

- Fibrous dry material (tinder) —Think light, porous, and dry: pine needles, dry grasses, very dry, rotten wood. Dry cedar bark in the northwest or the bark of ash juniper in the south works exceptionally well.

- Toothpicks—thin, dry sticks about the same diameter as a toothpick. Look for these on limbs protected by overhead boughs or leaves.

- Pencils—dry sticks (remove wet bark if necessary) about the same diameter as a pencil. This is commonly referred to as kindling. In the woods, it's rare to find thin, dry, flat pieces of wood, so for this exercise, kindling will be small dry limbs, thin, flat pieces of driftwood, or the like.

- Broom handles—small tree limbs. By the time we use these, the dryness will be less important, but avoid saturated wood. If it breaks apart in your hands, or the phloem (inner core) of the wood is rotten, it won't work.

- Logs—either rounds (sections) of a small, dead tree or branches. These will be the fuel for larger, hotter burning fires, such as cooking fires. The Boy Scout handbook refers to this wood as about the size of your wrist, and we think that's an excellent way of describing it. Large, heavy logs are inefficient as they require more energy to gather, and you'll have to refuel your fire every hour or so regardless of the size of the logs you add. Finally, gather your wood from an area outside your camp —leave the easy stuff nearby, just in case.

As a very basic (and rough) guide to fires and wood: Hardwoods are usually deciduous (lose their leaves in fall, found near water sources). They are generally harder to burn, and they burn hotter once they get going. Softwoods are usually coniferous (evergreen, found in areas of good groundwater and rocky earth in most climates). They burn easier, but are pitch heavy and burn quickly, though they produce less heat.

This semi-prioritized list considers the material's size in relation to its order in the fire-building process. It will take anywhere from a few minutes to several hours to gather as much wood as you'll need simply for one day, but to get started, your selection should look something like the list above.

A good way to determine how suitable any of this material is for fire starting is to see if it twists or shouts—when you try to break it, does it snap audibly, or does it just twist around? Leave the twisters and take the ones that shout. They contain less moisture and are more suitable for the fire-building process.

Things to Avoid (This is in bold because it's almost as important as things to look for):

Napkins—They don't burn well, and they fail to generate enough heat to light wet tinder. They generally waste your time.

Leaves—Leaves are basically devices for managing water. Even when they're dry, they lack the body for combustion. While they can work, better tinder is preferable.

Big pieces of wood—Bigger isn't better. It requires more calories of heat to start the burn and requires more to keep it burning. Start small.

Next, assemble the dry, fibrous tinder to create a tinder ball, which is essential to starting a fire without a lighter or magnesium. This is no small amount of material, especially before you shred it, but you'll need quite a lot as this process is very dependent on your skill at balancing the fuel/air/heat triangle.

Once you've collected your material, take the dry, fibrous grasses or dry bark and shred it. Your tinder ball should be the size of a major league baseball, or roughly the size of your hands held together as fists. It should be very loose and lightweight, with no areas densely compacted. The goal here is to allow as much dry surface area as possible. The tinder ball should easily catch sparks of flames and allow them to spread. Remember: as a part of your preparation, you should keep the toothpick- and pencil-sized materials close at hand. A curved piece of bark to hold the material as you set it alight will also be helpful; this accomplishes several things:

- It keeps the tinder ball insulated from the ground.
- It allows airflow from the bottom of the tinder ball.
- It allows you to move the burning material once it's lit.

You can make an effective tinder ball from shredded, dry grass, and dry, brown pine needles, with toothpick- and pencil-sized kindling laid atop. They will not burn if you just leave them like this; it's just for ease of setting up the fire once your tinder is burning. If you've found some dry wood, take some shavings and add them into the mix. This finely shaven material should be kept dry.

Once you've assembled your tinder ball and have your wood material handy, set the tinder alight—if you use magnesium, take care as it burns very hot and very bright. The first challenge here is managing where the sparks land. Smooth, quick scrapes work best. Once you see an ember and smoke, give it a little air. It can be tricky to provide airflow while not smothering the fire or blowing it out. Don't blow from your cheeks; blow from your lips and breathe in from your mouth, not your nose. If you breathe in from your nose, the smoke will get into your sinuses, and that sucks. Blowing gently with your lips will manage the air flow into a nice, even stream and won't overwhelm the combustion process or blow your loose tinder off the coals, slowing their heating. Oh yeah, if you're not lying belly-down in the dirt, you probably will be before long, so don't wear your Sunday go-to-town clothes.

Now that you've reached this point, don't give up—the task is not finished! Your fire may not continue to burn freely, and you might end up relighting it several times. This is the sun of your fire-building universe—everything else will orbit around this component, so make sure it's strong.

More important than flame is heat. If there is a good amount of heat coming from your tinder ball, it's time to start setting up the fire. There are a few different thoughts on how to accomplish this, but we're going to use the teepee method. In contrast, the hut or cabin methods disallow access to the interior component of your tinder, tend to collapse (which disrupts the heat distribution), and typically work poorly with smaller pieces of kindling. They do, however, excel if all you have available is hardwoods.

The Teepee Method of Fire Starting

The toothpick- and pencil-sized materials should be assembled as a cone with a circular base around the tinder ball. The materials should conclude in a single point atop the tinder. This directs the fire into a single point, which means your heat transfer is directional, and therefore somewhat controlled. Also, you can build upon this basic foundation, adding larger pieces in the same way until the fire is mature. As the fire becomes more stable, the lean-to method works well. To use this method, lean smaller pieces of wood perpendicularly against a larger piece, forming a shape similar to the teepee method. Once your fire is at this stage, continually add oxygen to it. As your fire begins to generate more heat, it will cause the surrounding sticks to warm and, ultimately, burn.

This brings the fire to the growth stage. At this point, it is burning unaided and will continue to burn until it is extinguished, or it runs out of fuel or oxygen. Use this opportunity to scavenge more wood from an area outside your camp, because this growth stage usually only lasts for fifteen to forty-five minutes.

It's important to gather plenty of wood in the "pre-fire" stage because you do not want to continually expend calories getting up, scavenging, dropping back down (and getting cold) in a chaotic sequence, never really accomplishing anything. You'll lose energy and heat, both of which are critical for survival.

To recap:

Select a suitable site.

Scavenge suitable material.

Prepare material for combustion.

Assemble material in a way that facilitates combustion.

Add material as needed and maintain.

Additional Techniques

There are a variety of substances that will burn in a pinch. Oftentimes, these are thrown out as suggestions for innovative survivalists based on some real loose footing. For example, it's often recommended that people carry cotton balls soaked in petroleum jelly. Another common one is carrying dryer lint as tinder. Here's the thing about these suggestions: they might work in the short term, but not as advertised. For example, while dryer lint will burn, it tends to be compacted, which wrecks it in terms of using it for a fire starter. Why not just carry some paper? Or better yet, carry lightweight meals wrapped in paper, such as MREs. This way, you have both food and fuel in one convenient package.

There are other methods, such as using lenses, that actually work pretty well. Binoculars or bifocals can direct the sun's heat and get things burning in a hurry. The problem is that you've got to have some direct sunlight. If your climate is frequently overcast, have an alternative method.

If we look at this realistically, what we need is a wide variety of information that we can verify works in the field. Doing this will give us options, and options buy us time and save us effort. While it's okay to know things like steel wool and a 9-volt battery can be used to start a fire, in all likelihood, there will either be better ways (lighters), or no other way and you'll simply need to know the primitive methods. The ultimate lesson here is this: Find the easiest method and keep it close…but know how to work without it.

Now, get out and try different methods of fire starting in different environments. Start with the teepee method and then try other ways. Challenge yourself. Try starting a fire one-handed or with only natural materials in the rain. When you need these skills, chances are you won't be at your best, so practice for the worst before it becomes reality.

WEATHER

Fieldcraft: Field Meteorology

Meteorology is an ongoing aspect of life that you can't control, and it's very often a major factor in how well we're able to survive in primitive conditions. A deeper understanding of this can help you predict weather for route planning, understand the ingredients for severe weather, and to plan for everything from a weekend getaway to natural disasters.

The Iñupiat people called the earth and sky *nunaa* and *sila* and believed both have a soul. As some of the world's most resourceful hunter-gatherers, the Iñupiat survived on a deep cultural understanding of how the earth and sky worked together to change the environment, and utterly without advance scientific explanations. In this section, we will discuss how folklore relates to some basic principles of meteorology, and how the shapes of clouds and colors of the sky can help you determine not only what's happening now, but what will happen in the future, and we'll use a combination of folklore, traditional knowledge, and science.

Folklore and Forecasting

Red sky at morning, solar radiation activating aerosols and lithometers 0.5 micros or smaller that are suspended in the mid-level of the troposphere to the east. It just doesn't have a ring to it. Many people have heard the saying *red sky at night, sailor's delight; red sky in morning, sailors take warning.* There are a mess of these old adages, and you might be surprised to find they have some science behind them. Often, people who lived and died by the weather observed patterns without understanding the science behind them. As a part of our broader emphasis on awareness, recognizing these patterns and knowing why they happen is an extremely useful skill.

First, let's take some extremely complicated scientific concepts and make them plain language:

The Causes

Weather is all about the exchange of hot and cold (large-scale differential heating, to the science-minded). To make these terms less ambiguous, we can say that −129 to +134 degrees Fahrenheit is the full range of temperature on Earth. We consider "warm" air to be around 80 degrees F, whereas "cold" air is around 40 degrees F. It's important to know that these temperatures are always relative to one another and relative to elevation, latitude, and geographic conditions.

Brief note: the verbiage discussed will be in relation to the Northern Hemisphere. In general, cold air flows from the poles toward the equator, and warm air flows from the equator toward the poles. This process is influenced by the trade winds—in the north: the prevailing westerlies (winds predominately from the west), and in the Southern Hemisphere: the prevailing easterlies (winds predominately from the east). In tropical, equatorial climates, there are different ways of forecasting due to the diminished role of the trade winds, so please understand that this is largely generic advice designed for people to build upon.

Principles of Air Masses

Cold polar air drifts southward as warm tropical air moves northward, and we call these *air masses*. Recall from physics a few properties of cold and warm:

Cold contracts and sinks while warm expands and rises.

A "stable" environment is one in which the cold air is on the bottom and warm air is on top.

As these air masses move, the cold air sinks, acting like a plow that throws warm, moist air upward into the atmosphere. As this happens, that warm air—now under less pressure as it rises—can expand and cool, and this is where it condenses into water droplets. The strength of this process determines whether we have simple cumulus clouds or full-on, midwestern style supercell convective complexes. If that previously warm, moist air is forced up and rapidly becomes colder than the surface air, we have dangerous instability.

What is a front?

A front is essentially the boundary at which cold air collides with warm air. There are three fronts in most classic instances: a warm front that pushes northward and brings warm air and southerly winds; a cold front that brings cold air and northerly (becoming northwesterly) winds, and an occluded front which occurs when warm air becomes trapped above and below by cold air, creating instability in the atmosphere. With this basic understanding, we can tell quite a lot about what's going to happen just based on the wind field.

Weather Effects

In addition to knowing some basics about how weather works, it's important to know that *temperature* isn't straightforward. Temperature can feel different depending on environmental factors. For example, strong winds or having wet skin can change the way temperature affects your body. Likewise, it can be difficult to hear wind speed and correlate it to actual events.

The Beaufort Wind Scale is the general guide to winds and should be looked at to fully understand the impacts of wind speed on structures and the environment. While somewhat subjective, if you spend some time observing wind speeds and getting used to the feel, it becomes fairly easy to guess the range of the wind speed and its direction. This is extremely important in limited data forecasting—especially in the field environment.

Reading the Sky

Most of weather observation is reading the signs in the sky. Here are a few of the most prominent and meaningful signs and explanations of how you can use them:

Watch for "horsetails" in the sky. Usually, they're a sign of moisture that's been forced up to the top of the troposphere… unless you're in a mountainous region where fronts are the primary cause for horsetails. They tend to be ahead of the front because the winds move faster up there (less friction).

Warm, moist wind from the southeast is an early sign of bad weather. When these winds shift more southerly, watch for their speed to increase to up near 15-25 knots; if it does, start planning for bad weather.

As the southerly winds pick up, watch for altostratus (flat, mid-level clouds that don't allow shadows). This is generally a sign that a front is twelve to thirty-six hours out. This isn't hard and fast, but it serves as a useful guide. Your specific area may have faster or slower moving fronts.

Pressure moves from high to low: high pressure is associated with stability (if it rains, it'll be drizzle) and low pressure is associated with showers and storms.

These are some extremely basic principles to keep in mind, and they need to be meshed with an ability to read the clouds. For now, let's focus on some of the signs and effects.

Folklore, Sayings, and Their Meanings

...Red sky at night, sailor's delight; red sky at morning, sailors take warning...

A red sky is a measure of how solar radiation interacts with gasses and particulates in the atmosphere. The red color of the sky occurs when solar radiation strikes particles and gasses and produces a certain wavelength of light. Most of the atmosphere is nitrogen and oxygen (which scatter to make the sky blue, a phenomenon called Rayleigh scattering), but at certain times of the day under certain air masses, the sun can hit just right and produce red and orange scattered light. Typically, pollutants, aerosols, and lithometeors (particles) are much larger than other atmospheric molecules, and therefore scatter longer wavelengths than naturally occurring gasses.

When you see this to your east (in the Northern Hemisphere), it means that light is scattering off trapped, mid-level gasses and the high pressure is moving off and will be replaced with lower pressure, less stable air mass. The opposite, red sky at night, means that the stable column of air is moving toward you and decent weather should result. They say that the coldest weather is generally forty-eight hours behind the passage of a cold front. That's because high pressure and stable air indicate that the cold air is below the warm air. Because of this, we can expect ambient cold, generally accompanied by some sunshine.

Bottom line without the geek-speak: Red sky in the morning, high pressure is moving out. Red sky at night, high pressure is moving in. Keep in mind that pressure is correlated with the weather—you'll need to know more to say what kind of change will take place, but it's a useful first look.

Note: Red sky can also be a sign that there are fires to your west (winds blow from the west), which can give you some lead time if there are fires coming your way.

...Dew on the grass, high pressure will last...

This is another adage with some backing in science. The observation of water particles on the ground indicates that subsidence (the settling of cold air) has pressed moisture to the ground. This is a strong indicator of high pressure and generally indicates that you're solidly under a stable air mass. If there's moisture nearby (coastal climate, near a lake, recent rain, etc.), this can be visible as fog or mist. Essentially, the high pressure traps the moisture, and light winds mix it up. Another way we can see this effect is when smoke fails to rise. When under the influence of high pressure, smoke is "pressed" toward the surface, whereas if your smoke rises quickly, the pressure is trending toward low.

Oftentimes, when we go outside and there is dew on the grass, we can count on a day of stable, decent weather. High pressure can also be a boon for those caught in survival situations; you can collect the water generated by this phenomenon, such as the "solar still," which can supplement your water intake. The bottom line: Dew on the grass is a surefire sign you're under high pressure, and weather should be stable. If there's a lot of moisture, you might see some morning fog, but expect the weather won't turn severe within the next day or so.

...If you can't see your shadow, rain is coming...

As light passes through various types of clouds, it can have different effects. Low clouds generally allow light to penetrate through to the surface, while very high clouds tend to be thin.

In the "mid" levels of the troposphere, where the temperature is cold enough to turn water vapor into ice crystals, stable banks of clouds are thick and very reflective. Because of this, light won't easily penetrate them, and you may not be able to see a shadow. These clouds, called altostratus (alto: mid-level, stratus: stratiform, or stable) often occur in warm fronts in which the environment is still largely stable. This happens predominately as a cold front approaches, so not being able to see a shadow can mean a front is approaching.

This can signify a significant weather change and more like than not, some rain, especially in the midwestern region of the US. This adage isn't without some hang-ups, however, and altostratus can occur without a weather change. For this reason, it's one of the less reliable indicators. However, when used in conjunction with other evidence of an approaching front, it can still be useful! The bottom line: Altostratus can indicate a front, but it can also just be clouds. Take this one with a grain of salt, and watch for our other, more reliable indicators.

...Rain follows Horsetails...

The very high wisps of clouds known as cirrus, or more commonly "horsetails," are really ice crystals that are in the upper levels of the troposphere. As cold fronts push water vapor aloft, the vapor freezes and comes under the influence of the fast-moving upper-level winds. These winds can launch the ice crystals up, and they occasionally override higher pressure ahead of a front.

Because of this, horsetails can be a sign that low pressure is coming. However, they could also be an expression of surface topography. Mountains and hills can lift moisture if surface winds are strong enough, so this one requires some knowledge of terrain. This is a reasonably reliable sign, but it's important to note a couple pitfalls of using this method:

Not all fronts are strong enough to produce bad weather.

Terrain can cause orographic lift, which is when terrain "launches" water vapor aloft. In mountainous regions, the front can also stall on the windward side (west in the Northern Hemisphere), leaving horsetails but not a front on the lee (east, in the Northern Hemisphere) side.

For these reasons, use this adage as a first "tip" that something could potentially develop over the next couple days. If you apply this principle with other signs (such as a strong southerly wind and rising temperature), you're going to be able to accurately determine what's coming with a decent lead time. The bottom line: If you see cirrus clouds, use them as an indicator that something might be coming your way. Watch for those southerly winds, an increase in humidity, and the emergence of altostratus. It could just be some trapped moisture, but it's a useful first look when used in conjunction with our other indicators.

With this knowledge, you can better understand what you're seeing when you look at the sky and how that relates to weather that could impact your plans. The objective is to give you a powerful tool in assessing conditions as you get out and spend time outdoors. Weather can be deadly, and shelter is one of our top Rules of 3 priorities. Understanding how and why weather develops is an important step to beating mother nature at her own game, especially considering her game is killing you.

Fieldcraft: Cloud Genera

In meteorology, cloud genera is a term we use to describe the types of clouds. As we progress, however, we learn that these types have significance; they tell us about the state of the atmosphere. Clouds are a language, and you can learn to speak the basics. In this section, we'll start with the very basics by breaking clouds down by their heights and the conditions that create them. Simply put, we start by identifying the height at which the clouds are in the atmosphere, and then considering whether the atmosphere is stable or unstable. While this section will give a general orientation regarding the clouds, please refer the the article "cloud genera" on ISG, or scan the above QR code for visual aids that will help you in identifying clouds in the field.

https://integratedskillsgroup.com/2021/06/level-up-cloud-genera/

Cloud Heights

Generally speaking, cloud height is broken down into three basic categories:

Low: These clouds occur from the surface (fog or mist) up to around the bottom of the freezing level. The majority of routine weather impacts are caused by low clouds.

Mid-level: Mid-level clouds extend from the freezing level, typically somewhere between six thousand feet to around sixteen thousand feet in the mid-latitudes. Mid-level clouds are largely those that indicate transitioning conditions, and they rarely cause significant weather events by themselves.

High: Clouds that occur above sixteen thousand feet in the mid-latitudes are generally considered high clouds. High clouds are ice particles and can indicate weather that's coming.

Cloud height tells us quite a bit about what's going on in the atmosphere, but before we get to that, it's important to talk about stability. Stability is relative, but it's easy to understand conceptually. Typically, when the temperatures increase with height, the atmosphere is conditionally stable. If the temperature cools with height, we have a conditionally unstable environment. How fast it heats or cools plays a part, as well. In general, we expect that the atmosphere will cool 3.5 degrees F (2 degrees Celsius) for every one thousand feet (305 meters). This is considered a neutral environment and is a useful reference. Clouds are a language, and you can learn to speak the basics.

Stable Cloud Types (Stratiform): Mild Weather
Stratus

Stratus is a low level, stable cloud that creates drizzle or snow. Stratus clouds tend to linger and drop a lot of rain a little bit at a time and are very common in coastal climates. The appearance of stratus is similar to a sheet; it appears as a smooth, covering layer.

Altostratus

Altostratus is a mid-level, stable cloud that generally doesn't produce much precipitation (although these clouds occasionally produce virga—rain that evaporates before touching the ground—especially in high desert environments). Altostratus clouds are frequently found ahead of fronts, provided there are no mountain ranges to interfere with them, and they can warn of an approaching front. They frequently bring warmer weather and higher humidity. Altostratus can be confirmed using a simple trick: If you can't see your shadow, there's altostratus present. This is because the clouds are highly reflective, and the light that passes through them is diffused due to the thickness and altitude of the clouds.

Cirrus

Cirrus is a solid-state cloud, comprised of ice crystals and situated very high in the atmosphere. These clouds typically appear under high pressure or during transitional moments such as post-frontal periods. Likewise, they can be in wisps (horsetails) or more uniform swaths (shields) that ride over high pressure. Because we know something has to be driving that lift, we should be cautious of a weather change when we see cirrus. Cirrus are often referred to as "horsetails" even though there are several types with slightly different appearances.

Unstable Cloud Types (Cumuliform): Changing Weather
Cumulus (CU)

Cumulus, which is Latin for *heaps,* are the puffy, popcorn-looking clouds you see during fair weather. If given enough time, they can develop into rain clouds and thunderstorms. Cumulus is typically a sign that the weather is fair, but be alert; cumulus like this generally mean there's lift and moisture present, which is often the first indication that a front is approaching. Cumulus commonly produce rain showers and snow flurries.

Towering Cumulus (TCU)

Towering cumulus clouds, or TCUs, create the core of a storm cloud as it forms. These clouds typically reach up in columns that can extend several thousand feet. TCUs themselves aren't major weather producers, though. What they are is a physical manifestation of a couple ingredients necessary for storm development: moisture and lift. TCUs mean the atmosphere lift, instability, and moisture are rising rapidly. However, they don't mean you should watch for storms unless there are a couple other things in play: dry air intrusion in the mid-levels (this can be determined by a tilt to the TCU). If you see a tilt, watch out for our last two clouds: enhanced cumulus and the cumulonimbus.

Enhanced Cumulus

Enhanced cumulus is that which is developing to a great extent and can produce significant weather but has not yet formed an anvil. An anvil occurs when the clouds hit the top of the troposphere—the portion of the atmosphere we live in—and the top of the cloud begins to spread out. Enhanced cumulus are often found in the mountains where cloud bases start at higher elevations and are formed by the terrain itself through a phenomenon called orographic lift. Enhanced cumulus can transition into a storm, but they often lack the characteristic anvil of a traditional storm cloud.

Cumulonimbus (CB)

The cumulonimbus, or CB, is the traditional storm cloud and produces strong winds, hail, lightning, and heavy rain or snow showers. Hail and lightning are only produced by CBs, so if you see those, you've got a storm on your hands. Tracking the development of the CB is a practical skill that can have serious impacts on your time afield. We discussed the necessary ingredients for the development of these clouds when we detailed the towering cumulus clouds. Remember the principles discussed earlier in Reading the Sky. They will help you understand how severe storms form, and consider the acronym MILE:

Moisture: the presence of available moisture in the atmosphere; typically represented by a high dew point, high relative humidity, and southerly winds.

Instability: Instability occurs when the surface of the earth heats rapidly and the temperature aloft is cold (remember the lapse rate discussed above and our principles from Reading the Sky).

Lift: Lift occurs when wind flow is interfered by topography (orographic lift), rapid surface heating (convection), and collision between air masses (frontal lift). Watch out for terrain effects! If you're near hills or mountains, lift is more likely.

Exhaust: This is what causes the tilt we can see in developing TCUs. If you think of the TCU like a calm, then what goes up must come down. Eventually, if there is no exhaust (and tilt), the mass will "choke" development, and the rain will fall straight down. If the TCU tilts, it can expand, and the rain will fall ahead of the updraft core. The exhaust will also cause the spread of the anvil, which occurs when the storm has grown so tall that it hits the extent of the troposphere. This is an indication of a strong updraft.

Strong thunderstorms are a matter unto themselves; they can cause many serious complications, including flooding, damage to structures and trees, lightning strikes, and of course, tornadoes.

TERRAIN AND NAVIGATION

Understanding terrain will help you with everything from finding water to navigation. Our emphasis here will be a discussion of how to relate the terrain to navigation, map reading, and overland travel, and understanding how terrain benefits or hinders your movement. Once the art and science of terrain reading is honed, you'll find your ability to dodge nature's wrath more complete.

Fieldcraft: Reading Terrain

Here we will assess terrain from a rural perspective, although the same features can be identified in urban environments. A firm grasp of how terrain influences runoff and vegetation can be critical in finding resources in an emergency, as well as ensuring you're not placing yourself in danger when you select a spot to hunker down.

The purpose of a topographic map is to easily translate three-dimensional features into two-dimensional representations; these maps use contour lines that act as lines of equal height, so being able to read one can be an excellent tool when planning for both urban and rural expeditions. First, let's discuss maps a bit.

Maps come in a variety of types, the most common being road maps and topographical maps. Road maps give information on roads and features of a city or town, whereas topographical maps show topography, or changes in elevation and features of the landscape. Like cloud types, this is most easily learned with visual association. If you're able, our article on integratedskillsgroup.com titled "Level Up: Reading Terrain", or scan the QR code above!

Major Terrain Features

https://integratedskillsgroup.com/2021/06/level-up-reading-terrain/

Hill: A hill is a high area where the ground falls away in all directions. Hills are represented on topographic maps by contour lines arranged in concentric circles. The innermost of these circles is considered the hill top. Hills are prominently visible features both on the map and when viewed from the ground.

Depression (not depicted): A depression is an area from within where you find higher ground in all directions. Lines denoting depressions differ from typical contour lines in that they have hash marks that look like barbs coming off of them. You may find the ground within a depression saturated or laden with dense vegetation or grass.

Saddle: A saddle is an area that features high ground on two sides and lower ground on two sides. The saddle commonly connects hills and provides a good path between them. To find a saddle on a map, look for a strip of land that has no change in elevation with tight topographic lines on either side.

Ridge: Ridges feature high ground to one side and lower ground to the other three. The ridge differs from the saddle in that the relief in the three directions of lower elevation is variable. A ridge shows up on topographic maps as having the shape of a tongue or a U shape, and while you're moving across a ridge, it may have a very gradual slope.

Valley: Valleys are, at their most basic, areas where the land slopes upward in three directions and downward in one. The valley differs from the draw in that it's generally a much larger feature. The valley generally hosts year-round water, which is fed by either a spring or mountainous region. Valleys can be identified by large expanses where the elevation changes very little between rapid elevation gains on at least two sides.

Minor Terrain Features

Draw: A draw is an area through which water cuts, carving a channel through higher terrain; When standing in a draw, the terrain will lead to higher ground in three of four directions. Draws often have residual water and dense vegetation.

Spur: A spur is a series of prominent points that fall away rapidly on three of four sides. The photo in the QR link above illustrates spurs (the spur can be seen in the upper leftmost corner).

Cliff: A cliff is a sheer drop off from which the terrain contours quickly come within close proximity to one another, and in some cases, overlap. The name for this occurrence is "carrying contours," which represents topographic contours so close that they can't be distinguished using the map's scale. The elevation is considered to be the lowest present numeric value.

Terrain and Weather

This section discusses the interconnectedness of weather and terrain, so it may be helpful to mark the section on reading the weather above, as the processes there will be directly related to the processes here. Here, we will discuss how terrain interfaces with the atmosphere, and how it relates to how we should select routes and shelter. If you keep these things in mind as you assess terrain, the tasks of finding shelter and resources will be easier:

- Cold air sinks, so valley floors tend to be cooler than lower elevation ridges.
- Mountains and significant hills create "windward" and "lee" effects; in the Northern Hemisphere, where the wind blows from west to east (prevailing westerlies), the west side of a hill is the windward side, whereas the east is the lee.
- The windward side of mountains collects rain, so be cautious when camping on west-facing slopes...especially in coastal climates.
- The lee sides (eastern, in the northern hemisphere) of mountains tend to be arid: rain falls on the windward side of mountains and creates a "rain shadow" on the lee. Little or no rain falls in these areas.
- Lee slopes typically have rivers and fresh water; however, they are often fed by mountain springs or snow/ice melt.
- Hills provide lift for storm development; when the wind flows perpendicular to mountains or hills, there is potential for cloud or storm formation.
- Lakes and standing water provide a source for both cloud development and animal/ insect habitat.
- Winds come from the mountains at night and valleys during the day (generally speaking).

- Following water will ultimately lead you to mountains or the ocean.
- Large rivers and beaches often have driftwood, which can be very useful for shelter construction.

Fieldcraft: Terrain and Travel

Terrain affects transportation in every way. It doesn't matter if you're on foot, horse, off road in a vehicle, or in an airplane, terrain features can change the way you travel. If you're moving on foot, your route is going to be substantially impacted by terrain and your ability to read it, and this goes for off-road driving as well. The things you'll want to look for is grade (how far up and how fast), water crossings (and the draws they live in), open, low-lying areas that get saturated easily, and so forth. The goal is to stay out of trouble, so avoid the following terrain features for the reasons explained:

Thick brush and undergrowth: Not only is this tough to pass through but also, if you're on foot, it's a great way to pick up ticks or wind up with stray sticks to the eye. Thorny vines can cause cuts and tear clothing and equipment. In a vehicle, body damage can occur, and the ground is often deceptively soft/uneven.

Steep or boulder-strewn hillsides: Avoid these! There are two predominant types of rocks we're looking for here: talus and scree. Both are loose rocks that result from weathering, and both are prone to shifting. Talus is large (if you need two hands to pick it up, it's talus, but talus can be boulder-sized, as well) and scree is typically smaller chunks. Both can cause dangerously unsteady conditions and are killer on vehicles and horses or pack animals. Flat ground is not a problem but be especially careful when a grade is introduced.

Marsh and low-lying areas with lush, short foliage (drainage basins): These areas tend to have significant populations of disease-carrying insects, and bacteria flourishes in the warm, stagnant waters. For foot travel in marshy areas, the big risks range from insect exposure to thermal injury and wet feet, which can lead to a condition called immersion foot (a foot injury caused by water absorption in the outer layers of the skin). When traveling by vehicle in a marshy area, you can quickly find yourself without a vehicle if you're not careful, as the inconsistent bed can give way and cause vehicles to sink. The water depth can be very deceptive, and what looks like firm ground can instantly turn to muck a foot deep.

Rivers and Streams: It goes without saying that fording rivers can be very dangerous, whether on foot or in a vehicle. Rivers act as natural barriers, but they are subject to nature's whim; watershed rainfall can cause quick fluctuations to depth and discharge which need to be considered before you attempt to cross. Locating an ideal spot is more important than saving time. If your ride goes into the drink, you'll be a lot worse off. In general, look for depths of no more than a couple feet, slower moving water, and bedrock ledges that provide traction or footing.

These terrain features take time, energy (either calories or fuel), and risk to negotiate. They also tend to be away from the natural lines of drift (obvious paths) that people will instinctively take. That can be beneficial, depending on the circumstances.

In a vehicle, being able to see terrain on the micro-scale can really make the difference between an easy off-road trek or a damage-causing nightmare. This is an art and a science, and it requires a high degree of familiarity with your vehicle's turn radius, height, wheelbase, and departure/approach angles.

Reading Terrain

Now that we have a baseline understanding for the terrain we encounter in the field, let's turn our attention to how we can use this to our advantage.

The first thing we consider when we're in the field is shelter. More than anything short of breathable oxygen, exposure to the elements has the most significant and immediate impact on our health. As such, we often need to be prepared to find shade, building material, fire-starting material, windbreaks, or insulation. It helps to know where we can find materials that will help us.

Grasses, Saplings, and Vines

Along with reading terrain is knowing what resources can be found in those environments, both for shelter and improvised resources. Grasses are useful as thatch, and sometimes they are able to be worked into nets or similar materials. Grass is generally found in low-lying areas and is short in length. Longer grasses can typically be found in most environments. Saplings can likewise be used for making thatch, fish traps, drying racks, baskets, and other items. Vines such as ivy can be turned into improvised cordage.

Moss

Moss can often be found in temperate climates, especially on the north-facing aspect of trees or rock faces. Don't think for a second you can use moss to determine direction, though. Moss grows everywhere, on everything, so you'll end up confidently lost trying to guess your direction by looking at it. Moss can be used as an impromptu hemostatic (a wound dressing that promotes blood clotting), but it is more wisely applied to improvised bedding.

Coniferous Trees

Coniferous trees (or evergreens) can be found in the foothills where there is little soil and rocky detritus covers the ground. The predominant evergreens in the rainforest are the Douglas fir and hemlock, and lower-lying areas near water can host cedar (the bark of which burns nicely). As you approach more arid climates, pines become more common. Pine are likewise common in the reaches of the Ozark uplift and southern Appalachia. Coniferous trees are considered soft woods, and they are characterized by flexibility, high amounts of pitch, and quick burning. Most importantly: Conifers have year-round boughs (hemlock, fir, pine) or sprigs (cedar, juniper, etc) that can be used as thatch for shelters and bedding.

Deciduous Trees

Deciduous trees lose their foliage in the fall and winter, which makes them less useful for improvising shelter, but the fallen leaves can still be used as insulated bedding in a pinch. The deciduous trees common throughout the United States are often found lining the low-lying areas around streams, rivers, and lakes. These trees are hardwoods that burn very hot and slow, and they make for stout building material. However, the less dense physical consistency of their coniferous cousins means they are harder to cut and shape. Stands of deciduous trees very often indicate that a water source is nearby, as these trees require ample amounts of water.

A note on wood: Do not try to burn sprigs, boughs, or leaves. This is a common novice mistake. They don't catch fire easily or burn long enough to be useful. They also tend to produce a lot of smoke (needles and sprigs in particular). Dried leaves can make a pretty passable insulation if you've got a way to bag them up. Just watch for bugs.

Stone

Stone is useful for a variety of tasks when establishing a camp; it can be used as structural material for camps, fire rings, and primitive tools. Thin slabs of slate can be used as impromptu cooking surfaces, and gravel is a useful component of the sand/charcoal water filter. Stone can usually be found in sites where there is terrain relief, such as hills.

Using Terrain Analysis to find Food and Water

After establishing a camp, the next priority is finding a source of water and food, which is harder than it sounds. Analyzing the terrain for potential flooding, fire hazards, and seclusion from the elements becomes critical. Likewise, access to fuel for your fire and suitable water will either increase your workload and calories invested over calories returned or decrease it.

Low-lying areas with deciduous trees surrounded by grasses almost always indicate water. If you're looking down on a landscape, finding this kind of area can be a resource for water, fish, and often game. In wooded environments, look for draws where snow melts and natural springs will naturally shed water. Game will often cut trails in the side of hills leading to standing water, as well.

The desert, especially the high desert, can be especially challenging. Finding vegetation can allow you to create a solar still that draws moisture from the plants and collect it in a receptacle. Even under the best cases, the solar still won't provide you with much. Between the moisture in the plants and the water vapor that often sinks to the desert floor at night, a person would be lucky to secure eight ounces. If you're forced to build a solar still, it would be wise to build several.

In coastal environments, water is often fairly easy to find, and fresh water means food and shelter tend to take the priority. In general, fishing is one of the most expedient and rewarding approaches you can take. Don't forget while we in the west scoff at eating bugs, they can provide nutrients in a pinch. The rule of thumb is *six legs or less, good; eight legs or more, pass.*

Additionally, many naturally occurring plants can provide some flavor and vitamins, such as pine needles and vitamin C. Scavenging things like fungi and even plants is extremely dependent on your location. Because of the dependency on location, there really is no responsible advice other than finding people who create foraging groups in your local area. Books can provide some basic overviews, but many poisonous plants, such as hemlock or nightshade, can look edible even though they are extremely toxic.

If you do attempt to determine if a foraged plant is poison, you can often apply a simple Boy Scout test by taking a small portion, touching it to your lips and waiting for 30 seconds. If it doesn't burn or irritate your skin, you can put a small amount on your tongue and repeat the process. If you don't experience numbness, burning, or any other unpleasant sensations, you can attempt to put the fruit or plant in your mouth. Eating a small amount and waiting to ensure there are no ill effects can give a good idea of whether something is edible. Again, please don't take risks without first properly educating yourself.

Conceptual Checkpoint

Next time you're out, take a look around and ask yourself "Where would I camp? What's my plan for food and water?"

Fieldcraft: Navigation

Navigation by way of map and compass is a dying art in the age of GPS. While GPS is fine for good times, magnetic fields and compasses will probably be around long after GPS and humankind have gone the way of the dinosaurs, so it pays to conceptually understand how to read a map and use a compass to get a bearing. When it comes to navigation, we'll discuss four equal, interconnected parts: terrain (which we discussed above), map reading, using a compass to determine a heading, and pace counting. What we're doing here is giving you a down-and-dirty working knowledge of the concepts, but navigation requires some technical skill and math; there's just no getting around it.

So, what is navigation? Essentially, it's the process of translating the three-dimensional terrain features we discussed earlier and accurately determining their direction and distance.

Basic Map and Compass

The most crucial element of map reading is to orient your map north before you start any calculations. We'll repeat this and give some justification, but if you begin by orienting yourself and your map to the north each time, it'll be easier to determine your location as well as shoot an accurate azimuth.

Map reading consists of two main parts; the legend, which describes the features you'll find on the map, and the scale, which relates the size of the grid squares on the map to their true size and allows the longitude and latitude to be read.

The scale is particularly important because not all maps work with all compasses. Baseplate compasses will work with maps produced for citizens, while lenstatic compasses are predominately used for the military grid reference system (MGRS). Make sure you've got the right maps for your compass.

Each type of compass has some specific and unique advantages and disadvantages. The lenstatic compass is capable of shooting a more accurate azimuth—a word that really just means *degree heading toward a known object*. When used with military maps, the lenstatic compass is very accurate and can be used to navigate on a scale that's too small for most maps. This compass relies more on taking an azimuth by using the sighting wire, and it allows greater precision when relating the terrain in the real world to that on the map.

The baseplate compass is lighter, has a built-in protractor, magnification, and is meant to be overlaid on the map allowing the navigator to view the compass and map simultaneously. Most baseplate compasses are also meant to be used with USGS topographic maps, which are predominant in the US, and you'll find quick references on the map for baseplate compasses to quickly adjust for magnetic declination, which we'll talk about later in an effort to explain the concept without people glazing over.

Reading the Map

As mentioned, maps have some common features you should familiarize yourself with. First and foremost is the scale, which you'll need to know in order to take an accurate reading and determine distance. Scale is expressed in a ratio, such as 1:100,000. The larger the number, the *smaller* the area it represents. It's important to know your map scale right from the start as it'll help guide you when it comes to making measurements and determining your latitude and longitude.

Scale is also represented by a bar. This black and white bar will show a fixed interval, usually an inch or five centimeters, that you can measure and use to represent a known distance on the map. For example, if the scale bar indicates that every one inch represents twenty miles on the map, then you can use a ruler to determine the distance between two points with some reasonable accuracy.

Next is the legend. This helps you determine what the lines you're looking at mean. These can be things like roads, train tracks, or terrain features, or they can be lines describing the terrain (topographic lines). Almost all commonly encountered maps will have a scale and a legend, as well as details such as the grid coordinates and latitude and longitude.

Latitude and Longitude

The backbone of navigation is the Geographic Coordinate System, which is the primary way we find our position on a map. It is comprised of parallels of latitude and meridians of longitude. Right off the bat, if you're ever confused which is which, just remember *lat* rhymes with *flat*. Flatitude. Has a nice ring to it.

In any case, parallels of latitude are lines that run east and west starting at the equator, and they are divided into equally spaced lines that go around the globe. The spacing of lines of latitude means each degree is equivalent to 69 miles (or 11 kilometers), each minute is equal to 1.15 miles (1.85 kilometers), and one second is equal to 101 feet (30 meters).

Meridians of longitude are lines that run north and south and, by contrast, converge at the poles, making them narrower the closer you get to the Arctic or Antarctic poles. Because of this, no constant distance is recognized for longitude, and this is also why we have magnetic declination. However, we still use degrees, minutes, and seconds to measure longitude. Meridians of longitude are relative to the prime meridian, which is 0 degrees longitude and runs through Greenwich, England.

Using the MGRS, you can easily use a compass and protractor to find your exact position on a map. However, this is something that requires both military maps and hands-on experience. For this primer, just be aware that the goal is to be able to find your whereabouts precisely using these tools.

Magnetic Declination

One of navigation's more head-scratching concepts is magnetic declination, or magnetic variance. The official descriptions of declination are the stuff of irreversible boredom, so here's the short version:

The magnetic North Pole isn't the same as the North Pole on the map. There's true (or geographic) north, and there's magnetic north. The difference between them is the declination. Magnetic north varies year to year, and because of that, the meridians of longitude change slightly with that variation. So, especially if you're navigating in the mid-latitudes, you'll have to adjust for magnetic declination, which can be done by either adjusting the compass or reorienting the map.

As we mentioned earlier, the first thing we do when we're navigating is to orient the map. If you know the declination, you can adjust your north by the number of degrees toward the agonic line. Many maps will have a diagram demonstrating the correct declination. Otherwise, when you take your bearing with the compass, you can adjust the bezel to compensate for declination by rotating it however many degrees are required to reach your true north. This is determined by your location in the world and must be researched individually, as Earth's magnetic field changes over time.

Science alert: If you're interested in cartography and the science behind declination, read on. If not, feel free to skip ahead to Using the Compass.

Maps that demonstrate the declination are referred to as isogonic, which means "lines at which declination is the same." On an isogonic map, there's an "agonic" line, or a line at which you do not need to adjust for declination at all. As you move east or west of the agonic line, the lines of declination will lean toward the agonic line, and the closer you get to the poles, the more they'll lean.

When we measure declination, we use degrees east or west. This is confusing in the beginning because it's in reference to which way the lines must lean in order to reach the agonic line, not whether you are east or west of it. So, if you're actually using an isogonic map, remember that if you're east of the agonic line, you'll be measuring in degrees west, and if you're west of the agonic line, you'll be measuring in degrees east! This reflects the direction the compass will have to be adjusted to reach true north, as opposed to magnetic north.

Using the Compass

The methods for using compasses are straightforward but intimidating. The very first thing to do when orienting yourself and your compass, no matter what type you're using, is find north and orient your map in that direction. Make this a habit, and it'll stick with you when you're cold and your fuse is short as you huddle around weak light trying to find a direction. Doing so will ensure that you're referencing the information you see on the map in a way that's "true to life." If you look at terrain that should be to your west, when you look west, you should be able to see it.

While the designs of the lenstatic and baseplate compasses are different, they have common elements, such as the needle and bezel. The needle will always have an identifying mark indicating north, whether that's a color or a pointed head (as on the lenstatic). When you set up to use your compass, you'll need to orient yourself and your map and take account of any declination. Once that's done, you'll need a way of determining the distance and then moving

that distance.

Pace Count

After orienting yourself, determining your location and destination, and choosing a heading, you'll need some way of knowing how far you're traveling. This is referred to as your pace count, and it's a crucial part of movement to your point.

Pace count is defined by how many steps are required to reach a known distance—usually 100 meters. An important note: your pace count will change slightly depending on your load weight, the terrain, and obstacles. Moving in a straight line is impossible when we're moving to a point, so we'll need to step off our azimuth, travel some distance, and regain it. Try to maintain your pace count when this happens.

An easy way to establish your pace count is to head to the local school's football field. Since they're usually graduated in increments of ten yards, you can walk the initial one hundred yards (if you're looking for a pace count in yards), or you can pace off the one hundred and double back for another ten yards, which will give you your pace count for one hundred meters. As you walk, count the number of times *one* of your feet hits the ground during the trip. Use whichever foot you lead with. This number will let you know when you've traveled a distance of 100 yards or meters.

One of the quick and recognizable issues with pace count occurs when you're traveling long distances. It's easy to lose track of how many times you've hit one hundred and reset. For this reason, there are a few tricks you can use. Some people pick up a small rock when they hit their count for one hundred. Others use Ranger beads, which allow you to slide a bead up or down a length of paracord and can account for one hundred and one thousand yards or meters. Whatever you choose, get out and practice. Start small and find local resources. There are navigation classes available that will at least get you on your feet. They that are offered by everything from local enthusiasts to chain stores like REI.

Navigation could be—and is—a book in and of itself. Like many of the topics here, we can introduce you to the concept and basics, but you'll need to get out and put in the work for the principles to work. With that said, the principles here, an understanding of terrain association, and a good idea where you can find further resources will go a long way towards understanding orienteering.

WATER

The good, the bad and the infectious

Let's start by defining the importance of water: Water is a non-negotiable, consumable requirement, and it's a vector for diseases —especially in emergencies. Water is a common theme in survival —it is unique in that it is both an absolute necessity and a looming threat at the same time. Behind breathable oxygen and shelter, it's one of the most critical elements on our priorities list, and we have just three days to ensure a clean, potable supply of water if we are to survive. This is an overview of the hard way of procuring safe drinking water—by creating a filter and boiling the remaining impurities.

Obviously pump filters, straw devices, and other methods of purification are faster—when they are available. However, we can't always count on technology, and so, here we'll talk about how to strain impurities and debris out of the water and kill microbes in the water. When determining how we'll come by water, there are several things to consider:

- Demand: How many people are you providing for?
- Source: Where will you get the water?
- Collection: How will you collect it?
- Decontamination: How will you make it safe to drink?

Obviously, some common sense also needs to be applied here: Don't contaminate water. Build latrines at least one hundred feet from your water source.

Stagnant water must always be purified. Warm stagnant water is even more dangerous.

Keep water resources separate. Douse water, cleaning water, and drinking water should all be separated.

Use only what you need. Keep stocks proportional: drinking water is always the priority, but budget for cleaning water.

Demand

When assessing the demand for water, figure that each person requires about three gallons per day in order to take care of hygiene and replenishment. Also, keep in mind that this is the bare minimum. In austere conditions, this requirement may well exceed five gallons, so it's imperative that you include this as a part of your initial assessment when you choose a site. Once you understand the logistic demand your party will have for water, you can begin considering what to do to procure it. Keep in mind, you'll need to rinse any cookware, clean your hands after using the restroom, and you may want to use some to wash your face, feet, and other areas that are prone to bacterial buildup.

Source

Your water source will depend greatly on a variety of things: your location, demand, duration of stay, and also, rainfall. Obviously, if you're only going to be in a spot for a night or two, you do not want to create a splendid purification system that cannot be taken with you. This is what lightweight portable filters are for. Pick one up to get you where you're going, and then apply these principles.

Collection

Water collection in most areas is relatively easy; things as simple as rain barrels or as complex as cisterns can be used. Water is heavy and difficult to transport—a single gallon weighs close to eight pounds, but it's important that your plans and equipment reflect the need to have some at hand. A three-pronged approach to water collection and purification is beneficial. A solid equipment list is the following:

A three-liter water bladder in a backpack for drinking water while moving.

A canteen or Nalgene bottle with a metal cup to heat, purify, and drink your water.

A folding water bucket for non-potable water.

This will allow you to scale your efforts up or down depending on the circumstances. Over the years, there has been a shift among people who decided that they really only need one of the above—usually a water bladder or similar piece of equipment that holds a good amount of water and makes drinking it convenient. This approach begs the question—how will you refill it? If you're on the move, how will you collect and purify water with only one reservoir? This is the logic behind carrying the canteen and cup. Strained water can be taken from the collection device, put in the cup for boiling, and then added to the canteen, bladder, or bottle.

A note on bottles and canteens: dummy cord them to your backpack. Murphy's law: If it can get lost, it will. Also, *canteen* is a generic term; a Nalgene bottle with a metal cup will work as well.

Water Science: Contaminants

Having briefly been a part of the nation's leading water science academy, I spent a lot of time training and studying water quality and safety in a variety of capacities. It's important to understand water as broken down into two categories: physical safety and consumption safety. There are major considerations that need to be taken into account for both categories. In particular, you want to be thinking about inorganic (dissolved solids, heavy metals, chemical toxins) and organic (viruses, bacteria, and protozoa) contaminants.

What we should make clear at this point is that there are places in the US where the drinking water has standards of treatment comparable to third-world countries. Flint, Michigan, is a recent, high-profile example, and another location is Love Canal, NY, where toxins in the groundwater caused widespread birth defects, miscarriages, and cancer in the late 1970s, so this isn't a ghost; it's a legitimate concern. We should only expect that this will get worse if we find ourselves in a state of emergency.

The second point to consider is the introduction of biological contaminants. The short version is this: If you get sick, you require *more* clean water. If you get sick with diarrhea, water will be required to sanitize the mess. Such illnesses cripple your ability to move, which is essential in disasters—which may compromise our access to clean water.

The takeaway is that water all across the US has contaminants, and it doesn't matter if it's groundwater or surface water. Additionally, it's often impossible to tell if the water is contaminated. It can have a pronounced signature (rust-colored deposition on vegetation, irregular color, etc.), but it may not. Further, bacteria from decomposing animals are impossible to detect. These problems are compounded by disasters, so plan accordingly.

Decontamination

This process can be drawn out and difficult. There are numerous ways to decontaminate water, and no matter how many people spin it however many ways, there's a basic, conceptual approach that is more important than any one technique. We'll get to that, but first, assessing water for potability:

Is it salt water? Yes? Find a different source unless you can distill it.

Is it stagnant? Fresh water? Is there surface muck (algae or flora) growing from it?

Is it too clear or discolored for its location/season? This could indicate the presence of metal toxicity/chemical/radiological contaminant.

Scout around. Is there anything dead nearby? If you can smell it, it's probably there.

Is there any other concern with the source? Is there human settlement nearby? If so, do they dump waste in this water?

Once you've determined that the source of water is not packed with chemicals, decaying organic matter, or salt, use the following principles in purifying your water:

Filter out large impurities. Get rid of pond scum, vegetation, or any sediment that might have been stirred up by straining through a medium. Here's where you can start using your imagination. To strain, you can use anything from a T-shirt to a coffee filter. Coffee filters are lightweight, cheap, and designed to filter out junk you don't want to drink. It might not get everything, but that's ok, that's why we…

Pour the water through the filtering medium into an actual filter. You can improvise a filter using sand or pumice and charcoal. If you're out on the road during an emergency, you've probably had to make your own fire. If so, save the charcoal and use it for your filter. Layer it in equal parts in a container—again, you can improvise with anything from a milk jug to a beer can. It just has to be able to hold the filtering media and have an outlet for the filtered water.

This is a simple, effective method that will work with almost any size container and can be constructed simply without many tools. Sound easy? It is. This is the "street fight" version of water purification—simple, effective, and meant to stop the crisis.

Important note: It's always better to have the right equipment than it is to improvise, and while we rarely make endorsements for specific products, the pump style filters have been the standard backpack kit for us for almost a decade as of the time of this writing and have shown themselves to be substantially better than straw types.

Improvising may become necessary for a variety of reasons, so just like primitive methods of fire starting, you should know how to do this without any special equipment.

First things first, here's what you'll need:

- A container through which to strain the water
- A cloth to put over the top of the straining bottle
- Sand and charcoal, in equal amounts, to fill the straining water
- A knife to puncture the bottom of the straining bottle and cut the top open
- A receptacle in which the strained water can be boiled.

It's important to remember that the straining container can be anything—a milk jug, a coffee cup or can, a five-gallon jug, or a 55-gallon jug—whatever you happen to have available.

Primitive/Improvised Solution

The simplest method of water filtration is a sand-charcoal filter. These can be improvised, usually with materials that can be found locally. As mentioned, to prepare this filter, you'll need a fine layer of sand and a coarse layer of slightly larger gravel. It's important to note that "slightly larger" doesn't mean pebbles or rocks. We are looking for something between the size of sand and pea gravel.

In addition, you'll need something that keeps the media out of the water; this can be anything from a shirt to a coffee filter. You'll have to improvise based on your situation—and keep in mind this is a stop-gap solution to get you *safe* water, not perfect water. To make this filter, you'll need two water containers. If one is metal and can be used for boiling, all the better.

Assembling your DIY Filter

Assemble the material and make your filter by putting the base layer of charcoal at the bottom of your improvised filter—this could be a plastic bottle, can, or jug—as long as you can create a way to pour water into and out of it and find enough media to filter the way. Again, make sure you put a filter of some sort between the opening and the collecting container.

Improvised plastic bottles work well. Cut some holes in the lid and wrap a coffee filter over the opening. Fasten the filter with a rubber band, tape, rope—whatever you have available. Once the cap is complete, open the top of your container and add in a layer of charcoal. This forms your base layer. Next, fill about half of the container with sand, layering it on top of the charcoal. Ultimately, you'll want to have a couple inches between the sand and the top of the container. Finally, add in about an inch of the pea gravel. At this point, you're ready to add water to the filter and collect your filtered water in a clean container.

Keep in mind that there may be discoloration to the water depending on how good your filter is. The charcoal will often cause the water to turn black; it won't hurt you, but as a precaution, you should boil the filtered water to make sure you've killed any biological contaminants not sifted out in the filtering process.

Don't take any shortcuts! You have to get your fire going and have a container that can sit on the coals at a lightly rolling boil for ten minutes. A jet burner system or similar can save you a LOT of time. Otherwise, it takes patience, but so does diarrhea.

At this point, we're trying to get rid of the bacteria that will cause infections and sickness. This is really a case of preventative medicine. Be very cautious about what you drink and eat—when you're in the wild, think of your water as you would meat…cook it!

Backpack Filters

It's always good to know how to improvise, but a purpose-built solution is always better. In the confusing world of disaster preparedness forums, blogs, or social media groups, you'll quickly be assailed with the following wisdom any time you recommend a good water filter: *Get a LifeStraw, they're twenty dollars.* These good people will talk you to death about their guns and how they'll survive out of their backpack once the electromagnetic pulse hits, but what they won't do is regale you with stories about how they got pinworms, beaver fever, or diarrhea from drinking water through an insufficient filter.

This topic is going to get heavy-handed quickly, and if you're inclined to look at reason and evidence, it'll leave you with no question as to the importance of a good water filter. If you're not inclined and you're banking on a twenty-dollar budget device for a worst-case scenario, well, at least you'll know the risks.

Budget Preparation

We get that not everyone has the money to drop on an expensive pump filter, so please don't mistake this as a jab at people on a budget. Our goal is to provide some evidence that you're going to be miles ahead by saving and getting a quality filter (which can be had from $75-$100), as it will last longer, perform its task more efficiently, and provide you more protection against what basically amounts to gut worms, diarrhea, and liquid cancer.

There are places where you can skimp. We've tested dozens of knives and backpacks. We'll gladly tell you that if all you can afford is a Kershaw and a surplus ALICE pack, you can put those to good use and not be all that far behind the guy with a $700 backpack and custom-made knife from whoever's popular. Oftentimes, skill and mindset are enough to overcome deficiencies in equipment. In the case of water filters, that's not true.

Also, if you've already grabbed a LifeStraw or Sawyer filter, we're not knocking you. Taking a step is better than nothing, but you need to have a realistic assessment of what you can expect if you have to press it in to serve in a post-disaster environment. For this reason, if you laugh at a $100 water filter but you've got a $1500 AR-15, now would be a good time to reconsider your priorities.

A last point on this: We often say that water is a non-negotiable, consumable requirement. What this means is *you can never carry enough*. Period. What you *can* do is have a method of preparing water you come across to make it safe. As such, if you can carry enough for a day or two and plan around finding more, we can address the problem of infinite requirement by having the right tools. So, here's the bottom line: If you buy a $20 filter, you're going to get twenty dollars' worth of protection for a resource that you're going to need throughout the duration of the situation and that, if filtered poorly, will make you sick with one of the deadlier conditions known to mankind.

Water in Emergencies: Floods and Swift Water

Floods are the kind of disaster that get the old ho hum from most people until it happens to them. They are deceptively common and fade quickly into obscurity for those not directly impacted. Where earlier we discussed some of the hazards of drinking contaminated water, here we will discuss threats to your physical health and safety. They're two sides of the same coin, but the way we mitigate the risks is entirely different.

Floods: Overview

Floods are one of the most frequent, severe, and costly natural disasters on the planet, and you really should be thinking about them. For one, they can happen anywhere. It doesn't matter if it's a desert flash flood or a coastal deluge, floods lack the regionality of other disasters like volcanoes, earthquakes, or hurricanes. They also often occur as a secondary effect from other natural disasters, such as rapid snowmelt from volcanic activity or flooding associated with hurricanes. What's worse, the population expansion has driven developers to take up riskier developments in known flood plains, which was put on display near San Antonio in 2015 during the Wimberley floods. It's okay, though. Local officials make flood insurance more expensive to compensate for the increased risk of living there. Sarcasm off: you're on your own. City planners aren't out there making sure you won't be swept away in a hundred-year flood, and that term is chronically misused. For this reason, we want to discuss the topic, so you've got a place to start if you want to harden yourself against floods.

"100-Year Floods"

When people throw out terms like "500-year flood" or "100-year flood," ask yourself, how were they collecting flood data back then, and whose job was it? The answer is, in most reliable cases, the USGS—which is an excellent organization with some extremely bright minds. We haven't been keeping good records for very long. We've had a decent system of recording some basic weather data for one hundred twenty years or so, but not much more. Looking at USGS's literature on the topic, the concept of a 100-year flood is somewhat misleading, and it doesn't mean that a flood of that magnitude will only happen once every one hundred years.

The 100-year flood projection is based on a per-year chance of water exceeding a known boundary of one percent. This means that from the data gathered, most years won't see a flood like that… but, as with all statistics, caveat emptor; percentages don't work like that. From the USGS website:

"The 1 percent AEP flood has a 1 percent chance of occurring in any given year; however, during the span of a 30-year mortgage, a home in the 1 percent AEP (100-year) floodplain has a 26 percent chance of being flooded at least once during those 30 years! The value of 26 percent is based on probability theory that accounts for each of the 30 years having a 1 percent chance of flooding."[4]

In October 2018, in Texas Hill Country near Wimberley and San Antonio, the Llano River rose ten feet in twenty-four hours, causing some massive flooding. Since weather patterns tend to shift gradually, record floods can happen over short periods. Using the Wimberley example from 2015 and this 2018 situation in Burnet and Travis County, Texas, we have two major floods in reasonably close proximity within three years. While they didn't affect the same flood plain, there's a good chance those same areas will have similar floods before another hundred years pass. Don't slip into comfortable complacency because "hey, it's a 100-year flood plain!" It's tricky phrasing that opens the door to dangerous development practices.

A Word on Prediction

Floods, like most other weather phenomenon, aren't predicted accurately with much lead time. A good forecaster with the right tools can generally see the conditions coming three to five days in advance, so like other weather emergencies (heavy snow, hurricanes, wildfires), you've got a Type II emergency, often with a few days of lead time. While that can be greatly beneficial, taking some steps now will significantly boost your chances of a positive outcome. You can streamline certain aspects of preparedness by:

- Having equipment staged in a common area.
- Having a solid load plan for the equipment that fits your vehicle.
- Creating a plan and checklist for who's responsible for loading what. A clipboard near your supplies works well.
- Discussing a plan ahead of time that includes a PACE (primary, alternative, contingency, emergency) location your family can move to if displaced by a disaster. Think about low roads with flooding!

Paying close attention to the areas affected to adjust your route, ensuring you're not caught up in a mass exodus or the path of destruction.

Getting out ahead of the crowd.

More often than not, simply being ready to do these things is enough. Likewise, we know that people have low confidence in meteorologists. Try to keep in mind that those forecasters are putting almost unimaginable amounts of data together to provide you a free, cautionary service. While most truly have your best interest in mind, allow for the fact that meteorology has become a reality TV show on most stations. If you want the weather without the fluff, go to the National Weather Service and the Storm Prediction Center.

Swift Water (and Some Rescue)

If we like one thing, it's nerding out on our readers with facts and making them approachable. Water weighs eight pounds per gallon and sixty-two pounds per cubic foot. This water exerts constant force, which means fatigue quickly sets in. Along with cold and debris, we want you to take away a key point: The more time passes, the lower your chances of a successful recovery.

We also like honesty: You can't learn this from a blog, article, or books. That said, we can help you make good decisions around swift water so that you don't need to be rescued. One of the first things they teach you during swift water rescue is the force water is capable of generating. It creates a dramatic amount of force, but what we want to focus on is the *bathymetry* (underwater topography) of a flooding channel and how to read the water surface to detect threats.

Reading the Water: Flow

When we discuss how water flows and determining left and right banks, we always look downstream. The banks themselves define the waterway's *control*, or the mechanism keeping it bound. Controls aren't important for causal interest, but once the waterway exceeds the natural controls, it enters flood stage. Next are some of the hydrological features we see with rivers, and what they mean.

Hydraulic: A hydraulic is a condition created by water circulating downstream from an obstruction. There are many types of hydraulics, but for now, just keep in mind they're dangerous and you want to avoid them. Weak hydraulics are referred to as holes.

Laminar Flow (A): Marked by flat, consistent velocities free from eddies and turbulence, laminar flow is typically a sign of no trouble. Even if you're in swift water, laminar flow can be used to swim hard to shore. However, laminar in man-made structures, like waterways or irrigation canals, can still be very dangerous and difficult to escape, especially when there are strainers, which we will discuss next.

Strainer: A strainer is an obstacle in the water that has the potential to "catch" a victim, pinning him between the force of the water and the obstacle. Common strainers are fences, downed trees, and guardrails along the sides of roads. It's typically advisable to go feet first if you find yourself in swift water, but if you see a strainer, swimming hard and deliberately toward it with the objective of going over the top is the best chance of survival. Strainers are one of the most threatening obstacles encountered in swift water rescue, and they often cannot be seen from the surface. It's important to understand that once caught in a strainer, the force exerted by the water increases substantially; that is to say, it takes a tremendous amount of strength to open a vehicle door or move your body over a strainer once you've become immobilized by one.

Riffle (B): Riffles are an indicator of shallower, wider areas of flow. They're often found immediately upstream from a hydraulic, below which escape can be difficult (or impossible). Riffles generally occur in very shallow water, and if you see them during flood conditions, they should be a big red flag that you need to get to shore or prepare for a drop. These drops on roadways often include strainers, so your best bet is to get out as fast as you can.

Frown (C): The frown (as viewed looking downstream) indicates swift water dropping sharply, which can push you under and keep you there. Frowns can capture a victim and trap them in the hydraulic. This is more of a concern the deeper the drop, and the strongest reversal of the current occurs on the sides where you can easily be pushed toward the faster flow in the center. A smile, conversely, has faster flow on the corners, which can provide a path around obstacles or hydraulics.

Turbulence (D): Turbulence is created as the gradient increases and laminar flow is disturbed. It doesn't always indicate trouble, but it does mean there will be irregular currents.

Eddy/Eddy Line (E): The eddy line is the boundary where the flow reverses and velocities drop off sharply. The eddy can typically be used to get out of the water, rest, or grab ahold of some *terra firma*. Short of being tossed a rescue device, the eddy offers one of your best chances for self-rescue. If you can, swim hard to get to the eddy line. Even if you can't find a place to pull yourself out, you'll likely be out of the path of debris and more dangerous water.

Boil: A boil is a spot of diffluence in upwelling that pushes against the current and downstream, creating a "roll." These often indicate loose or shifting bed, but boils can occur downstream of hydraulics and low-head dams, and they can trap a victim underwater. If you see a boil, try to avoid it, as it signals rapidly sinking and rising water.

Other Water Hazards

There's a lot to consider with flow and the hazards swift water creates, but it doesn't end there. Some of the more obvious hazards to consider are debris and thermal injury, but it's important to know that hydraulics can exist behind low-head dams and drainage culverts. If you find yourself in one, chances of survival are slim, so as difficult as it is, you have to be aware of what's coming if you're trapped in floodwaters.

Low water crossings are likewise a major concern; every time there's a flood, some dunce tries to cross the water in a Prius thinking it's probably not as bad as it looks. It's likely worse than it looks, and *any* water crossing you undertake should be done with as much information as possible. If you do have to ford a water crossing, knowing the depth and width and having a general idea of how swift the water is will go a long way in determining how much danger you're putting yourself in. The adage *turn around, don't drown* isn't a joke, so if you're unfamiliar with water crossings and you didn't plan ahead by having an alternative route or destination, don't make your situation worse by sacrificing your car, equipment, or life.

Secondary Concerns

In addition to the hazards we've already identified, we need to keep in mind that there are also mudslides, sinkholes, and contaminated standing water to consider when we look at water hazards. Don't forget the impact that the Type II emergency has on availability of resources. During Hurricane Harvey, gas was in short supply from Dallas to Fort Hood and east to the gulf. The stations that had fuel limited quantities, leading to long lines for less fuel. Closer to Houston, many stations were sold out completely. Second-order effects from disasters should always be figured in!

Topographic maps are easy to buy these days, and establishing a firm understanding of your local area's likely water traps is a wise preventative measure. Keep in mind that floods can happen anywhere, whether they are the product of volcanic snow melt or torrential rains. This section illustrates that of all the emergencies people ignore, floods are probably the most complicated, common, costly, and significant. No one wants to talk about them because they aren't exciting (if you're not dealing with them), and we get bored with things that aren't outlandish. Don't become complacent.

Localized flooding is a classic Type II emergency with embedded Type I emergencies, so give it some thought. The preparations we make to dodge severe flooding are common with the other Type IIs, so apart from familiarizing yourself with the specific hazards and getting some topographic maps, gaining an understanding of this material is easy lifting. As well, we discuss water as a hazard because it's on our "rules of three", but you may be asking "why aren't other emergencies discussed in detail? The reason is we encourage people to look at how the event impacts access to critical resources, rather than the event itself. With that said, we have several write-ups that discuss the specifics of natural disasters that can be found by following the QR code here.

https://integratedskillsgroup.com/2021/06/water-in-emergencies-swiftwater-and-floods/

FOOD

Every book that discusses survival throws a bone to how to clean and skin small game and how to dress out a deer. It's a gesture so the authors can say they checked that box and readers feel like they basically know what's going on. This usually continues into how to make snares and the like. We're not going to give you diagrams for making traps or skinning animals—there are other books specifically for that, and there's truly no substitute for practice. It isn't something you're going to want to learn on the fly, and this chapter isn't going to save you. It will give you some ideas, but it's up to you to turn the principles into useful, usable concepts for your location. What this text can do is give some useful guidelines on how not to waste your time when you're a few days in and getting hungry. As with all things in cheating our bony-handed adversary, you win or lose the battle in advance.

Metabolism Overview

Without getting too far into the weeds in the science, your body is home to cellular power plants that metabolize oxygen and carbon-based life into energy. Understanding metabolism at the most basic level is crucial to staying ahead of the curve when it comes to calories. While chemical processes involved in metabolism are complex enough to be their own book, right now we're interested in only few critical elements.

One of the most important things to start with is also one of the simplest: How many calories do you need? To know this, you should also consider how gender and phenotype (physical build) affect calorie requirements. Predictably, your gender and size play a huge role in determining calorie requirements. Men and women differ in terms of their body composition, with men typically carrying a lower percentage of body fat. Fats, which are essentially stored energy, don't really require much upkeep, whereas muscle does. Therefore, the more muscular a person is, the more calories are required to keep their body from initiating a catabolic process that deconstructs existing mass for energy. Your body stores glucose as an energy reserve in the blood, and in a normal adult, that reserve will last between six hours and two days. Like all the Rules of 3, after the first third of that period, your body is going to be protesting heavily, and the deficiency of calories can lead to a host of side effects that you should be aware of.

To continue supporting your resting metabolic rate (your most basic function), a woman will need approximately 1400 calories, where an average man will need 1800. So, what happens if you start dipping below that resting metabolic rate? After your supply of glucose runs out, brace yourself. Your brain's primary source of energy is glucose, and as it's depleted, the brain starts turning to ketones. This process is defined by the feeling of being hungry and angry due to the brain's inability to efficiently use ketones as it does glucose. It's also important to note that these are the absolute minimums a healthy adult needs to sit around all day. If you're physically active or performing difficult labor, those caloric estimates should be doubled.

During their unconscionable reign, Nazi scientists discovered that with less than 1500 calories per day, humans began losing emotional and cognitive function. This loss of function made them less susceptible to revolt, less able to plan or attempt escape, and unable to draw upon an energy reserve to survive if they were able to escape. Because of this, prisoners in concentration camps were limited to 1700 calories per day (2150 if they were involved with hard labor). Children, who are utterly reliant on proper nourishment for proper physiological and neurological development, require significant calories. Rachel Roth's book *"Here There is No Why[5]"*, and attending exhibit at the Wagner College Holocaust Center goes into this in detail.

Conceptual Checkpoint:

How many calories do you need to find each day to keep your family from starving?

Ask the following:

- Without supermarkets, where would I get my food?
- Could I get enough to meet my family's caloric intake for one week? Five weeks? Twenty-four weeks?
- What can I do to offset the demand placed on the grocery store? What can I grow or where can I get locally sourced food?

Look at which foods offer the highest caloric density per pound and consider which you could easily store over long periods of time. We will return to this topic, but for the time being, grab a piece of scratch paper, write out what your family needs per day. Imagine you're in New Orleans and the levees have broken. You're stranded for the next five weeks with no supermarket. Where do you get your calories?

Physical Starvation

If you find yourself starving, your body will slowly break down stored tissues (fat and muscle) at a roughly equal rate. During catabolism (the breaking-down aspect of metabolism), your body is burning tissues that chemically need very little conversion to become energy, and for a brief period you may feel very alert and vital. Shortly after, when your body runs out of fat reserves, organ dysfunction and heart problems set in due to electrolyte imbalances caused by a diet devoid of fats. This most often leads to fatal cardiac arrest. If you suddenly reintroduce solid food into your diet after periods of starvation, the sudden gradient of glucose, proteins, and carbohydrates can offset the balance of electrolytes available for metabolism. This causes the body to expel the food in the form of vomit or diarrhea.

This is crucially important. As the body expels the food, it further depletes the body's supply of water and electrolytes and can cause muscle spasms, delirium, and can result in cardiac arrest if sufficient amounts of phosphorus aren't present in the blood. When reintroducing your starving body to food, start with broths and liquids and ease into solid foods by eating light, tender foods that have been baked or boiled, and be sure to keep your water intake up.

Take this knowledge with you. While starvation and the long-term effects of malnourishment and diseases such as pellagra, marasmus, and kwashiorkor aren't common in the first world, you should be familiar with them as things in our world continue to change. Now, let's discuss how to avoid this fate to the best of our ability.

Fish First

If you're in an area that allows you to pursue fish and game, fish first. Not only are fish reasonably abundant and nutritious, but they can often be caught with a simple net or trotline tended at intervals throughout the day. This means the methods of catching fish aren't labor intensive, and they're high reward. A simple trotline can be tethered to a bank with a floating end and an anchor, or it can be placed using two anchors and two floats. Connecting the two points is a rope, off which fishing line with a baited hook are attached. When considering bait, remember that the fish you're after eat things from the natural environment. Bugs, worms, flies, and even entrails from smaller fish can be used as bait.

Anything buoyant (such as empty milk jugs) can be used as the floats, and the anchor weights don't have to be complicated. Tin cans filled with cement and an eye bolt can act as an anchor. The depth of the water should be known so that the distance between the anchor and float keeps the float sitting on top of the water.

When the floats dip, it's a good sign a fish has taken the bait from one of the hooks.

Fish traps are likewise easy to make and can be passive systems. A fish trap might be a net or a series of sticks that allow entry but make exit difficult. In streams where crawdads are present, you can lure them using shiny metal (no lie, they'll go right for it) or meat/guts from captured fish. Simple, improvised fishing poles can be made with fairly basic items, such as paracord and a safety pin. When fishing, try to find natural bait that lives near the water source where you intend to fish. Things such as periwinkles, grubs, maggots, and worms are all tempting bait for fish.

Fish tend to hide out in places that are hard for predators to find them, and that's not always deep water. Often, its root clusters near the shore. Try finding a spot that's deep and provides protection from predators, and "jig" for fish—that is, place a baited hook in the water and bob it up and down. This motion tends to draw fish who feed largely out of reflex rather than conscious thought.

Fish are easy to clean with a minimum number of tools. For most, simply cut the head off right behind the gills (this can be used to make soup). Then, insert the blade into the anus, staying as parallel to the body as possible in order to avoid puncturing the organs. Cut until you reach the neck, and remove the guts with your hand, a spoon, or a stick. The fish can be cooked and eaten in about twenty minutes over an open fire.

Foraging

Of all the skills associated with finding your own food, foraging is one of the most intimidating. Not only is it extremely specific to your location, but often the consequences of misidentification can be poisonous or deadly. For this reason, it's best not to take the advice of a book that merely skims the topic. If you are interested in learning more about foraging, buy a book that's dedicated to finding edibles in your area. There are often local groups that teach foraging, as well.

With that said, there is a general test for determining if something is poisonous if you're forced to foraging. First, watch for what the animals eat. The berries they can eat will often be safe for humans. With wild berries, squeezing some juice on to your lip and waiting is a good place to start. If your lip doesn't sting or burn, place some juice on your tongue. If it's not bitter, acrid, or causing discomfort, then it's very likely safe to eat. Berries that are very firm are not usually edible for humans.

Scavenging

Scavenging is a fancy way of saying looting. Make no bones about it, it happens, and it might happen to you, and it might be you who's desperate enough to loot. When an area is impacted by a large-scale disaster, stores and shops are picked clean in the immediate aftermath, which means that most of the resources left to be looted are from private residences.

Those who have the ability or forethought to evacuate ahead of the disaster (if possible) often leave their valuables loosely secured and without adequate policing to enforce laws against looting, theft, and trespass. This is a moral conundrum that you need to take up before you're placed in that position. Do you starve and be a "good" person, or do you loot and steal from others?

Our take? Neither is the best option. Planning ahead here, like all things we try to do to cheat the reaper, gives us options. So, consider looting and the way it will impact your area during a major disruption and understand how it creates a security problem as well as a moral question…but try not to find yourself in that position. Furthermore, keep this in mind: If you are fortunate enough to have a place where you can keep some animals and a decent garden, those things are usually outside. What's your plan to defend them? How will you do that without power? Scavengers will know in short order if you have backyard chickens. Anything you leave unattended will be stolen. Be aware that if you keep dogs in your backyard for security, they're likely to be poisoned or killed.

Subsistence Gardening

The title sounds intimidating, right? No worries. While you might not become completely self-sufficient in food production, there is much you can do. The old saying goes that a journey of a thousand miles begins with a single step, so here goes.

Obviously, you will need a plot of land for your garden. The size of your garden plot depends on what is available to you and how much food you want to grow. A good size for each of your garden beds is four feet wide by twenty-five feet long. That makes your beds each one hundred square feet, which makes calculations easier. Your garden needs to be in full sun; that's important. Once you have a suitable garden plot, your next step is soil preparation. When you build a cabin, first you construct the foundation; it's the same with your garden plot. To maximize your garden's yield, you need fertile soil. Take the time to properly prepare the soil before you start planting. Some patience and labor are required.

Soil and Compost

What kind of soil do you have? Is it mostly clay or mostly sand? There is much to know about soil. There is sandy loam and loamy sand and many other variations. If you have poor soil or even little or no soil, you can amend it or even replace it as needed. If you have the time and inclination, double-digging your garden plot is highly recommended. Proper soil preparation provides fertile soil initially but keeping it fertile requires periodic soil amendments.

Depending on the quality and workability of your soil, this is the ideal time to add soil amendments. You want to add organic matter to your soil. Compost is excellent if you have access to quality compost. Avoid the cheap stuff in bags that you find at big-box stores. Check with your county extension office to learn about compost availability in your area. If there is a master gardener association nearby, ask a volunteer and you'll get sound advice. Some master gardeners are willing to make a site visit to assess your situation and make valuable suggestions.

In addition to compost, you can add peat moss to the soil, which is considered a nonrenewable resource. Coir—ground up coconut fiber—is a great alternative to peat moss, and its renewable. If you have eggshells, fruit, and vegetable scraps from your kitchen, add them to the soil and bury them at least a few inches down. Rotted leaves (leaf mold) are good, too. Add them if you have them. The plants take nutrients from the soil, and these nutrients need replenishing.

Conventional In-ground Gardening

Conventional in-ground gardening is time-tested and reasonably straightforward. Prepare the soil and amend it as needed to create rich, fluffy soil. Get rid of big rocks and stones. Double-digging is recommended, but many gardeners do just fine by loosening the top twelve inches or so of soil. If you go that route, carefully avoid allowing a hardpan (densely compacted soil layer) to form beneath your soil layer. It is okay to use a rototiller for initial garden preparation, but don't use one after that. Not only does it chop up valuable earthworms, but it encourages that hardpan to form. If you decide to loosen and amend only the top twelve inches of soil, by all means at least break up the subsoil below to encourage good drainage. You can do this with a pickaxe, broadfork, or gardening fork. You want good drainage to prevent your plants from getting "wet feet" and rotting.

Here is another valuable tip: Avoid walking on your garden bed. If you must do so, create a walking path by laying down a wide piece of plywood to distribute your weight evenly and avoid packing down the soil.

Climate Zones and Growing Seasons

When you purchase seed packets, you'll find helpful planting information on the packet itself. Use this information to help you plant and grow a successful garden. The information will include planting time, which varies depending on your USDA climate zone (based on the USDA Plant Hardiness Zone Map). It will also tell you how deep to plant your seeds. Some seeds are barely covered with soil, while others are planted at various depths. The seed package should tell you. It will even tell you what to do once the little seedlings emerge; if you thin them according to seed package directions, it ensures that each plant has sufficient growing room and is not crowded out.

Some vegetables are not well suited to direct seeding. For these seeds, start them in trays and gently transplant them into your garden when they are big enough. Some plants do well in colder weather, while others prefer warm weather. The seed packet will explain when to plant based on your USDA climate zone.

Understanding growing seasons is important. The further north you are located, the shorter your growing season is likely to be. If you are situated near a coastline, this may extend your growing season. If you live in, say, Alaska, Montana, or North Dakota, your growing season may be one hundred days or a little more. In parts of south Texas or south Florida, you may be able to garden year-round. For most plants, one hundred days is sufficient time to reach harvest maturity.

Watering

Here is the rule of thumb: water infrequently, but water deeply. Plants love rainwater because it does not contain chlorine. Collect, if you can, rainwater from the roof of your house in a bucket or other container (do not drink water runoff from a composition roof). Watering with a garden hose is fine, though. Check for soil dryness every day or so, depending on the weather. Stick your finger into the soil to a depth of a couple of inches. If it feels moist, you do not need to water. If it is dry, water deeply. Deep watering encourages deep root growth. This can be anything between two and four inches for shallowly rooted plants, such as lettuce, or as much as eight to twelve inches for fruiting trees. There's no hard and fast rule to define deep watering but be aware it is an option that may help you in your location. As always, check with local authorities, such as your county master gardener to establish best practice.

Mulching

Mulching your garden is important. Mulch keeps the soil cooler in summer and warmer in winter, and it helps the soil retain moisture. Mulch also breaks down gradually and feeds the soil. For this reason, use fine mulch instead of large pieces; you want it to break down as a soil amendment. Avoid those attractive-looking, color wood mulches. These often include dyes that can absorb nitrogen into the soil. Quality mulch should be available in your area, but if you have trees that shed leaves in fall, you can also use them as mulch. Rake and bag the leaves and store them for use later. Run them over a few times with a lawnmower to break the leaves up before bagging and use the broken-down leaves as mulch.

Do not apply mulch right up to the plant stems. Allow a few inches of space around the stem of each plant. Applying right up to the stem can introduce too much moisture too closely to nutrient rich roots (which certain insects find to be a perfect combination), and it can also put high concentrations of necessary minerals too close to the root clusters. This can cause fertilizer burns, which will harm your plants.

Composting

Mulch consists of organic matter that has not decomposed. Compost, on the other hand, is decomposed organic matter; so, while mulch is applied on top of the soil, compost should be mixed into the soil. Both compost and mulch basically accomplish the same thing, but compost goes to work enriching the soil right away, while mulch must break down, which takes more time. Composting is highly recommended for serious gardeners. There are many commercially available composting units from kitchen-sized to much larger, yard-sized tumblers. The principle to remember is that you need to periodically disturb the compost to ensure that microbes and, if you choose to have them, worms can find their way to the un-composted material. Building your own compost bin can be as easy as building a frame with a lid and dumping your compostable scraps into it. Stirring it with a pitchfork or shovel every few days or once a week should keep it moving along.

Additionally, there are certain things that are fine to compost and others you'll want to avoid. Meat, the feces of carnivorous animals, and citrus can introduce contaminating bacteria, parasites, flies, or acids that will kill the beneficial worms. Organic matter like coffee grounds, vegetables, eggshells, and such compost nicely and produce less waste. Shredded paper can likewise be decomposed, provided it isn't laminated or laden with colored ink.

Compost tea is a beneficial snack for your plants, and you'll likely notice a difference if you use it. You can spray it on your plants or use it as a soil drench around the plants every few days. To make compost tea, fill a 5-gallon plastic bucket with water, and let it stand in the sun for a few days to dissipate the chlorine. Then, add a generous scoop of compost, stir it thoroughly, and let it stand for another twenty-four hours. You can also make manure tea the same way—but put the manure in cheesecloth and soak it in the water. Discard the cheesecloth and its contents, then use the manure tea like compost tea. Caution: Not just any manure is good. Avoid canine and feline manure, and remember that horses, cattle, goats, and donkeys may have been fed hay that was sprayed with chemicals while it was growing in the field.

Fertilizing

Plant roots take nutrients from the soil, and you can replenish those nutrients in several ways. A preferred way of replenishing those nutrients is to add compost topped with mulch to your garden at least once a year. Just as when you're laying mulch, you want to ensure that you keep this away from the plant stems.

Bagged fertilizer is a fine option for your garden if you find it more convenient. By law, there are three numbers on each bag of fertilizer (e.g., 10-10-10). The first number gives the nitrogen component as a percentage of bag contents, while the second number is the amount of phosphate, and the third is the amount of potassium (potash). Check with your county extension office to learn the approximate levels of each in your native soil. For a more accurate report, purchase a soil test kit (available from your county extension office), and follow the instructions on the kit. You'll mail a sample to be tested, and a couple weeks later, you will receive a written report with exactly what nutrients to add to your garden soil, and in what amounts.

While the three main components are the most important, plants also need small amounts of trace minerals. A quality fertilizer product should contain these, and it will be on the bag label. Apply the product according to label directions. Fertilizers come in organic and inorganic versions, with organic fertilizers being more expensive. A typical bag of organic fertilizer will contain far less nitrogen, phosphate, and potassium than an inorganic fertilizer and will probably be more expensive. Here's a tip: the plants don't care.

Please understand that we are on the subject of fertilizers, not herbicides and pesticides. Try to avoid herbicides and pesticides because they can destroy beneficial insects, and you probably don't want to eat harvested plants that were treated with chemicals without thoroughly washing first.

Critters

You will have unintended visitors in your garden. It is important to remember that there are beneficial insects (e.g., ladybugs), which is why avoiding the use of chemicals is desirable. Pollinating insects are required for the health of your garden and fruit-bearing trees. To keep out deer and small wildlife, put a fence around your garden and line the bottom foot or so with wire screen. Watch for signs of digging around the fence. Be vigilant and remember that the insects and animals are just trying to make a living. It's fine, and sometimes necessary, to share some of your crop with them.

General Gardening Advice

If you have an interest in growing some of your own food, gardening can be highly satisfying because you will see the results of your efforts. Feeding your family with food you grew is rewarding. In-ground gardening requires some stooping, kneeling, and hands-in-the-dirt. To protect your skin, purchase a pair of gardening gloves and wear them. A wide brim hat is essential in warm climates and at high elevations. It's also a good idea to wear a long-sleeve shirt and long pants.

One final point: Without over-dramatizing this, glyphosate (the principal ingredient in Monsanto's Round-Up herbicide) has found its way into trace amounts into America's food and water supply. Researchers have assured us that these are safe levels, but one must always ask who funded the studies that produced those conclusions. Monsanto (now owned by Bayer) is defending lawsuits alleging that Round-Up is toxic to humans. By growing your own produce, you will know exactly what went into your harvest. When you do shop at the grocery store, it is worth considering the higher cost of certified organic produce. If you shop at a local farmers market, ask each vendor if he/she is part of the Certified Naturally Grown movement, a voluntary self-policing group of small-scale farmers who practice organic growing techniques but individually cannot afford the expense of becoming certified organic.

Yard Birds: The Basics of Keeping Chickens

Chickens are the quintessential animals for a homestead or farm. Not only are they delicious, but hen eggs provide a daily boost of protein that can supplement your family's diet. Our experience with backyard chickens spanned several years; going in, we read countless books and blogs and shopped around for the perfect little chicken tractor. Here's the bottom line, up front: None of it really helped.

You wouldn't expect it, but chickens are actually pretty good at providing for themselves; you just have to keep them from being eaten. Don't worry too much about having the perfect roost or nest set up and don't waste your time and money on some expensive chicken tractor. For the best results, you'll need a yard that you can fence off, and whatever you do, don't listen to the people who say chickens will eat bugs off your garden. They will, but they prefer to eat your garden.

Urban Gardening with Chickens

An herb spiral, a small bio-intensive gardening spot, and some chickens are a good addition to any backyard. Check with your city's ordinance if you're in an urban area, but otherwise, there's not much of a reason not to keep chickens. Even if keeping birds is not allowed by your town, you can often present your case to the city and win, as hens don't make any noise, do any damage, or carry much in the way of diseases. Often, such ordinances are more from ignorance of these facts.

Rookie Questions

Being in the city, we got all sorts of questions about having chickens, and nearly always, they'd come from someone looking nervous about asking a "stupid" question. It's perfectly fine to ask questions when you don't know, so here are the answers to some of the questions that askers seemed hesitant to ask:

If you only have hens, you'll never get chicks. Eggs left unfertilized are just like the ones from the grocery store. Without a rooster, you can't get chicks.

Chickens do really well in a wide variety of temperatures, provided they're healthy and well-tended. With food and water, they'll be fine at temperatures as low as about 20 degrees up to around 110 degrees. Below 20 degrees, make sure you get a heat lamp on them and make sure their coop is free from drafts and water intrusion. The birds can survive very low temperatures, but they'll require more food, water, and their productivity will drop significantly. Hens go through a "molt" period where their laying slows dramatically. Don't worry—there's nothing wrong with them, and they'll resume production before long. This usually occurs in the transition seasons, but we've had it hit at unexpected times, like late winter while it was still cold.

Roosters are the noisy birds. Hens tend to cluck and coo but are no louder than most ordinary birds. Don't expect hens to be silent because they're chatty, but there's no comparing the chatter you hear from hens to the crow of a rooster. Hens won't keep your neighbors up, but there's no hiding a rooster.

Eggs won't make you sick, but the bacteria that covers them can. Make sure you wash them well before use. Leave the eggs unwashed until you're ready to use them, as the coating of bacteria actually helps keep them from spoiling.

Don't be nervous about eating eggs or meat from your chickens. Both will taste different, but if they are cooked well, there's no hazard.

The eggs themselves can sit awhile outside before going bad, even if it's warm or cold. They keep surprisingly well.

There are occasionally blood flecks in the eggs. It's not dangerous or gross. You can still eat the egg.

What to Expect

Chickens are pretty easy to maintain, but they can do some weird and messed up junk; we had one bird who would crack the other birds' eggs. She wouldn't eat them, but she would damage them, and the "pecking order" is a very real thing. If you start with a flock and add birds later, the new birds will be bullied, sometimes indefinitely.

The eggs themselves can get thin if the birds aren't well fed. Hens are generally pretty quiet, but we had one that made a strange cooing sound, sort of like a really obnoxious pigeon. She'd do it at all hours, too. Another annoying habit they had was when they were free ranged. They would climb up on the roof of the house, and since they're chickens, they couldn't help but scratch. Not only did it keep us awake, but it tore up our roof shingles. So, for all the talk about "cage free" …meh. Chickens have brains the size of a pea; as long as the conditions of their pen aren't dangerous to their health, cage free is honestly kind of silly, considering they'll eat your garden.

They also turn any ground you range them on into muck, and the sludge gets worse if you live in a wet climate. The slurry of poop, mud, and bare ground can make a nice garden space if you cultivate it wisely, but it takes work. You want to confine your chickens to a specific area. Ranging is great if you've got twenty acres, but if it's your backyard, you don't want to come home from work and have nothing but sludge out there. As well, allowing chickens to range if you *do* have acreage will expose them to predators. We've had better luck keeping chickens in town than in rural areas because there are fewer foxes, skunk, raccoons, or other predators to eat them. As it turns out, pretty much everything that eats meat likes the taste of chicken.

Long story short, expect the unexpected. There's a reason farmers cage them, feed them, and forget them. As weird as it might sound, though, they all have personality.

What They Need

Chickens need a roost up off the ground and some sort of barrier between them and predators. We ended up just repurposing a kid's swing set that was damaged in a move. The approach was basically this: we wrapped it with chicken wire and made a door.

We hung hanging water and feed where the swings originally went, so the chickens had a reasonably safe place to hide out and still had access to food. Make sure you have a square foot or so per bird. In our case, the chickens naturally went to the modified swing area to lay at first, but it was crowded with four hens, so one bird started laying under the deck. The swing set coop was to get us on our feet and it worked, but for more than a couple birds it just wasn't big enough.

Chickens are going to destroy whatever ground you put them on, so having something you can fence off and move is of benefit. The good thing is that their poop is a great natural fertilizer, and their scratch turns the ground and reduces weeds, making the old site perfect for a garden the following year. Provide them with a fenced area (so they don't wreck your yard), a roosting area that's up off the ground and out of the elements (keep cedar and other soft wood chips away. Birds are prone to respiratory problems and coniferous wood can give them diseases) and feed/water them. We used the anchor points from the swing set to make hanging feeds which worked pretty well. However, doing it over, keeping them a little higher off the ground and covered to keep the feed from getting soaked during rainstorms would have been a good play. The food will mold in hot or wet climates. We hung a water feeder in nearly the same way, and it worked just fine.

Protection from Predators

The problem with chickens is that *everything* knows they're delicious, so you're going to need to make sure your coop is overbuilt. Other than that, don't overthink it. From raccoons to dogs, all carnivores are going to try their hand at eating your chickens and their eggs. Certain breeds of domesticated dogs (for instance, German Shepherds) are known for killing them, so while your dog can provide an alarm system for other predators, be careful about leaving the birds to hang with the dogs.

Some predators will dig, so if you can, wrap the bottom of the coop with chicken wire, as well, and secure it along the seams as tightly as possible. Either place a trim piece over the joint of the wire or tack it down with screws and washers. The farther out you are, the more wild animals you'll have to contend with. Keep in mind most of the predators will be nocturnal, so keep the birds up off the ground and the coop wired tight. If you range your chickens, they're going to get eaten, especially if you keep only hens. Not only that, but snakes, raccoons, and dogs will all eat eggs if given a chance. If it happens to be a domesticated dog, it can be a real problem because it's exceptionally hard to break them of the habit. Some people have gone to great (and slightly disgusting lengths) to stop their dogs from sucking eggs (more on this in a minute) or killing chickens. I heard of one family that tied the chicken's corpse to the dog's collar until it decomposed as a way of discouraging the pup from killing their chickens. In our view, it's best to just keep the chickens locked up and separate from the other animals.

A Final Note

Here's a bit of useless information. The origination of the phrase "that sucks" actually started as a permutation of the phrase "egg-sucking dog" in the early 1900s. The first attribution of the phrase dates around 1906. An egg-sucking dog was a pretty lousy thing to have if you were working on subsistence in post-Civil War America, so it got truncated to "this sucks eggs," and then "this sucks." It's not a reference to what most people think. So, what we're saying is, keep your dogs away from your eggs unless you want to risk starting an avalanche of slang that lasts for over a century.

Book 2: Mental

MINDSET

The Strength of the Pack

We think of the Integrated Skills Group community as a pack, an homage to Rudyard Kipling's famous "The Law of the Jungle," in which he wrote "the strength of the pack is the wolf, and the strength of the wolf is the pack."

What is strength? How do we assess such a thing, and how can we cultivate it, both in ourselves and for our pack? As we continue, we will look at what we believe is the skeleton of any successful organization, and we'll dive into the meaning of Kipling's "Law of the Jungle" and discuss how it relates to us.

Strength in Intelligence

If we examine the root of what makes humans *strong*, we can look at two different perspectives:

We're not biologically blessed with sharp teeth, talons, stunning speed, or strength.

Our principal strength is our ability to solve problems because we have thought.

Giving homage to thinkers before us, this concept has deep roots throughout Western history. The story of Epimetheus and Prometheus defined humanity through civilizing thought. Kipling's "The Law of the Jungle" itself is a poetic descendant of Aristotle's classic quote, "the whole is greater than the sum of its parts." Even Google devoted several years of study and millions of dollars to determine why some teams composed of leading professionals failed while teams of less imminently qualified individuals seemed to perform well.

The ultimate takeaway from these examples of classical wisdom and modern studies is that trust is extremely important when it comes to working within a group. Acts that compromise the trust of your fellows are tremendously caustic to team efforts, and acts that emphasize commitment to a group's productivity embolden other members and often encourage them to be more dynamic. This is to say, we must often set our egos aside—especially in emergencies.

Panic Is Contagious, But So Is Composure

When we say the "strength of the pack," we mean intellectual flexibility, accountability, honesty, and trust. It means that each individual who is bound by these expectations to a group will lend his strengths to that group, and the group as a whole is stronger for it. We can't arrive at these conclusions without acknowledging that the flip side, the weakness of the pack—selfishness, ego, instability, dishonesty, and deception. If we are to be trusted leaders in any endeavor, we must be trusted beyond a doubt to act in the best interest of those in our care as if they were our family—our pack.

Paul Howe often says, "panic is contagious, but so is composure." One interesting example of this was the tale of the *Grafton* and *Invercauld*, two ships that crashed in the Auckland Islands about five hundred miles from New Zealand. Either story alone would be very interesting, but these two ships crashed on the same island at nearly the same time. Their fates, however, couldn't be less similar.

Thomas Musgrave's *Grafton* struck rocks and required jettison. At great personal risk, Captain Musgrave tied a sick member of his crew, a man called Raynal, to his own body and was nearly pulled into the surf during the daring rescue. Raynal himself expected to die of the illness before becoming shipwrecked.

The *Invercauld's* crew likewise was abandoned, but the crew panicked, leaving a young man named Tom Page to die. He was last heard crying for help, pleading, "Please, God, don't leave me!" Page, along with 88 percent of the *Invercauld's* crew, perished. The men lied about scouting, failed to find ways of killing and cooking the ample seal population that abounded on the island, and only escaped fate when a ship called *Julian* anchored off shore for repairs.

Raynal made a full recovery. He went on to assist in the building of an elaborate longhouse, a double chambered forge with bellows, and was instrumental in the creation of a life raft that was used to sail to New Zealand and initiate a rescue operation which resulted in all of Captain Musgrave's sailors being saved.

Even if they become ill or injured, our commitment to our people is a bond to our group, and our treatment of our weakest members reflects our true selves. In times of hardship, it's easy to become preoccupied with one's own safety. It's easy to panic, and panic is contagious, but so is composure. Cultivate trust and composure as if your life depends on it. Someday it might.

Applied Situational Awareness and Schrödinger's Cat

Training yourself to apply situational awareness.

Awareness is, at its core, taking in information. But is that enough? Not if you can't make that information actionable. You need to be able to accurately recall the information on command for it to be useful. How often do you see someone and panic internally, trying to remember their name? Do you ever try to subtly get a friend to spill the information you meant to memorize? In this section, we're going to discuss the difference between "awareness" and "applied situational awareness." We will look at how multiple aspects of awareness must merge to create an actionable, useful ability.

First Blush

A lot of us cruise through life without ever really becoming victims. At first blush, that might look like luck. If you really look at it though, there aren't many people out there who are really, truly bad. Most of the violence or crime we encounter is interpersonal/social and easily avoidable. Even in rough neighborhoods, you're as likely to get away without injury as not if you can manage space, treat people normally, and be aware of your surroundings. So, when instructors say things like *be aware of your surroundings*, it's expected that people around them will know what they mean. Do we?

The truth is, awareness is the Schrödinger's cat of the tactical world. In Schrödinger's thought exercise, he imagined if a cat were in a box with radioactive material that would eventually break, the cat had an equal chance of being alive or dead. From the outside, we would know there were only two outcomes at any given time: the cat is alive or it's dead, but it couldn't be both. He speculated the outcomes were mutually exclusive. Schrödinger was wrong, as his theory applied to quantum mechanics, and we're being dorks here, but it would be wrong here, too. Here's why:

Someone who is actively paying attention and remembering the building layout, the hostess's name, and the daily special, but who has their head buried in their phone looks less aware than say, a bouncer who's not really paying attention to people at all but has his head up and is looking around. In reality, awareness can be active and passive, but until it is challenged, it's either *on* or *off* to the observer.

In this way, looking like you're paying attention influences whether you're seen as perceptive regardless of how aware you are, and even if you're paying attention, if you don't look like you are, people will assume you're not.

Applied Situational Awareness

Awareness is the process of actively absorbing information from your surroundings. This topic gets more lip service than just about anything else in the training/self-reliance world. Situational awareness, or SA, is a common topic, and it's universally regarded as necessary to make sure you don't end up a victim. But is that true? More importantly, is that the limitation of SA? The answers are yes and no, respectively, but what we're interested in is applied situational awareness (ASA).

ASA is like the quark of the mental world. It's the thing all other things are built from. ASA happens when you use information you've been gathering your entire life to apply to situations you encounter on a daily basis. It's also important to note that awareness, when taken to its extreme, results in fixation. Fixation is extremely detrimental to your overall awareness. Think about it like concentrating on something closely versus taking a broad view.

Think about that for a second. The more information you take in, the more capable you'll be of making situations work to your advantage, but this requires being able to focus as quickly as information presents itself. Like a language, the more words you know, the easier it is to learn. This is conceptually important because we all know that it's possible to have *too much* information, and that's a recipe for inaction. This is discussed more later, but for now, we should understand that knowing how to receive and organize the things we see around us into risk categories is of use.

With that said, what we want to do is establish a baseline and then look for things that don't belong. Once we've established that, we can take a closer look at those things and start collecting information.

Transitional Spaces

There are a number of articles on this subject, and while there are a number of examples of what transition spaces might be, there isn't much of a definition; it's incredibly hard to define what makes a transitional space. However, defining the space is less important than how it affects you. What we're concerned with are places that:

Limit our visual field along lines of approach.

Limit our mobility or require that we follow a predetermined path.

Divide our attention or require that we devote our entire attention to a specific task (examples: elevators, doorways, fountains, vending machines, bathrooms, ATMs, car doors, drive-thrus).

Transition in this context refers more to our transitioning between actions than being in a physical place. Thinking of it like this turns the attention from the space we're occupying toward how that space forces us into an action. For example, in a hall with doors on either end, the hall forces you to open a door (taking an action) to leave. So, for our purposes at ISG, a transitional space is all about how the space affects your ability to move and not about defining an actual place.

Applied Awareness and Angles

Angles apply to everything from grappling to driving, and transitional spaces are no exception. If you understand how angles and awareness interface, you're well on your way to understanding the deep, unifying principles of ISG. Being able to observe others safely while denying them information is tremendously valuable.

When considering angles, which are geometric features of our surrounding environment, you want the greatest amount of visual information with a minimum amount of exposure. Most often, angles present themselves as directional changes in buildings (think hallways joining larger rooms) or features of our environment (such as staircases, foliage, or other natural or man-made visual obstacles). It's not all about having the back corner seat. That silly display of pageantry just won't die, so let's just called it out now: you're not Wild Bill Hickok and having your back to the door isn't likely to get you killed if you live a normal life. If McCall hadn't shot Hickok in Nuttall and Mann's Saloon, he could have done it some other time in some other place. Keep in mind there are probably more glaring vulnerabilities in your daily life than where you sit in a restaurant—but that doesn't mean you should drop yourself into "condition white" or a mental state where you're oblivious to your surroundings.

Back on topic: Let's say the priority is to see as far as possible along avenues of approach. For example, consider your field of view if you park directly in front of a store. Can you see around the edge of the building? How about if you park farther back?

Kim's Game and Applying Awareness

There's a way of testing and building your awareness: a game called KIM, or "Keep in Memory." While I learned this as part of the military skill set, I was surprised to learn that Kim's Game was actually derived from Rudyard Kipling's novel, *Kim*, in which the hero was training to become a spy by memorizing elements of his surroundings.

The object of Kim's Game is to notice as much about a given area as you can. For example:

Look at the vehicles parked out front. What stickers or custom plates do they have? Are any particularly notable? Why?

Look at the people surrounding you. Are they telling a story about themselves by the way they dress, their choice of food or drink, their tattoos, or their equipment? Pay particular attention to shoes. Look at the interior of the building and try to memorize aspects of it. How many steps does it take to cross it? What color are the walls? Are there paintings?

Put this information together and see if you can draw the correct conclusions. Use those conclusions as an excuse to start a conversation. The worst thing that can happen is that you're wrong in front of a stranger. Either way, you get a chance to practice perception and apply it to social interaction. You might never verify whether you're correct, but it's still a good mental exercise.

Another thing that bears mentioning is this: often, being courteous to others puts you in a better position for gathering information. Holding the door puts people in front of you. It gives you a chance to look around without looking weird. Holding the door for someone can politely take them from a position in which you can't observe them, to one in which you can. It can also give you an opportunity to look around before entering a building, so you can take note of anything out of place or spot check to see if someone is following you. Verbally greeting people is both polite and disarming. It shows a willingness to extend courtesy and opens the proverbial door for others to do the same. It also allows you to directly control the position of people around you without being rude, pushy, or obnoxious. This may sound judgmental, but there's some very important nuance here. Let's dive into that.

There's a difference between judging people because you think you won't like them and noting obvious behavior anomalies that have are common, predatory behaviors. You don't owe anyone your trust. Period. Here's permission if you ever needed it: make trust a reward, not a gift. Do the same with respect. It doesn't mean you can't be decent toward others—you should be and that's a mark of your character—but you don't have to give in to society's demand that you trust and respect everyone equally. If your gut tells you someone might be a threat, keep your guard up. There are people who don't think like you do, which means you can't just expect civility and reason.

Awareness and judgment could easily be the difference between life and death if you find yourself confronted by a person on the street or in the presence of an active shooter. So, trust your gut, be respectful, capable, and prepared to handle the problem... mentally, physically, tactically, and technically.

Behavioral Warnings

There are a few major indicators in a person's behavior that broadcast their intent. Some of the more notable indicators that someone is about to initiate an attack are:

Noticeable shifts in balance (loading the weight onto one leg or the other).

Movement around the waist—tugging at trousers, belt, back of the pants, reaching into pockets.

Grooming cues—stroking the face, pinching the bridge of the nose, scratching the eyes.

Threat glancing—looking over their shoulder to see if anything has changed in the pre-attack environment.

Learning this can help you set the curve when it comes to reacting to violent encounters. There are two other major areas of concern relating specifically to women and children.

Some lesser behavior cues would include staring, loitering, trying to strike up conversation using leading questions (*Hey, you got the time?* Or *Can I bum a smoke?*) which forces us to break our concentration and puts us in a transitional task (fumbling through your pockets or looking at a watch). These make us more vulnerable. The problem is, sometimes these aren't preludes to an assault, so we can't just assume anyone asking for the time is waiting for his partner to clobber us over the head with a brick as soon as we look away.

Predatory Behavior and Women's Safety

The National Institute of Justice has published an infuriating report on the prevalence of violence against women and children. Before we address how to recognize the behavior, let's look at some statistics from their report.[6]

- Nearly 18 percent of women surveyed reported being victims of rape or attempted rape. Of them, 21.6 percent said they were under the age of twelve when the attack occurred; 32 percent were between twelve and seventeen.

- 22 percent of women reported being assaulted by an intimate partner.

- Most violence against women is perpetrated by an intimate partner: 64 percent of the women who reported being raped, assaulted, or stalked were victimized by a current or former husband, boyfriend, or someone they dated.

- 32 percent of women were injured during the course of assault, meaning that in one-third of the cases of rape, the woman was physically assaulted as well.

- About 8 percent of women report being stalked—the majority of these women seem to be college-age females.

While there is no foolproof method of eliminating the risks of victimization, we can make some statements regarding self-protection. The first thing we've got to say is that you can't underestimate the seriousness of stalking behaviors—especially if you're female.

- Stalking is a predictive behavior of violence; if a person is stalking you, you should assume they have the capacity to hurt you.
- Stalking is done through physical means (surveillance, following, planned encounters), as well as through technological means, such as GPS, unwanted communications (calls and texts), or digital means such as on social media, online information brokers, and illegal access to your computer.
- Minimizing available information can protect you and your family from such efforts. Make your social media accounts private (LinkedIn as well) and be alert for suspicious activity such as friend requests from people you don't know.
- Threats to children, dependents, or family are serious warning signs and often result in violence.
- Once stalking has begun, protective orders are largely ineffective (35-39 percent of stalking victims report the behavior continues after obtaining a protective order).
- Physical assaults—especially against females—are more likely to result in injury.
- Firearms or knives can be great equalizers that require special attention, especially for women.

The types of attacks women are likely to face occur at very close range against an aggressive, enraged male who likely has a weight and strength advantage. Don't fall for women's self-defense stuff from fashion magazines or retired police officers. There are some excellent female thinkers in the self-defense world, such as Tamara Keel and Melody Lauer. If you're looking for advice, a necessary first step is to find someone whose life circumstances look like your own.

When facing stalking behaviors identified above, awareness and vigilance are extremely important. Another frustrating aspect that you should expect before it comes up is that the police are largely helpless. Even if they believe you, they can't respond fast enough when you need them. Expecting help from the court systems is a long wait for a train that doesn't show.

Stay alert. Pay attention to people and your surroundings and trust your gut! Prevent the situation from getting dangerous if at all possible.

Travel with a friend whenever possible. Don't be shy about asking for an escort from coworkers/classmates/friends if you're uncomfortable. Ignore catcalls or remarks. Side note: Guys do this to guys, too. It's a way to start a fight. Responding in any way is an invitation to trouble. Don't invite the challenge, and don't think one-liners will work. They don't.

Get some training in Jiu Jitsu. There are other acceptable styles of self-defense martial arts, but Jiu Jitsu works extremely well to overcome a strength disparity—strength is less of an advantage against someone skilled in Jiu Jitsu.

Keep your personal information off the internet. Make this a habit.

Stay honest with yourself. If you choose to get some training, keep in mind most self-defense techniques are equal parts humorous and awful…vet your instructors.

Don't surrender if you're attacked! In the cases we reviewed, the women who escaped victimizing simply didn't stop fighting. No technique or class was as important as simply fighting with everything you have.

Children's Safety and Abduction Prevention

In the Escape and Evasion section, we will touch on a topic that's both difficult to read and painfully common: kidnapping. Before we do, we want to have it clearly spelled out. As your family's protector, it's your job to organize your family's risks. Regardless of who you are, child abductions are a frighteningly common occurrence. This section was added as sort of a wake-up call to dealing with situations of illegal captivity. The people we need to reach the most clearly aren't young, healthy men who spend their free time on Jiu Jitsu mats or at the range. They are women and children.

While doing research on the topic, we came across some numbers[7] that were stunning and truly deserving of their own topic.

Whether or not you have children, a firm understanding of the modus operandi of a kidnapper could prevent someone else from losing their child. While we often hear things such as "not my problem" in the self-protection community, one in five abductions were stopped by an adult intervening. It's hard to express just how impactful this one act of courage could be in the lives of the parent and child being victimized. We believe in being prepared to help others; it is a source of great contentment and purpose. So, as we move through this topic, whether you're a parent or simply a bystander, be ready to identify some of the marks of the abductor and how you can interfere with their plan.

Abduction, by the Numbers

It's hard to describe the love a parent has for their children. Children embody not only our hopes for the future, but they are living vestiges of our ancestry; they're the hereditary success of hundreds of thousands of years of human life. We just generally agree that children are precious. However, viewed in this light, it becomes a little more clear what's at stake.

We have already discussed threats that women face, so let's draw on that and look at how abductions occur and how we can approach teaching our children to be wary of them. With that said, it should be tempered with the knowledge that not all kidnappings are the same. Let's look at some of the facts surrounding abduction:

- 68 percent of attempted child abductions involved a vehicle.
- Approximately 31 percent of the attempts happened when the child was going to or from school (or a school related activity).
- 34 percent of *those* attempts occurred during the hours of 2:00 p.m. and 7:00 p.m. —the hours children are least likely to be supervised.
- According to the statistics, the most likely means of abduction (68%) will be someone approaching the child from a vehicle.
- The child is most likely to be approached when traveling to or from school during the hours when parents are usually at work (2-7 p.m.).
- The child will likely be female (64%) and between the ages of 10-14. Most of the time, when a child is able to escape, it's by running, with attracting attention helping in almost 1/3 of the incidences reported (29%).

Now that we have established some facts, we can start planning some ways that your child can make themselves a harder target.

Training

It's miserable that we have to think about this, and the grim realities often go ignored because it's emotionally taxing to give them the attention they demand. After all, most people go through their lives without being abducted, so why stress over it?

Well, as we have mentioned, women face this kind of nonsense their entire lives. Instilling some habits for awareness in them now will likely mean they're less likely to make some of the mistakes that traditionally result in attacks or abductions later in life. For our sons, discussing these hard realities with them may give them the presence of mind to detect and perhaps even assist in stopping an abduction. Taking the time to give them some information is a benefit, regardless of their risk category.

While there are organizations that specialize in women and children's defense and awareness, we will discuss some of the measures you can take to "train" your child to prevent them from being victimized…starting at home.

Security at Home

First of all, good security hygiene at home is a great place to start. Reinforce that your children should never open the door as soon as they hear a knock or a doorbell, and they should wait for an adult. Ensure that children have locking windows in their room. You can take it a step further and purchase some door and window alarms if you don't have a security system that covers you already.

If you use security cameras, don't set them up to use your wireless network; they are vulnerable to hacking. Use hard-wired cameras that can't be accessed by someone with technical knowledge. This allows you to have footage of what's going on in your home recorded and saved without risking compromise or unauthorized access to your "secure" networks. Remember: if it's wireless, it's available to anyone so long as they know how to collect it.

Deterrent Strategies

Often you see things like *don't let them walk home alone* or *don't get into a car with a stranger* in advice articles. Okay, those are nice thoughts, but can you control the circumstances your child faces to such a degree that is possible? Everything in life is a risk versus reward metric. For example, while ride-share services such as Uber and Lyft have spotty track records, it's important to note that abuses are really pretty rare, even though they do happen. Let's look at some strategies we can use to harden our families against criminal selection.

Responsibility: This is one of those issues that will mean different things depending on the child's age. While anyone who lived through their teens will recall that not being one hundred percent honest is a big part of it, talk to your kids about trust and its importance. If your child feels comfortable calling you for help, it can go quite a way toward a good outcome if they find themselves in a pinch. Table the disappointment if they're up to no good. It's better to be disappointed than bereaved.

Recognizing danger (lures, ruses, and grooming): Talk to your children about the methods adult predators use. Encourage your children to trust their gut. Children often have an innate sense of uncertainty around people. Encourage that. You don't own anyone's unhurt feelings, and neither does your child. You do own your child's protection. Discuss with them how a person approaching in a car offering candy or to show them a puppy could be doing so in order to lure them into a vehicle.

Be sure they understand that just because they've met someone once or twice doesn't mean that person isn't a stranger. Talk to your children about grooming and playing games like house or family with older kids or adults. These behaviors can be used by predators to build trust or to make a child more comfortable with inappropriate behaviors.

Finally, make sure they understand that if they're approached by adults, they should always default to "Let's go ask my mom/dad if that's okay." Teach them to say they're scared of dogs or that they don't like candy. Teach them to play Kim's Game. Shut down the approach.

Awareness and Avoidance: We can't stress it enough: being aware is one of the biggest advantages you can deal to yourself, from driving to home security. Discuss with your kids who is at the park when you go. Simply being aware of other adults can help both you and your child have a running threat matrix.

Fight back! This could mean a lot of different things because there is a huge difference between a four-year-old, eight-year-old, twelve-year-old, and sixteen-year-old child. For any age, however, yelling, biting, kicking, and screaming are appropriate. Get them to yell like you just grounded them. Martial arts can also be a solid benefit. As we discuss later in the Fights section, they'll get fitness and technical skill out of it. It might not turn them into a wrecking ball, but it will at least give them some confidence, physicality, and experience with opposing will.

Vary routines: Part of predatory behavior in humans is what is commonly referred to as stalking behavior. Having a routine that's predictable and usual makes it easy to be followed. In addition to throwing a potential stalker off, you can use your habits to help identify potential stalkers. If you think someone is following you, making three right turns can help verify that they are. The odds of someone making the exact same loop as you to get back in the direction you were just heading are low.

Additionally, if you are on foot and suspect a car or person is following you, change your direction. Again, it'll be very obvious that they've *also* changed direction, and you can confirm your suspicions of danger. It will also take time for them to change directions discreetly, which may allow you or your child time to escape.

Tracking devices: These days, everything from Gizmo watches to cell phones have GPS tracking installed. For your kids, leave it on. While we entirely get the privacy concerns, the risk versus reward in the case of your children is worth it. While they might resent it, you can still respect their space while having their location in case something does happen.

Online Presence: *Especially* as children age, be aware that cyberspace is worse than the bar scene from Star Wars. All sorts of scum and villainy lurk within. Discuss with your children that they shouldn't use social media to make friends, but rather to keep in touch with the ones they already know. Have them set their profiles to private and viewable only to friends. Don't use location services through social media or its image sharing features. Simply not handing out any of this information to potential predators could result in criminal de-selection.

Drugs and Alcohol: While we might not want to think about it, it's going to happen. Be real about drinking and the effects thereof. We're mainly talking about younger children in this section, but the threat doesn't just stop once they turn eighteen. Teach kids the effects that drugs and alcohol have on judgment and how people take advantage of that. It's okay to talk to them about it.

Self Defense and Escape and Evasion: In the case of Samantha Josephson, it was revealed that the man who abducted her after she mistook his vehicle for her Uber used child locks to prevent her escape. A simple tool for breaking glass could have been the difference between this young woman being held captive in the vehicle and escaping. There are various devices that can be used for escape: glass breaking tools, improvised tools like spring punches, or hard substances like aluminum oxide ceramic, so look into a solution you think will work for you. Remember, if it's not on you when you need it, it might as well be on the moon. Most of the commercially available products are a bit gimmicky and have questionable effectiveness on hardened windows. A center spring punch has been one of the most consistently useful glass breaking tools we've found, but there are others, such as safety glass breakers. If you're the type who wants to test your equipment, find a junkyard. If you pay them, they'll likely let you test your glass breakers on windows to prove their effectiveness.

Self-defense, as we've discussed, is a lot less about winning a fight and a lot more about losing as little as possible, especially for women. For people who are smaller framed, Jiu Jitsu is arguably the most effective form of self-defense for keeping a stronger opponent from overpowering you. It'll be difficult, but all things worth doing are. When it comes to skills like escape and evasion, those most likely to need it are women and children, who disproportionally face abduction and illegal custody in the modern west.

This is a difficult topic that amounts to every parent's worst-case fear. While we spend most of our time discussing how to make you more resilient, we have to trust that you'll pass on the relevant lessons to those in your care. As with most of the things we discuss, there isn't an easy, cut-and-dry solution that guarantees the outcome we want. What we can do is give a spiderweb of approaches that allow you to interrupt the attack cycle by using good awareness, social judo, and making yourselves difficult to target by using good security practices.

While we often hope that these things won't happen if we ignore them, everything at ISG is based on the reality that bad things happen to good people all the time for no real reason. Once we accept that, things like this become no different than a fire drill: a low probability, high impact event that you don't want to think about for the very first time when some stranger has you trapped and at his mercy. Be smart, plan ahead, and be safe.

PRESENTING YOURSELF

Signature: Presenting Yourself Publicly

The term signature is used to define the amount of attention you draw to yourself. There are ways of making sure everyone knows how awesome you are. Tattoos, flashy or esoteric equipment, logos, footwear, and eyewear—all these things give away significant details about who you are and, more likely than not, what you do for a living. It's common these days to attempt to stand out by emulating things you identify with, but this can be a serious detriment. Having an obvious appearance, especially one that is threatening or overtly "martial," identifies you as either a source of protection or a threat. What you wear and how you present yourself will go a long way toward establishing your role within whatever situation you're in. That's not something to take lightly, and it's important to give a significant amount of thought to how you are perceived, how you'd like to be perceived, and what is most beneficial given your abilities and disposition.

To the person new to disaster preparedness, the world of training is a black hole. This might sound hypocritical, but it's true. There are a few classes that are built with the citizen in mind, but they stop right after "concealed handgun" —which is a pretty myopic view of what a real emergency will constitute. You might be better learning how not to use your handgun. The techniques you can learn during low-light training, rifle training, or whatever other skill set you might want to build are not made for you unless you're on an entry team in a combat arms military unit or you're a police officer who can radio for backup. Training venues aren't to blame for this—it's not even a bad thing—but considering what we may face, it becomes increasingly important to have a realistic view of what we can do. If you're a healthy adult, 99 percent of any altercation you're going to find yourself in can be solved with non-lethal resources.

The point here is this: if you're overweight, middle-aged, and going to carbine classes instead of improving your fitness, consider what the US Army determined during WWII: The single most important aspect in surviving combat was soldier fitness. Not only can the other skills be learned easier if you're fit but working on skills like fighting with a rifle is like searching in the least likely spot first. Bad guys aren't going to attack you from three hundred meters with atlatls and war drums. Further, violent situations often unfold in very unpredictable manners and have multiple solutions. If you're in your car and you get into an altercation, most of your pistol work is out the window, unless you practiced nontraditional firing positions, retention, and you understand how serious it is to have a piece of lead ricocheting around the inside of your car while you're defending yourself. So, why not punch the accelerator, or better yet, use applied situational awareness to avoid the situation all together?

While it doesn't make you feel cool to take courses that are physically taxing or more difficult, anything worth doing is difficult. Don't fall for the promise that you'll be a better *whatever you want to be* by attending a course or school. The goal is to be flexible.

If you choose to carry or own a weapon, take classes where you're challenged with obscure and realistic shooting conditions (sitting at tables, in cars/through glass, with people/family around you, response to active shooter scenarios, shooting from supine while on stair steps, while being attacked, etc.). If you're not in the training world, it's a great time to start looking at your perceived weaknesses now so you don't start wasting money on irrelevant or discretionary training.

Thinking like a Good Guy

A chief failure of the training industry and of the organized "good guys" across the nation is they *feel* like good guys. They think like good guys, and they live in insular societies of good guys where bad guys are reduced to anecdote more often than not. As such, the tactics and techniques employed by "good guys" tend to reflect this. There are a few examples of this that bear scrutiny:

The FBI uses a flashlight technique (discussed later) where they suggest that holding the light way away from the body will draw bullets toward the light. I'm not sure where they're getting this information, but most bad guys are going to run away or give up if they don't feel like they have a chance of winning. They're not going to just spray bullets at a light—that's a *military* approach, and the FBI is drawing on information gleaned by military operations. Criminals are not an adversarial military. They're just people with radically different values and ways of getting what they want.

You've probably heard this or something very similar to it: "I carry my gun here because when a bad guy demands my wallet, I'll pull my gun and shoot him instead." This is a particularly useful example because it shows how mindset shapes tactical approaches; unfortunately for Joe Gunslinger who's carrying his gun by his wallet, bad guys don't ask you for your stuff from twenty-five feet away, giving you just enough time for that perfect draw and shoot drill you see people practicing all the time. Strong-arm robbers realize that this puts them at a disadvantage, so don't expect them to do it because it's convenient for the way you've been trained. Expect them to follow this basic template: get you to drop your guard, distracted you, have someone hit you from behind. You've seen *Jurassic Park*; you know what happens next. So, while you shouldn't train for the "best-case" scenario, you should train yourself to keep your tank full so you don't have to stop on some seedy road after dark and increase your risk.

Here's another common anecdote: "I keep my gun unloaded because when the bad guy(s) hear the slide (loading the gun) they'll reconsider" …or some variation thereof. The problem with this line of logic is it's not true. What it does, first and foremost, is telegraph exactly where you are, what your disposition is, and that you're armed. Before we get to how the person reacts to that, it's important to identify exactly what this means: it means you gave away information. A lot of information. If the person decides to bail, that's good for you. If they're determined, you just put yourself at a tactical disadvantage. That bad guy doesn't care about your training, what kind of gun you're using, or who you trained under. You just told him you're intent on hurting him, so you better be as serious as a heart attack because this might work, and it might not.

If you want to keep your weapon unloaded because you don't feel safe with it loaded or you've got little ones bumbling around and for some crazy reason don't have a way to secure it, that's different (and if it's the second, please fix it). There are plenty more examples of this type of thinking, and the underlying point here is to think critically about ideas regarding your security. Do not just take them for granted because they came from an authority. It's important to realize that expertise in one area of security/protection/warfare does not inherently imply competency in other areas. Look for ways to test and evaluate the suggestions, find cases in which the proposed solution or method was tried, and observe how and where it succeeded or failed.

As to criminals, they are not, regardless of how Hollywood movies make them look, carefree, loser archetypes who don't care if they live or die and who are perfectly willing to just go out in a hail of gunfire. More often than not, what sets them apart is simple: their willingness to break the social contract. But that doesn't make them reliant on overly simple approaches that rely only on violence. They think. They're complicated, and they're predictable —just like good guys.

You are probably neither a good guy nor a bad guy, regardless of what you want to believe. If you're not a police officer, you're a bad guy until proven otherwise. Don't believe it? Go shoot an active shooter and come out with your pistol in one hand and concealed weapons permit in another. See how you're thanked. It'll be with a face full of cement, handcuffs, and a trip downtown. Does it matter that you just saved a school or mall full of kids? Nope. They are going to treat you with this bias because that's how they survive. It's not a bad thing—it just is. Be square with the fact that society does not trust your judgment. This begs the question: why, then, do we choose to train like police, or worse yet, military? And moreover, why do we adopt their thinking when it comes to how we view criminals?

"Bad guys" exist, but many of the people who would victimize you are in thralls of addiction and they're just after your stuff so they can sell it at the pawnshop. They're not looking for a confrontation unless you're in gang country. This might be a relief or a frustration, but either way, you probably know the perpetrator or are separated by one degree (they know one of your family members, friends, or some other person you're in direct contact with). The reason you're being targeted is likewise simple—it's not because they hate you and want to roll the dice on seeing if they can victimize you as a person. It's because you left an "In." It's as simple as that. You were texting your BFF in the car at the gas station when someone saw you weren't paying attention. You left your house unlocked and a random crime occurred. Someone found out you won a few bucks on scratch tickets—the examples don't matter. What matters is how you deal with two aspects of the criminal MO: Closing the "Ins," and managing the opportunists.

Closing the "Ins"

This is largely comprised of the stuff you wouldn't really know unless you've ever had to break into a place or have had your place broken into. The very first thing to consider is the direction your doors face. It's much harder to kick in a door that opens outward. A door that opens inward is easy pickings and knocking out the hinges makes the lock inconsequential. It sounds obvious, now, doesn't it? A security door adds a layer of complexity.

Most break-ins occur through windows. Doors are generally high visibility, and people have the discipline to lock doors. Windows, especially in hot climates, are easy to forget about. You open them often and leave them so for longer periods of time. Making sure you have ways to keep windows shut tightly is critical. Dowels and such make a difference, but if you can get the window open a little, a clever thief will be able to get through. This is assuming they don't just break the window, which brings us to another point: barring your windows. This is a contentious issue because who likes living in a house that looks like a prison?

You've got to weigh it for yourself, but having the ability to secure your windows in a pinch is something worth looking into. Your nice neighborhood now is going to look like a plump turkey to the poor neighborhood across the street if things get bad. Also worth considering is whether you live in an area in which disasters confine people to their homes. Hurricane Katrina kept people stranded for days in their attics and roofs. Prioritize based on your likely situation. You don't want the bars to lock you in.

Managing Opportunists

The notion that you can manage opportunists has to be viewed from two different perspectives:

You have to be *capable* of managing opportunists.

You have to be responsible for maintaining the capabilities.

We're all aware of the simple ways of keeping bad guys out—locking our doors, keeping valuables secured, avoiding bad areas after dark. This type of "official" sounding advice is not particularly practical. Let's talk straight here: Locks only stop honest people. Security (be it physical or cyber) is a myth, and if you are known to have valuables, you're a target. You have to be an inconvenient target. In addition, in an emergency, be ready to adapt because the gang model could easily replace the standard, non-violent B&E (breaking and entering) model. How, then, do we manage the opportunists who would test our security?

Redundancy, Discretion, and Discipline.

Redundancy is a common, easy to understand term, but with regards to physical security, it can be a little confusing. Redundantly locking your door with four or five locks, for example, is basically just a cosmetic announcement that you're paranoid. Having a lock and a dowel in your window is more practical. Having physical barriers between a thief and your valuables is practical redundancy. This is self-evident, but thieves operate on a timeline. Unless they're also planning on using violence, most thieves want to be in and out of your house with your property in the time it takes the cops to get the call and get to the neighborhood. The harder you make it for them to get your stuff, the better your chances are retaining your valuables.

Discretion covers two large and overlapping concepts in security. First, keep quiet about what you've got! Flaunting wealth or assets to someone you trust might seem innocuous enough, but that person might tell his wife, and his 16-year-old might overhear. Then, the kid goes to school and talks about it to his friends, and for initiation night, the local bangers decide to go out and find your house, thinking you've got some specific valuable. I can't stress enough that this also requires that you keep your valuables, and any components that might signal you own such valuables, out of sight. Any professional that comes to your home knows the "normal" things that they see in houses all the time. If you leave a coin bag out, food surplus, a box of ammunition, or expensive equipment all over the place, you're trusting that person's character and assuming that they won't make mention of it to anyone. While in the vast majority of instances that's probably a safe bet, there is a caveat; we're not talking specifically about ordinary circumstances, and we can't be sure that people will not talk. It pays to be discreet. There is no benefit in flaunting; it makes a person look pretentious and telegraphs their valuables.

Second, be discreet about who you let into your home. Don't open your door without checking to see who it is first. If it's someone you don't recognize, don't stand in the doorway to talk to them. If you intend to talk, shut your door behind you and speak with them outside. Now you've created redundancy—you have your person and your door between you and who/whatever you protect, and that's a good way to start discouraging thieves.

Discipline, like discretion, has a few components worth evaluating. Make your security habits second nature and stick to them. Put your valuables in a safe and keep it locked. Visually check your security and ensure you've done everything you can to secure your property. But, also be disciplined and stick to the efforts of redundancy and discretion. All the efforts in the world won't do a bit of good if you don't have the discipline to keep up with them. These are a good *first step* because they cover places which we feel are ours to secure: our home, car, office, or business. Moving on, we will talk about the more involved task of securing your person.

Personal Security

Personal security is largely a measure of three things: skill set, mindset, and tactics. This can be summed up in three basic questions:
What skills do you possess?
Are you mentally alert and prepared for hardship?
How will you react to the various types of emergencies?
Since these are all covered in previous or subsequent sections, let's talk about a few orbiting issues relating to personal security.

Fitness: Your Single Most Important Habit

Personal security is generally considered the ability to keep your physical person safe, but it easily extends to matters of family. To begin with, the most effective method of keeping yourself safe is, simply put, physical fitness. Studies conducted during World War II showed a definitive correlation between physical fitness and survival in combat. The recruits who were more physically fit were better at evading fire, managing stress and injury, and simply put, they could maneuver out of harm's way. Physical fitness is critically important to personal security, but unlike other "important" skills, physical fitness will help you in every aspect of your life, good times or bad. In addition to all that, you'll reduce your likelihood for things like cardiovascular disease and obesity (with all its lurking co-morbidities). In addition to being more likely to survive and delaying disease, you'll feel better, and it'll improve your quality of life.

The standards used to judge physical fitness are widely varied, and as such, they don't give a composite view of your overall health in many cases. However, most incorporate an evaluation of muscular strength, cardiovascular endurance, and muscular endurance. While this topic could take an entire book itself and there are "revolutions" in fitness every few years, this topic can be distilled to a simple, practical, and effective core:

Anaerobic Fitness

Muscular fitness is a measure of how effectively you're able to exert force. Muscular strength is wildly subjective, but as with the rest of this book, the notion is practical, simple, and efficient. While these types of exercises can include other anaerobic exercises such as lifting weights, interval training, or sprints, there are a few basic calisthenic exercises that are widely accepted to be an effective measure of your strength:

The Pull-Up: The pull-up is an exercise where you hang from a bar with your arms fully extended and pull your body up, bringing your chin over the bar, then lowering yourself to the starting position. Repeat this motion as many times as you can while maintaining form. The pull-up assesses the strength of the upper back and shoulders—an extremely important ancestral element of human fitness for reasons discussed later.

The Push-Up: The push-up starts with the body straight and the person being evaluated balancing on their hands. When the exercise begins, they lower themselves as close to the ground as possible without touching it (arms passing 45 degrees) and then press the torso up to the starting position. A push-up for a man will be roughly the equivalent to doing a bench press with two-thirds of his body weight. In addition to being a strength exercise, the push-up is a measure of your endurance.

Squats/Squat Jumps: The squat tests the strength of your legs. Another important attribute in the human arsenal is the ability to quickly rise or lower your body; staying balanced is a fundamental fitness task. Adding a jump to this exercise can test the explosive power of the legs. To perform a squat, stand up straight and lower your body by bending the knees and keeping your weight in the heels of your foot. Return to the starting position to finish one repetition. To perform a jump squat, simply jump as high as you can while preforming the return to starting position. Upon landing, be sure to bend the knees as needed to reduce strain on them.

Sprints: The sprint is a total exertion exercise where you go at your maximum speed over a short distance. Your ability to sprint is the glue that holds all the other fitness tasks together. Sprinting one hundred meters is a general standard, with four hundred meters being a better overall measure of your ability to keep your speed up over a more extended distance. Approximately fifteen seconds is a decent median, with "competitive" being approximately eleven seconds or less. Four hundred meters should take an average runner about sixty-five to seventy seconds. Competitive would be approximately fifty seconds or less.

Cardiovascular Fitness

Typically, these events include aerobic events such as distance running, bicycling, and swimming. These represent one of the human being's core attributes—the ability to outlast their prey. Humans aren't stronger or faster than similarly sized creatures; we have intelligence and endurance. We could scare prey animals into stampeding, and when they dropped from exhaustion, we could kill and eat the animals left behind. We can graze or forage over scores of miles if need be. Running is a very personal skill; it's difficult to say exactly how fast a fit person can run a set distance. For that reason, try to run a set time—twenty, thirty, or forty-five minutes—and increase the distance you perform. This will give performance-based results, which is a good practical method. Forty-five minutes of running should give a fit person approximately six miles in distance. With swimming, a distance of five hundred meters is probably sufficient, and accomplishing this distance in less than fifteen minutes would indicate decent fitness.

All of these exercises are easy to fit into your lifestyle and require very little time, so don't worry about doing something excessively intense—they may create great results over the short term but can be costly in terms of joint, back, and rehabilitation costs if/when something goes wrong. Outpacing the reaper isn't about being the best; it's about being good at a variety of tasks. Make sure you don't over train in one particular event just because it's easy for you—the harder things are to do, the more they demand your attention. Also, it's easy to get wrapped up in buying workout gear. Stairs and a pull-up bar will go a long way toward your overall fitness goal.

Conceptual Checkpoint:
Of the events described, can you perform each? How many repetitions? In how much time?
Would you be able to perform each in sequence, doing your personal maximum number of repetitions?
What do you do on a daily basis to improve or maintain your physical health?

PERSONAL DEFENSE

It can be said that laws only stop honest people. Implicit in that thought is that dishonest people won't be dissuaded by laws. That's what we will be talking about here. The only way to govern "bad people" is to force them to look elsewhere for victims or be able to match—and exceed—their aggression should they choose to push their chips forward anyway. The latter option should be approached by asking yourself one question: Am I in better shape than a 23-year-old parolee? If your answer is no, you should start a physical fitness regimen right away, or start closing the "Ins."

The ability to keep your physical self secure is often the highlight of most peoples' training and preparedness plan. It's also continually mis-evaluated based on perceptions and priorities. As alluded to before, you're more likely to die from improper weight and health management than by a group of marauding raiders during a zombie apocalypse. Personal defense starts with the ability to manage the interaction between three things: your personal space, contacts around your personal space, and unwanted encroachments on your personal space.

Defining Personal Space

Your personal space is not a fixed concept. People get the notion in their head that between cramped city busses, movie theaters, and city streets, their personal space is inside their head. While circumstances can force you into close proximity with others, you can still take precautions to keep your person secure.

Because it's so difficult to manage personal space, it's crucial to understand the elements of being judgmental; when someone makes you feel nervous, they're in your personal space. That doesn't always mean they have mal-intent, but it definitely means you should start listening to your gut. On the other side of that, sometimes when people get in your space bubble it is totally accidental or the result of inebriation or poor judgment. Being wary of how people make you feel is an underrepresented element of personal space, so while you should try to keep people at an arm's length, they can be encroaching from much farther away. Don't neglect that.

Guarding your Personal Space; Managing Contacts

Secondary to mindset, having the ability to keep people out of your space is paramount. This can be done by managing contacts, and this task breaks down into three categories: non-hostile, hostile, and unknown.

Non-hostile contacts are generally easy to stand down using a combination of a polite request and body language that says, "I really don't want to be messed with." Presenting yourself this way means standing up straight and walking with your head up and eyes forward. Look people in the eyes when you speak. You don't have to puff yourself up to look intimidating. Plenty of people make it a goal to look hard. More on that shortly, but regardless of how you look, you're going to have to work with it. Just don't look like you'll go tumbling down the sidewalk if the wind picks up. You want to be confident in yourself. Improving your skills will build and instill this confidence. Test yourself often, be honest, and improve. There is no more essential way to build confidence than by understanding where your limitations lie and knowing that you can overcome them.

When someone approaches you and starts working their way into your space bubble, it's time to take some action. A verbal request for the person to stop where they're at through a defensive but neutral posture will, in most cases, do one of two things: get the person to go on about their business (possibly thinking you're weird), or force them into telegraphing their intentions, which might range from selling you a timeshare (proving their evil intent beyond a doubt) to distracting you while someone clubs you over the head with a bottle and takes your money (possibly less severe than the timeshare, but also undesirable).

Keeping your surroundings in mind is going to go a long way toward orienting you to the type of contact. After initiating contact verbally, don't just stay where you're at, fixated on the person of interest. Find a position that affords you as much peripheral vision as possible and disallows someone to approach you from behind. If you're outside a bar and it's 1:30 in the morning and the contacts are walking around in a pack mumbling stuff like "look at this shithead," you can skip the verbal request and start maneuvering to a position that will prevent them from getting you from behind and won't trap you between them and a chain-link fence. You know they're looking for trouble. These guys are hostile contacts. Don't try to explain it away like they might have been talking to somebody else. Be ready to fight.

Another useful skill is recognizing a ruse. More intrepid criminals who're looking for a buck rather than a bar fight have taken to using a ruse to get your attention by using good Samaritan approaches such as "Hey mister/ma'am, you dropped this," while displaying a few bucks. As you approach, their accomplice accosts you, and all of a sudden, you've gone from a normal day to a Type I emergency. There was a similar ruse in England in 2014. One man would throw and break a bottle. When the victim stopped to identify the sound and orient himself, a second man blindsided the victim with a punch and knocked him out. He lay in the street unconscious for hours.

These are the unknown contacts, and you need to be able to manage them by creating and maintaining personal space and awareness.

Protecting Your Valuables

With valuables, don't leave them in the obvious spots. For men, carry your wallet in your front pocket. If you carry cash, get something less obvious, such as an empty Chapstick tube and put your roll of money in there. Keep a few bucks wrapped in a plastic bag under the sole of your shoe in case the worst happens, and you do get rolled. This way, you've got some holdout cash for a cab, phone call, or first aid supplies. If you forget about the bag, expect the cash to be pretty nasty; under your feet is a pretty nasty place to keep just about anything. At home, false outlets, books, or ice cube trays conceal things nicely. There are numerous options. Just find what works and isn't out of place, and again…keep it to yourself!

Book 3: Tactical

URBAN FIELDCRAFT

The art of slipping the net.

Let's talk about *urban survival*. People ask about it, they make videos about it, and they post on internet forums about it. Listen to one of the many experts discuss what it's like to live in these conditions, and they'll show you videos of them walking around in a hoodie with a backpack, facing down armed robbers or the like. Be wary when people who've never missed a meal in their lives start telling you how to survive.

Urban survival is, above all other things, about people. Managing them, interacting with them, avoiding them, and being useful to the right ones. So, let's dig into this and talk about resourcefulness, budget, and dealing with surviving in the concrete jungle.

You want to talk about what it's like living in the urban landscape during a collapse? Here's some real talk: it's right here, in front of our faces. The ghetto, the barrio, the slums, the projects…they are collapsed societies. We say that an emergency happens when access to critical resources is compromised. It's easy to forget that in our home country, there are places where a meal isn't a three-times-a-day occurrence and the biggest trouble isn't trying to figure out what sounds good. There are places where education means a teacher quelling fights long enough to give homework that she knows no one will do all while being called all sorts of heinous names.

This is a tough topic to get rolling because it hits some personal nerves—personal enough that it's difficult fitting all my thoughts into a series of sentences meant to be read. So, if we accept that an emergency is a state of resource access being restricted, meaning you can't just get things the way you normally do, we can frame the magnitude of what *urban survival* means using an analogy: If I asked how to become a hunter-gatherer, how would you respond?

Even if you were one long ago, it would still be difficult. We're talking about nothing short of an utter redefinition of how you live, your identity and role in society, and entrance into a new culture. How does one prepare for that?

Preparation is a niche industry and, as such, it tends to peddle low quality stuff for high dollar prices to people who are looking to buy their way to a solution. This chapter won't be a shopping list. It'll be some hard lessons learned from personal experience. It's going to be gritty, sickening, and challenging to accept. At times you might even feel a pang of respect for people who you would shoot without hesitation and who would likewise victimize you. Such is the way of reality. These are old lessons from lives that seem long gone, but we'll tell them, anyway.

This subject is somewhat near to my heart. As a young person, my family fractured and found its way into some pretty deep poverty. It's difficult for me to remember things like living in a vehicle, having honk codes for the bridges that family members lived under, or staying in a rotted-out trailer with rotten floorboards and mice tugging at our hair, much less think of them as urban survival or budget preparedness. It was austere; it was gritty; it was poverty, and it wasn't all that different than what we think of as an emergency—something like being a refugee, having no set place or continuity.

In these situations, the day-to-day challenges won't be your chance to make a name for yourself by being a superhero. More likely than not, you'll find yourself dealing with stuff like someone with you overdosing or accidentally stabbing you with a dirty needle while you're trying to calm them down and convince them that police helicopters aren't looking for them. You'll deal with people wanting to jump you for invading their turf or because some distant relative of yours pissed them off.

You might think this is far-fetched, but put yourself out of your job with nowhere to go during a protracted catastrophe like an economic collapse. Who are your kids running with? How about extended family who know you've got your stuff together? The harder times get, the greater the desire for release, and there are always people willing to show them the way. At its most basic, drugs and gangs represent the id of mankind: the desire for power and pleasure.

When society is stripped of its rewards for following the rules, morality is often the first casualty. Because of this, we think this is an essential topic to discuss a few things:

Making some preparations doesn't have to be expensive, but it does have to be realistic. Short of having money, you're not going to be able to fully beat collapse at its own game.

You can get by with way less than you think if you build some skill and resourcefulness.

Urban resource acquisition is something that almost no one talks about because almost no one knows anything about it.

You'll need to be able to manage your circumstances to a degree that allows you to improve your position.

Background

The attending problems that come with this lifestyle are never far from my mind, so as we look at this topic, it will be with an empathetic view that you might not be used to among "boot strap" conservatives and libertarians—a group to which I belong. Though this might be hard to swallow, let me say a quick word on it:

Circumstances beyond your control could instantly turn you into a felon and that stigma could ruin your life.

Put yourself in the following position for a couple minutes: Imagine you're driving from Philadelphia to New Hampshire, both states that permit concealed carry. To get there, you have to pass through New Jersey, Connecticut, and Massachusetts, all of which prohibit concealed carry. Let's say you're stopped for improper lane change or some other minor infraction while in New Jersey. The officers find out you have a concealed pistol in the vehicle (even though under the Firearm Owners' Protection Act you should be protected) and you're charged with a 2nd degree felony. You're taken to jail and arraigned. Let's say you're convicted, lose your job, and now wear the brand of felon. You can no longer vote, and many professions are now closed to you. Through no fault of your own, due to laws that are unarguably unconstitutional, you can be reduced to second-class citizenship.

For many people, this plays out on a much smaller scale—petty moving violations, court dates, failures-to-appear, and poor education and employment opportunities make this a common problem and make the legal system a revolving door. It's easy to say *you should have just fixed your car and paid your insurance*, but how would you respond if someone says, *well, you shouldn't have been carrying your gun*?

If you've never had to choose between electricity, food, and insurance, it's easier said than done. Cold and hungry are just words if you're warm and full. Further, legislative whim could make you a "bad guy" tomorrow, and the rank and file of humanity wouldn't know you from a garden variety thug if they saw you on the nightly news.

Police

Briefly on this: whereas cops are a source of assistance and security for the middle and upper classes, for the people with incomes below the poverty line, police can be like bees—always looking to sting you for getting too close to the honey. We aren't against the officer, but you should be wary that people in lower socio-economic statuses may have possibly had nothing but bad experiences with police. While a traffic stop is a minor headache for you, for others it could mean scrambling to find a relative to take your kids while you're sent to jail for a couple days and your car is impounded. Going back to the traffic stop story from earlier, if you're now wearing that felon brand, every traffic stop is going to look a little different than before.

TEOTWAWKI is an acronym popular in survivalist culture meaning "the end of the world as we know it," or an event so disruptive that our lives fundamentally change. It is a term analogous to our Type III emergency. Every day is TEOTWAWKI for people in impoverished areas all around this country.

It's not uncommon for police who suspect a homeless person (or a known local in a low-income area) to give a shakedown. This generally means the person is stopped and questioned to put some heat on them. Sometimes it's to get them to move on—a subtle way of saying *we're onto you*—and sometimes it's because the police anticipate a bust. Either way, as a person experiencing homelessness, your interactions with the police will be very different. While a person experiencing homelessness will lack some agency that the upper classes have (let's face it, it's unlikely that they are going to show up to testify in court because what's their mailing address again?), police will often be respectful to them and can be a source of information. It comes at a cost, though, especially if you're male. Talking to cops is often a major taboo.

The Culture of Poverty

It's important to say that poverty is less of a racial matter than it is a cultural one. These ethnic subcultures differ. They have their own codes, languages, and social norms. You won't be able to navigate them by mimicry, but categorically they recognize *real*. They'll intuitively know if you're a fake or are vetted in violence. They know if you're being respectful or not. You see this among warriors as well.

What this means is they will know if you're bullshitting faster than you recognize it in yourself. Lying equates to lack of confidence, which is weakness. Weakness will get you killed. If you're trying to project an image, they'll crack you like a nut, which in that environment could mean you get an educational beatdown or even killed. Take this into consideration in your day-to-day actions now. Do you try to come across as a hard case? If so, have you ever really been punched by an adult who wants to hurt you? As my grandfather used to say, "It's not the size of the dog in the fight, it's the size of the fight in the dog."

As a regular, middle-class citizen, the monkey dance might work. But in the urban slums, it's not a game. In the self-protection world, it's common to hear people delineate between what happens in the gym and the streets. The entire line of reasoning is asinine because it's generally used by guys who might as well be saying "on Mars" for their lack of first-hand perspective. Let me tell you a story about this:

There was a martial artist who was something close to famous for getting drunk and starting fights at a bar in Mississippi. He had a thing he'd do for the pageantry of it all—he'd tear off his shirt before throwing down. Here's a guy who was technically proficient, aggressive, and fit…our archetype fight winner. One night, he started getting himself worked up over some bikers who came to his bar, and he got territorial. It's been a while, and I can't remember which motorcycle club it was, but it wasn't one known for screwing around. Before long, this martial artist stepped outside, yelling, cussing, and generally getting himself worked into a lather about it. Then that moment came; he strode forward, tore off his shirt, and before he got in over his head, one of the bikers pulled a filleting knife, slashed him across the belly, and spilled his intestines.

The moral of the story is this: don't try to put on a show. If you're really an asshole, then don't be surprised if all the Shotokan's horses and all the Shotokan's men can't put your intestines inside you again. Those bikers packed up and rode off. They know how to shut up when the police interrogate them because they live that life. If you don't, it's naïve to think you can beat them at their own game. Lesson Number One: Be Real.

Necessities

Let's briefly circle back to the Rules of 3. Just like primitive survival, urban survival also entails the need for oxygenated blood, shelter, water, and food. In the urban environment, we need to know where to get those things. But there's something else first.

We need a code of ethics that emphasizes humility, courtesy, and honesty. Whoever you are today, regardless of your position of the socio-economic chain, it will improve both your life and the lives of others to embrace humility, courtesy, and honesty. While we advocate stoicism and stoic readings, simply having some code of ethics will make a major difference in how you're perceived socially. Make up your mind that there's a right way to treat people and live by it.

This doesn't mean that you cave in or be nice to everyone. It might mean breaking someone's jaw. Our first necessity is our reputation for being real. You need to be someone who's known to be chill, who doesn't start shit, but who doesn't take it, either. If someone else starts it, you're going to get hurt either way, so you better damn well fight. In this environment, no waif with ironic glasses and an overpriced coffee is going to chide you about toxic masculinity if someone decides to stomp your head into the ground.

Acquiring things in the urban environment can mean anything from sifting through dumpsters for leftover food to performing on the boardwalk for enough change to eat. Having a water bottle goes a long way in a post-disaster environment. Most restaurants will allow a person to take water for free. In cities, many downtown areas won't let you use the bathroom unless you buy something, but those standards relax a little on the outskirts. You might be able to use restaurants or truck stops to clean up, which will go a long way toward presenting yourself like you're not planning on staying on the bottom. Keep in mind that this will cost you with other street people. You know what a clean-cut person on the street looks like? A narc.

Even in this situation, a sustainment bag will be crucial. What you want is a low-profile bag that can be used to acquire whatever you may need, and one that can keep you from freezing, drying out and dying, or withering away from lack of calories.

Shelter

The first thing to consider is what's going to happen when the sun goes down—especially if you're in a cold climate. Just like rural survival and shelter building, we're looking to create dead air space, maintain heat, and minimize exposure to moisture and wind. This can take a few forms: from abandoned buildings to the tunnels in park play areas. We have to be open-minded when it comes to where we hole up. What areas reduce wind and grant insulation?

The part of the bridge called the beam seat is often made of concrete and situated up out of the wind. Oftentimes sheds or outbuildings that are unoccupied serve as temporary shelter, which can again put you in trouble with the law for trespassing or vagrancy. Cemeteries and parks often have trees and green spaces that can be decent places for makeshift camps outside the eye of the decent folk and off the path of the other urban homeless who tend to clog the interchanges.

Living in a Vehicle

If you're lucky enough to have a car, there are some options and complications when using it for shelter. Living and sleeping in a car means that you're going to be restricted mainly to roads or trails, many of which have laws governing them and people who are either nosy, looking to steal something, or suspicious.

Walmart parking lots are havens, not only for the mobile homeless, but also those affected by wanderlust who drift through towns and live and sleep in their vehicles. Church parking lots are often well-lit and undisturbed, as are highway rest stops. Avoid places like gas stations (stop and rob, especially), residential neighborhoods and condos, and malls, all of which tend to have one extreme or the other—criminals or officers. Parks often have daylight hours rules or times at which they close to the public, and they're frequented by juveniles looking for a quiet place to burn or chill, and thus, they are frequented by police, too.

Staying warm in a vehicle can be tough. Having a dedicated sleeping platform restricts your space unless you're able to build or fashion some sort of organization. Items that you don't often think about in a home (laundry, trash, food, etc.) start to become a major issue when combined with a twenty-square-foot home. Finding ways to organize so that you don't have to have dirty clothes and garbage riding shotgun comes in handy. If you've got kids, space will get full very quickly. Couch surfing is also an option if you've got friends or family.

Another point to consider: It's obvious to a seasoned thief when a vehicle is being lived in, and as such, if you own guns or anything expensive, this can be a major liability. Not only is car prowl a common occurrence, but those who are staking out your rig know you're going to need to go into that McDonald's bathroom to shave and wash your face. This makes security a very live issue.

Finally, the basics of vehicle maintenance and driving will be more important than ever. Don't be that twit who drives around with the oil light on until your only source of transportation and shelter blows up. That'll cost you social capital, no matter your sphere.

Getting Food

Survival has changed, but survivalists haven't; they're still living in a John Milius commie-killing fantasy. Forget the squirrel trapping nonsense of yesteryear if you're in a city with nowhere to go. If you're planning to grab your trusty hunting rifle and head to the woods in a large-scale conflict, you'd best be careful, as this is the era of drone strikes, and you'd be crazy to think that technology isn't going to advance. Further, people in the country probably resent you for imposing your ways on them through the modern American city-state. Most urban survivalists would be better off with fishing line and a slingshot. All this said, it still pays to know how to dress out small game and fish.

Let's think in terms of scavenging. Think about places that have both perishable and non-perishable food. Many bakeries throw their bread out as soon as it's not marketable. Picking through dumpsters for stale bread isn't appealing, but neither is a situation where you're trying to survive against the odds. While there are opportunities to kill small animals, chances are there won't be enough squirrels to go around, and next up are dogs and cats. Another place people don't consider is schools. Elementary through high school…they all dump TONS of food at the end of the day. Often, it's cartons of milk, wrapped fruit, or other packaged food that you can eat without too much worry. Humbling to think about, isn't it?

When thinking about this, divide the situation firmly between uncontrolled circumstance and disaster. If you're made homeless while the world is functioning well enough, focus on getting back on your feet. If the world is not functioning, nothing short of having a community will help. When urban survival experts talk about how you can't survive in an urban area, they're wrong. You can. But it'll be tough as hell to grow enough food, and you'll have people everywhere trying to steal it. If you don't have some real firm footing in your community, and if they're not on the level, it'll be a disaster. If you're on the streets in this situation, don't give up. Just know that you're going to have to fight tooth and nail to keep from sinking. Hustle in any way you can; offer to take out the garbage for restaurants in the city. You might be able to scavenge or collect some tip money. Think in terms of work—your labor is your ultimate form of capital.

Lesson Number Two: Be Respectful

Churches, Soup Kitchens, and Outreach programs

Regardless of how you feel about social welfare, these programs and organizations exist for people who are truly struggling. Many churches run food banks; if you're already predisposed to faith, you may know this. If you are, get involved now and do good things. Not only will you help someone, but you'll familiarize yourself with their struggles, and that could come in handy someday.

If you find the local department of state health services, chances are you'll qualify for food stamps or temporary assistance. This may wane in a collapse, but it could be the difference between offsetting three hundred dollars in food costs each month and not. Obviously, when you're living on next to nothing, three hundred dollars a month is huge. If you're frugal, you can stock some away (and/or trade).

Public libraries typically have internet access points that you can use to locate local resources. Don't shy away from that. They can also direct you to temporary housing, though it'll likely be austere and first come, first served. If you're not involved with drugs, have some manners and don't screw people over; you will stand out. It can also be a decent line to the black/gray market, as you'll be around people who take the law as shades of gray.

The Streets and Getting Money

Hustling money right now is pretty easy. A panhandler can make a livable wage by excising their pride and dignity and just holding a sign by the side of the road. But during a collapse, expect no such charity.

Things shift quickly, so while playing guitar on the sidewalk might be a decent hustle for a modern vagabond, don't count on it if you find yourself in the midst of a disaster (Type II) or catastrophe (Type III). This is where skills come in handy, and this doesn't mean being handy with a gun or having extra booze to trade. You actually need to be able to produce something: functioning vehicles (to include producing fuel), power production, medical skills, or similar make tough times go around. Do you really want to be known as the guy with the guns and booze if there are no laws? You'd better have some hard bark if you do.

There's a lot of self-selection at ISG, so if you're reading this or have spent any time at ISG, you might be surprised to learn just how incompetent the average person is. Few people even know how to dress a wound or change anything more intense than a bandage, so don't be surprised if you're viewed as an "expert" just from having taken a first aid course or biology class.

In Afghanistan, I often helped local nationals in exchange for information. Daiwa tablets (medical tablets) for someone's sick kid often meant they'd both trust you more and feel indebted. Yes, even in those cultures, people have similar and basic understandings of social debt. Oftentimes your generosity can come back to serve you. Closer to home, immigrants from Latin America or the former Soviet Bloc often come to America to find that their credentials are worth about as much as their currency. No lie, I met a physicist whose only gainful employment came from teaching Russian Language privately. What is the takeaway from this? If you have to flee your home country, your profession isn't going to mean jack shit in the place you land. Your ability to do odd jobs, generally be useful, pick up language and culture, and not get bogged down in legal trouble will mean everything.

Theft

If we're calling it like it is, theft is a huge part of the lawless world of the transient, addicted, and general street culture. Prominent marks that are easy money are work trucks with tools in them, common cars with expensive equipment (souped-up Honda Accords), and homes that are known to have drugs or expensive electronics. Thieves typically hit people who are within a degree or two of separation for a couple reasons:

Oftentimes, those people are themselves on the wrong end of the law.

Plausible deniability. If you set up a score, you can shrug and said you didn't have anything to do with it.

For most people, this isn't so much of an issue, but if you find yourself down and out, be careful who you associate with. Don't ever talk about your valuables. While there's credibility on the street for having expensive jewelry and such, our goal—should we end up there—is to get out. If you have valuables in your vehicle, they need to be double locked. Chain them down. Cover them in a way so there is nothing obviously valuable. If you've got a truck with a canopy, don't think for a second it's secure because it's locked. Those things can be picked with ease, and they break even easier.

Pawn shops are a commonplace to fence stolen goods. They're also a good place to get stuff for cheap. Typically, they are a good place to meet people who can get you stuff. Keep in mind this approach is an issue and is absolutely a gray space that can easily turn black if you're not careful. The bottom line is this: Theft and fencing goods through pawn shops is a daily occurrence, especially in drug communities. With the increasing tide of opioids in more affluent communities, wealthier families are finding themselves targeted by addicted family member, friends of family members, or neighbors. Humility isn't something we harp on because we're pious. Staying off the radar will always benefit you. Lesson Number three: Be resourceful.

The Dark Reality

When it comes to this stuff, we all kind of know but we don't talk about the fact that socially, you're negotiating from a position of weakness. There's a lot of predations that occur in these environments. Favors for sex, drugs, alcohol, and other contraband add to the desperate circumstances of the homeless person. Especially for women, being alone on the streets is rough, and there's a constant threat of violation—not only from other street people, but from norms who view the homeless as demi-human. A further consideration is how this can contribute to the spiral of legal problems that pushes you further and further from freedom.

In addition to situations like this, keep in mind that hygienic issues disproportionally affect the homeless. Even those who don't have IV drug habits tend to suffer from ulcerated feet after prolonged periods of cold while in boots, have higher incidences of infections, and are at higher risk for respiratory disease. They're at heightened risk for rape, STDs, and diseases like hepatitis (C, specifically).

Lastly, street-level respect is very different than what you know. While polite society thrives on the anonymity of their vehicles and the use of veiled language, on the street, intentions are blatantly obvious, and if you think you can be sarcastic or condescending, you're going to get your face pushed in. The people you'll deal with on a daily basis may have done time in prison. They'll have killed, robbed, and stolen for what passes for a living in their world: respect within their community and enough money to not die. You're not going to be able to call for help from the police, which is the ultimate sign of weakness. Keep in mind that smashing your head into the concrete means they spend the night in county, warm and fed. Call the cops and you're a snitch. You're going to instantly and irrevocably close doors and people won't respect or do business with you. So, "self-reliant" as you might be, you probably don't understand what it means when you're living on the bottom of society's heap.

If you find yourself down and out to the point where you're homeless or a refugee, there's one bit of good news: There's only one direction to go…up. Be ready to work hard, be humbled, be treated poorly, and to have no protection from the authorities or representation from the justice system. You'll need all the resourcefulness you can muster, as well as interpersonal skills that gain you access to resources that will still trickle in, even to urban areas in a collapse.

Don't listen to those who say urban collapse is not survivable. They don't speak from experience, and you can bloom where you're planted. It'll just take work. Obviously, in the meantime, take the necessary steps to avoid finding yourself in that situation. Ultimately, the kinds of emergencies that people discuss are end of the world fantasies, not realistic assessments of what's likely to happen in the most common disasters. Understand emergencies. From there, you can start stacking the deck in your favor.

ESCAPE AND EVASION

The act of escape and evasion is a touchy subject. Many of the skills involved can get you arrested, injured, or worse. Some of the commonly used tools for escape and evasion could be illegal where you live. Please understand that, as with all other topics fitting these criteria, you accept responsibility for any actions you may take with this information.

Escaping illegal detention is a serious matter. Kidnappings are a business in many parts of the world and for a traveler abroad, you may be seen as a target of opportunity for ransom-seekers, political groups, or ideological militants. 2014 gifted us IS (or ISIS, or ISIL), and showed the world that severing heads wasn't as twelfth century as we all thought. In the Americas, violent drug trafficking organizations have been using torture and abduction as a political and physical weapon since the 1980s.

All this violence starts with one simple act: illegal detention. Any time someone attempts to take control over your ability to move or make decisions for yourself (without legal authority), you must not cooperate.

The Area Study

As with all things, being aware of your surroundings and situation will go a long way in preventing someone from successfully accosting you or your family members. If you're traveling outside your home country, don't go crazy trying to figure out all the ways you could possibly get hurt, killed, or accosted—but do take a minute to familiarize yourself with the active criminal or political climate of the destination. Are there groups of radicals with a history of violence or abductions? How active are they? Are they targeting groups that you belong to, whether racial, ideological, or cultural? What methods do they use in their attacks?

This is generally referred to as an area study, and you should absolutely sit down and take the time to do one for both your home area and any place where you intend to travel. As you analyzed these things, keep in mind that infrastructure overseas is rarely what you expect in the Western world. Police responses and court proceedings are significantly different, and while you're looking into how the foreign culture will impact you, also look at what you can do to minimize your footprint. It's best to try to blend in and be a gracious guest. This mentality will take you a long way and may even save your life against captors who are not intent on hurting you. Take a look at the local dress, customs, and diet, and do your best to learn a few phrases, especially those that constitute good manners.

The following are some questions to consider for your Area Study:

You're traveling to a region with known political upheaval, and your nationality is targeted. How would you treat hotel stays? How would you get around? What will draw attention to you, and how can you mitigate it?

Some critical things to ask: What is the MO of the politically hostile group? Abductions? Ransom? Execution? How will you react to unexpected knocks on your hotel door, suspicious packages, or people loitering around your car? How can you prevent abduction from being successful?

Alright, says you, what the hell does this have to do with escape and evasion? Well, this is the most important avenue of E&E—making a small target of yourself. The better you can blend in, look like you've been there before, and remain inoffensive to the local population, the more likely it is that you'll be able to conduct your business without an excess of burlap sacks over your head, pistol whippings, and demands for stuff you probably can't provide while tied up.

Conceptual Checkpoint:

Pick a random country you'd like to visit. What's the crime rate of that nation? Population? Predominant religion or cultural heritage? Has there been political or ideological crime?

Describe any economic or political turmoil that has occurred in the last five years.

In this country, do you have anyone you know and trust who lives there? Are they a natural citizen or an immigrant?

If you were forced to leave the country due to circumstances (political upset, war, etc.), how would you get out? How would you finance your escape without access to checks, debit, or credit? Can you keep the monetary resources secure while you travel?

Pick a country you'd hate to visit. Ask the same questions. You've just done a cursory risk assessment.

Escaping Restraints

Illegal restraint is a surefire way to damage a victim's sense of control. Being immobilized can be maddening, especially if you're being waterboarded or otherwise subjected to discomfort. Restraints come in a wide variety, but we'll discuss three, predominately.

Handcuffs

Handcuffs are the staple restraint device for officials in most places. They operate by having a spring-loaded locking cam interact with an armature that features "teeth" that can only move in one direction, so long as the locking cam is not released. The cam is released when an object places torsion (rotational pressure) on it.

The handcuff has a few main components:

Single Strand: This is the armature that features the teeth that set the diameter of the cuff. It is made of a single piece of steel and is riveted to the double strand.

Double Strand: This is the part of the cuff that holds the key post, pawl, and rivets.

Links: The links form the chain that connects the cuffs to one another.

Hinges: Hinged cuffs have a hinged metal bar instead of a chain. This connects the cuffs without allowing the wearer much range of motion (and can make it very hard to escape).

In order to remove handcuffs, we have to have an object to perform one of two actions:

Lower the teeth inside the double strand, also known as the cuff body, or

Create a surface that disallows the teeth on the single strand and the double strand to interact.

Apart from simply keeping a cuff key on your person when traveling, a few improvised objects can be used to accomplish this task. The examples given are by no means the only objects that can be used to escape illegal restraint. They represent the simple and common solutions that can be kept without much hassle.

Cuff Stacking

Experienced police, especially when dealing with high-risk suspects, will tend to stack the cuffs, which means they orient the suspect's hands so that the palms are facing out, and they'll cuff them with the keyway facing in. This makes it extremely tough to pick the cuffs, especially when dealing with hinged cuffs and double locks.

The bottom line with handcuffs: Most of the time they aren't used as effectively as they should be, and if you look like a problem, an experienced captor will take extra time to make your escape difficult. Most criminals aren't going to be using cuffs. They'll use rope, or more likely, duct tape. If you're dealing with illegal detention at the hands of a state level actor, put on the act. Give up completely and entirely, stick your hands out in front of you, and meet them halfway in doing their job. You may find this gives you some agency in how you get free.

The Pick Method

In order to pick handcuffs, you must first have a piece of metal strong enough to raise the lever inside the key post of the handcuffs. For this, bobby pins cut in half and shaped with pliers to make a 90-degree angle work very well. There are three key steps to escaping handcuffs:

Insert the pin into the key post so that the pick's body runs the length of the double strand.

Lift the pick straight up until you meet slight resistance.

Rotate the pin into the key post very slightly until you meet slight resistance. Apply a little more force and then press against the single strand. The arm will release.

The Shim Method

Shimming handcuffs relies on interrupting the teeth between the single and double strand. With this method, you must further close the single strand in order to release your hand. This means this method may fail if the cuffs are very tight to begin with. Also, if they are very tight, you may have to shim the cuffs more than once. All of this costs time, so the pick method tends to be a simpler solution. To shim a handcuff:

Insert the shim into the space between the single and double strands.

Apply forward pressure to both the shim and to the single strand. Place your thumb on the back of the shim and press firmly. Pull back on the single strand to release the hand. This will release the single strand and the bound hand.

While obviously the desirable outcome is to fully free yourself, if you've really got to make a run for it, slap the cuff onto your other wrist and get out of Dodge. It's better to run around with cuffs on your wrist than it is to get captured and show that you're capable of escape.

Flex Cuffs/Zip Ties

These devices have come into favor for situations when many people are captured at one time, but they're also a potential restraint used by criminals or terrorists intent on taking hostages. The good news is they're nothing to breaking free from. Zip ties function very similarly to handcuffs—there's a small plastic tooth that allows a one-way passage of teeth on a length of plastic. Even heavy-duty zip ties work this way. Sufficient force will break this tooth and allow the zip tie to be pulled back out. Fully extending your arms and pulling them down onto your chest with all your strength will break the tie and free your hands. In addition, friction can melt the plastic, so finding a taut rope, sharp edge, or anything else to rub the ties against will heat the plastic, which will then weaken and become easy to break.

Escape

Freeing yourself from restraints is only the first part of the equation. Orientation and situational awareness are going be critical. There are a number of things you can do to prepare for escape. Take a look at your surroundings. Memorize details about your captors. What are they wearing? How are they armed? What kinds of shoes do they have? If you've done a bit of planning before getting into the mess, paying attention can tell you details about the level of professionalism, financing, tactics, and affiliation of your captors. Keep quiet, keep your signature low, and learn—if you can't avoid the situation all together.

Non-Destructive Bypass: Picking Locks

"Locks only stop honest people." My father told me this ages ago, and it's true. The idea behind most modern security is to slow down potential thieves, keep them scouting for easier targets, or disallowing them access to your valuables.

Weapons-based skills don't cross cleanly between different professions. With lockpicking, we have a universally important, useful, and time-saving tool that, when employed by people who have some ethics, can be helpful whether you're out exploring or locked out of your hotel room. So, what do we mean by non-destructive bypass? We mean developing the skills necessary to get past padlocks, door locks, deadbolts, and vehicle locks without destroying the locking mechanism or some other element of security. We focus on these types of locks because they are typically the common points people lock themselves out of and have to call a locksmith. If you're a thief (or if you're in a serious emergency), it's far easier to just break stuff. Non-destructive entry, in general, means you care enough to not break the lock. As we'll see, locks don't even stop honest people anymore.

Ethics and Practicality

Our entire culture at ISG is based around things that are inherently dangerous; from rappelling to shooting guns, we find that the difficult skills are the ones most worth pursuing. With them comes responsibility, so while we agree with many of our peers that certain skills should be kept "private," we also want to skim the surface of security bypass. This means we're putting our trust in you that you'll follow the applicable laws…and more importantly, that you'll use these skills ethically. Here's what we'd like to ask in return: Please don't steal. Don't pick a lock without permission. Don't use these skills to trespass. Know the laws in your area regarding possession of lock picks. We're presenting information on this topic knowing that laws don't stop dishonest people and robbing good people of information only makes them more vulnerable. With the ethics disclaimer out of the way, there's still a feeling of revulsion in a lot of people when we discuss bypassing security. Often, people reflexively ask why anyone would need this, or worse, why we would teach this. The answer is manifold:

- We can't teach it. It's experiential. Bypassing security requires hours and hours of dedicated practice beyond instruction.
- This information isn't "state secret." It's all available commercially or free from media sharing platforms.
- Understanding how to bypass security leads to a greater knowledge of how to secure your valuables.
- Bypassing security can sometimes be necessary, such as when you're locked out of your home, locked out of your vehicle, or if you lose keys to padlocks.
- Illegal restraint is a real issue. Especially for young women, the ability to recognize threats and having some basic escape and evasion skills goes a long way.

There's nothing inherently wrong with being able to defeat security. Like many of our other skills, when you can pick locks, you'll find that you're a lot less reliant on others and that your friends and coworkers appreciate it when you can help them out.

Tools

Your security is only as good as your weakest point. Training for security bypass can start pretty simply: Got an extra lock with no key? Start a box. Changing out locks on your house? Keep the old ones and build a lock tower. As for what picks to start with, there are tons of options, and as with anything, what you get will start with asking what you want to do. Here are some of the kits and tools that the ISG team has used to great effect while out and about:

Bogota Entry Toolset: A simple, durable, and effective toolset, the Bogota provides a lightweight option with a limited magnetic signature. The picks themselves each serve as a tension wrench and feature a probe and rake that are good enough for most types of locks. The Bogota tools have been our constant companions for nine years now, having traveled most of the US and overseas with us. While they'll handle most jobs, for high-security locks or those that require top-of-keyway (TOK) picking, they just won't do.

Sparrow's Creeper Toolset: The Creeper picks up where the Bogotás leave off. They offer more tools in more sizes to address the less common high-security locks. ISG Team members view the Creeper toolset as a standard entry grade piece of EDC for those with some skill and interest in lock picking.

Plug Spinner: The plug spinner is a tool of convenience. On some residential locks, you can pick the incorrect way, which leads to cylinder release but no actuation of the lock itself. That means you picked it, but the lock isn't going to budge. A plug spinner can save you the hassle of picking it again by rotating the cylinder so fast that the pins don't have a chance to reset. While good picking technique is preferable, the plug spinner can save you some serious time. Anyone who says otherwise has never picked residential locks under pressure in the field.

Training and Practicing

When people learn you are able to pick locks, a normal first assumption is that you're either a criminal or spooky. When I tell people that lock picking, out of all the skills I've cultivated over the years, comes in handy more than any other, there's almost always a non-committal *huh* and a shrug. The truth is that bypassing locks is not only useful for criminals and special operators; there's a practical element to it that can help you save time, money, and generally be more efficient.

Let's be up front though: for disaster management, picking locks is one of the least expedient methods possible. Unless you're a pro, destructive bypass is far faster, but we oftentimes want to get into places without leaving a trail of broken stuff. These days, it's usually an abandoned site or a residence—not the kinds of places you want to bust up. Likewise, if you're in an emergency situation, non-destructive methods take a long time. Each lock is different, and it takes time to learn them. Cultivating some picking skills is great, but don't expect you'll be able to step to any lock you encounter in the field and pick it. The lock's condition, age, security rating, how its mounted, the light conditions—these all conspire to keep you out.

A person who can reach an intermediate skill level with raking and single-pin picking can expect they'll be able to get into most low-security padlocks, safes, and residential doors. As a part of your training in defeating locks using non-destructive methods, it can be helpful to make some basic training aids. If you're interested in a DIY project, consider building a lock tower.

A simple lock tower can be made with a drill (and hole-saw blades), and some extra residential locks. This will only help you address residential style locks and doorknobs, so also look into what Sparrows offers. They have basic practice locks as well as security cut-away locks for spool pins and serrated pins. These can be great assets in learning how to work your locks and refine your technique, from beginning to advanced.

Likewise, it's best to focus on practice when you train for non-destructive bypass. Don't watch TV while trying to pick locks. You'll find distractions cause you to tune out the subtle sounds and feels of learning a lock. Once you've got a lock down, sure. But when you're first learning, truly set aside some time to mentally map and methodically pick the lock. If you find that you can't, set it aside and return to some easier locks to stay in practice.

How It Works: Lockpick Types

There are a variety of different picks that can be used to open locks, but here's a very sensible set that will work for the majority of the locks you'll encounter. Here's a very basic description for the types of picks you're likely to encounter.

Bogota (3 hump) or Triple Peak: The Triple Peak works well for 6-pin padlocks without security pins.

Bogota (2 hump) or Twin Peak: These rakes (often referred to as Bogotás) are among the best "general purpose" rakes out there. Frequently used for padlocks or low-security residential doors, they'll also work well on certain canopies and deadbolts.

Worm Rake: A little more gradual than the Bogota, the worm rake can be used with slightly smaller keyways, but still works well on standard-sized locks.

City Rake: The City Rake is called such for its "cityscape" profile. It's less for raking and more for setting in the key and see-sawing, which can be useful for certain types of locks (padlocks, mostly).

Short Hook or Probe: Probes are the tools with which we feel around to determine the number of pins, their setting order, and how we lift them into place when single-pin picking (SPP). The probe is a tool for more difficult locks with security pins that defeat attempts at raking or scrubbing.

Offset Hybrid or Offset Half Diamond: These probes are good for smaller locks that require a bit more delicacy. Often, these tools are paired with a TOK tension wrench in order to free up space in the keyway.

Torsion (or tension) Wrench: This device allows us to rotate the cylinder slightly while setting the pins inside the lock. Torsion (rotational tension) is the first technical aspect of picking to pay attention to; over-applying torsion is a common cause of keyway binding. Imagine light pressure would be such that if you were applying your finger to a thumbtack, you wouldn't draw blood. Heavy pressure would be about as much as it takes to press a key on a keyboard. Wider, more rigid wrenches will give you more feedback and control when picking locks over thinner, springier wrenches.

Flat Bar Torsion Wrench: These are applied within one of two main spots: bottom of keyway (BOK) or TOK.

0.40" Dog Ear Flat Bar: These smaller-width flat bars are made for applying torsion to the TOK on higher security locks with recessed cylinders; this means that the body of the lock protrudes past the keyway, making it harder to get a standard torsion tool in there.

A quick word on types of lock picks: typically, a rake and probe are all you'll really need for most of the locks you're likely to encounter. However, you'll need quite an assortment of torsion tools to manage the variety of keyways! Keep this in mind. The pick tools get most of the attention, but the torsion tools handle most of the variance.

Anatomy and Mental Mapping

The basic pin tumbler lock is something that should be understood in order to be defeated. High-level pickers talk about "mentally mapping" the lock. It's really easy to overlook the importance of this because it's difficult, and it's easy to convince ourselves that we can just rake our way through easy locks.

When you start to encounter difficult locks where SPP is required, you'll have cheated yourself if you've not spent any time working on understanding what's happening inside the pin tumbler lock. Here's what to look for when mentally mapping a lock:

Cylinder Rotation/Counter-rotation as you set pins. This rotation can mean a few things, but it's mainly important because it tells us we're dealing with a security pin. Because security pins are "cut" in the middle, the taper allows the pin to wobble, which tells us it's trying to straighten itself.

The Binding Order in which the pins will need to be picked. When setting pins, they often bind as cylinder rotation is applied via the torsion wrench. This is because the pin channels aren't arranged in a line (when looking from the top of the plug). They are staggered, and because of that, there's an order in which they have to be picked. The first pins to bind the cylinder are the last pins to be picked.

Techniques for Picking Locks

Locks can be picked using a few different methods, but the most common types are raking, single-pin picking, and rake walking (also known as scrubbing).

Raking: Raking is the process of randomly popping the pins up and down while applying tension (or torsion) to the keyway. Raking works well for low-security locks without security pins. Raking generally requires a sawing motion, starting at the back of the lock and working your way forward, then back again. If there are security pins, raking often accidentally binds them, forcing you to start over.

Single-Pin Picking: This is the process of selecting pins in a sequence, setting them to the cylinder's sheer line (or the point at which all the key pins have been elevated to the height allowing the cylinder to turn), and unlocking the lock using a deliberate technique. This is required for higher security locks, as raking won't work well when security pins are present. When single-pin picking, we audit the lock for binding order, security pins, rotation and counter-rotation, and false sets. Without practice, the knowledge won't do you much good.

Rake walking/scrubbing: This technique takes a hook, probe, or half diamond to strum the pins while applying some light torsion. On some locks, this can work like raking.

Common Problems That May Occur

Security Pins: Security pins are a feature that makes it more difficult to set individual pins in place, especially against raking. Though it's possible to rake security pins, it often requires us to stop and single-pin pick the lock.

Overset Pins: Overset occurs when the key pin passes the shear line of the cylinder. In order to open the lock, you'll need to drop the key pin back below the shear line—but not so much so that the driver pin has a chance to snag.

False Set: A false set occurs when a security pin feels like it's in place and has been picked. Generally, this occurs when a security pin, like a spool pin, has been set incorrectly.

Torsion: Torsion (rotational application force) is often mistaken from tension (linear application of force). Whatever you call it, one of the most common problems with picking locks is "monkeying" the torsion. This happens when the impulse to use force overwhelms technique. There are some really great resources on lock picking out there, and we'll paraphrase some of the instructors who've mentored us: Heavy pressure on the torsion wrench should be no more than what it takes to depress a keyboard key. Light pressure would be so little that if your finger was pressed against a thumbtack, you won't puncture the skin.

Like most of our skills at ISG, a tremendous amount of time can be spent developing your picking skills and they're very perishable. If you plan to build the skill, plan to maintain it periodically, as well. Please use this knowledge responsibly, as we're not responsible for misuse the information we've provided.

Destructive Bypass

If you find yourself in an emergency in which a lock is blocking your safe escape, you probably don't have time to pick it, and anyone who tells you otherwise is wrong. The adage *if you can't rake it, break it* was made for the emergency.

Again, don't go around breaking locks that aren't yours for no reason, but if you do have to bypass a lock quickly, breaking it is, more often than not, a far more certain option than picking—and that's if you just can't go around it by other means.

Types of Destructive Bypass

The usual methods for destroying locks come in three basic, functional varieties:

Breaking the shackle via mechanical means such as bolt cutters.

Destroying the internal mechanism and latch through harmonics or tools like the Ramset.

Cutting through the hasp/destroying the door itself (bypassing the lock altogether).

Lately, there's been a lot of dark art mysticism about destructive bypass, for example, melting the internals of a lock. The reason we've taken a hard line against stuff like this is that it doesn't work well, it doesn't work fast, and it doesn't work consistently. Does it help to know you can melt the internals of a lock? Sure. But it helps more to know that the alloys inside most common locks require a melting temperature of anywhere between 2500-5000 degrees, which you're probably not going to get to quickly without specialty tools. It helps to know that the locks being melted in these demonstrations are super-cheap locks with plastic internals. These facts often aren't mentioned because there's a vested interest in making bypass look like mysticism. It really isn't. Just like improvising a weapon, there's no real secret to it. Bolt cutters, grinders, and Ramsets all work pretty well when it comes to destructive bypass.

VEHICLE EXPEDITIONS

Ages ago when I got my first 4x4 vehicle, a 1994 Nissan pickup, my dad said to me, "4-wheel drive is to get you out of trouble, not into it." While I didn't listen, I made enough mistakes to now recognize the wisdom in that advice, so the ISG approach to 4x4 and off-road travel is loosely based around it. We want to be able to get far enough out, set up a camp that keeps us safe, hygienic, and minimally invasive, and of course, we want to be able to get back again as necessary.

Off-Road Driving Techniques

With most things, the techniques you'll need when off-road are largely built on experienced driving: being able to read the terrain and place your wheels where they're least likely to slip or list. Your vehicle is part art and part science. There are classes for developing these driving techniques, but before you get to that part, here are some things to be aware of:

Brake and Gas: If you're like me, your dad told you never use the gas and brake at the same time, but when you're off-road on tough terrain, it's a mandatory skill. When working against gravity and RPMs, you'll need to get used to using the foot brake while goosing the accelerator enough to keep your vehicle from rolling back or stalling. It's a bit counterintuitive at first, but it's a simple practice.

Reading the land: One of the most experiential skills in off-road driving is knowing where your tires are without seeing them. Once you can understand their relative position to the road, managing ruts and irregular terrain, you'll be less likely to damage your vehicle.

Takeoff, Departure, Break-over angles: The break-over angle is how far your vehicle can drop when the front and rear are unequal without damaging your running gear. These angles could be a study in themselves but lets paraphrase it like this: When you're coming up to or down from terrain, the degree of the grade (steepness) can cause you to scrape your front or rear end on the ground. It's even worse if it's isn't a cut-and-dry "hill," and you've got rapid changes in terrain. At that point, the "break-over" comes into play. The break-over angle is how far your vehicle can drop when the front and rear are unequal without damaging your running gear.

Just remember, it's on you to do the hard work: Learn how to drive by getting out and building experience. Start with the basics. If you can't master them, you'll be useless off road. Once you have a good understanding of how to be a solid asset behind the wheel, look into the more advance defensive tactics of road work. Not shooting out your windows or throwing yourself under the car, but how to think about fights around vehicles.

Finally, give some thought to how weather is going to impact your movement. One of our friends recently lost his rig during a high-water crossing. Know what to look for when dealing with swift water!

First Steps

When it comes to off-road sports or adventure, it's important to size up what you want to do. There's mudding, rock crawling, wheeling, trail riding, off-road expeditions. There's overland travel and all sorts of in-between. These all require something just a little different of the driver, but there are some universal principles.

We'll need to plan for food, fuel, sanitation, weather, and of course, terrain.

Once you have an idea where you're heading, it's time to start planning. This doesn't need to be complicated. Start with a roster of who's going and any relevant licensing or responsibilities. After that, start looking at the environmental conditions for your route and time of travel. Between the US Geological Survey and National Weather Service, you should be able to get flood and weather hazards for your route. This can help you plan around water hazards and weather in case you end up in an area where water crossings might be necessary. Once you've sorted out how long you'll be gone and what you can expect weather-wise, the next step is planning meals and budgeting space. Don't forget the other end of meals—sanitation. Don't trash the trail by leaving garbage or waste.

Finally, assemble the trail gear you'll need. If you're going out in a group, you probably don't all need a snatch block, winches, or chainsaws, but communicate with your crew to establish who's carrying what and where it'll be when you set your trail order. You definitely don't want to jog six cars back to get the saw for a downed tree. A good hi-lift jack, spare tires, spare fuel, some basic tools, and fix-a-flat all make good additions to your gear. Once you've got the necessary goods together, start playing Tetris to make it all fit.

Convoy/Caravan

This might seem like a stretch, but really, any time you go somewhere with friends in multiple cars, you're in a convoy. Most people just get in and go, but with a little planning, you can move effectively as a group.

Lane and Space Domination

A big thing when traveling in a group is staying together. Good use of signals is a good start, and so is predicting movement. As a driver, you're going to need to watch ahead and see who's likely to do what. Once the lead vehicle signals its intention, you should do the same, but get over as quickly as possible. You want to dominate the lane you intend to change into so no other vehicle has a chance to interrupt your convoy. If the rearmost vehicle does his job, he will block the lane while the convoy vehicles ahead of him switch lanes to pass or avoid obstacles.

Intervals

Generally, this isn't something you'll need to worry much about if you're outside of a war zone. Interval is a reference to the distance between you and the vehicles you're following, or that are following you. Generally, you want to leave a car's length between vehicles, but when dealing with freeway travel, you may want a little more to allow for the braking distance of the vehicles weighed down with supplies. Off road, you may need to leave substantially more so that each vehicle has maneuvering room while negotiating an obstacle.

This concept was first introduced to me by convoy operations in the military. If counter-vehicle measures, such as mines or VBEIDs are a problem, a larger interval can be used to decrease the likelihood that greater damage can occur. It's the same with danger/ambush areas along your route. The more room you have to maneuver means more chances to make it out and targets are also more spread out.

How does that relate to the regular world? It allows for more time to react. Giving yourself a little distance typically means you have more time to act or react in traffic. You can control this as a method of forcing cars to slow down (and therefore making them want to get out of your convoy) or speed up (to block a lane so the convoy ahead of you can move over to get around a slow-moving vehicle).

In the civilian or overland capacity, a shorter interval when moving over flat, even ground is good, but when you hit tough terrain or water crossings, opening up a bit gives a chance to learn from the prior vehicle's path and minimize risk to the group. Intervals can also dramatically affect your ability to change directions in response to accidents or road closures. You want to give yourself some space, but not enough that someone else can steal it.

Composure

As a driver, you need to be able to roll with the punches. Stuff goes wrong. Things don't go according to plan. Accidents happen. Just get used to the fact that even when you're serious about doing things quickly and correctly, problems will come up, and you're a part of a team that has to solve them together. Remember, your chances of being an asset to your group are greater if you're not the guy who complains all the time or gets pissed when things don't go as planned. As a leader, consider ways to keep people focused and on task, as well. Just like in regular traffic, everything from vehicle damage to tempers will still apply.

On the Trail

The most important thing you can have on the trail, perhaps, is a good trail lead who can act as scout and spotter. Not only will you learn a ton from the lead, but they'll help you work through obstacles without destroying your ride, getting swamped, or finding yourself permanently stuck. One good ground guide can really make the difference in terms of helping the drivers overcome the angles of rough terrain. If you watch any YouTube videos of people working off-road, you'll notice there are probably three spotters for every driver. That's because they aren't doing it right. The spotter's job (just one spotter so you're not getting confused by several people telling you where to go) is to give the driver simple directions using audio and visual signals so that the driver can both hear and see when he gives directions.

When relaying directions, the spotter does so relative to driver's side or passenger's side to eliminate confusion about who's left and right. This mitigates risk of damaging either the vehicle itself or the vulnerable sidewall of the tires while moving through difficult terrain.

Obstacles are another concern; you'll often encounter either water problems that cause you to reroute or fixable situations like downed trees. As part of your planning, make sure that the people with the tools for obstacles are toward the front of the convoy. Things like medical kits should be spaced so that you're never more than a single vehicle from a decent kit, although ideally there should be a medical kit in every vehicle.

If you need, cross-train each other on the skills to stop bleeding, predict and understand the environment, and deal with problems like winching and recovery. It'll go a long way in building your resiliency for the trip, as well as your friends' skill base for hard times.

Practical Approach

As a matter of practicality, having an off-road vehicle can be an excellent hobby and skill set that reinforces some of the crucial skills we hold at ISG; vehicle maintenance, driving, teamwork, camping and primitive skills, and of course, regular old adventure.

The skills you'll need to escape an emergency look nearly identical to those that you'd need to get out of the rat race for a couple weeks and live out of your rig in the mountains.

Setting up Camp

Establishing a camp can take a number of forms depending on your company, goals, and how long you intend to stay. On longer trips with more destinations, you may end up camping in a different spot each night, making a fast, efficient, and well-organized packing space absolutely imperative. Alternatively, you might find that you're driving to a campsite to hike or camp in one area for a weekend or so and don't really need to worry so much about setup and teardown. Keep this in mind for your planning but having a good system that meets the needs of both can be done pretty easily! Let's look at some of the lessons learned for setting up a camp.

Cooking

Among the most important aspects of traveling off road is a decent kitchen. Whether you pool resources and share or have everyone do their own, there are a few required items:

- A stable platform for preparation and cooking
- A method of keeping food cold (a fridge or cooler)
- A set of utensils to prepare food, as well as for serving and eating
- A way of collecting and cleaning the utensils
- A way of transporting water

Something as simple as a large plastic storage bin can easily contain and organize your cook stove, some propane, some canned goods, plates, utensils, a small basin to clean up, and some paper towels/cloth towels. The benefits of having something you can keep in the vehicle can't be understated. If you've ever camped before, you know that critters are going to be on your garbage by the time you finish zipping the tent. If they could, they'd make off with your potatoes. You can put together a pretty serviceable setup for under $200, which will help a lot when camping or in an emergency, or you can go all out and drop $1500 on a fridge alone. The best bet is to start small with gear that you can use camping first, and then upgrade as you find deficiencies.

Sanitation

With the prevalence of those absurd toilet paper commercials, nobody wants to hear about going to the bathroom, but if you've ever lived in a field environment, you know it can get rank in a hurry. Portable toilet setups can go a long way, and the waste can be transported in thick bags that can be placed inside ammo cans. This keeps waste from spilling or causing a stink if you're remote enough that there isn't infrastructure for sanitation.

Digging catholes for sanitation can work, but if you've got a larger group, or are camped too near water, it can be a lot of digging. As gross as it might sound, packing out your waste can be done without being disgusting. Simple popup tents can add some privacy, take up little space, and are easy to set up, as well.

Toilets

There are also portable toilets that do a good job containing waste. These devices use two separate tanks: a water tank and a waste tank that allow the user to clean the toilet with fresh water and hold the waste securely in a watertight container. Coupled with another plastic bin that seals up (and maybe a trash bag), you can have a sanitary option that's comfortable, contained, and easy to use for those who need it most (women and children). A final note: oftentimes these toilets have chemicals that break down the waste over the course of a few days, making them easier to clean. Spoiler, though: Cleaning them is never fun. Don't use high pressure water to start the cleaning process. If you do, wear a mask.

Trash

Another aspect of sanitation is trash management. If you don't have a sealable container, something like the Trasharoo can help compartmentalize waste outside of the cabin where you're driving (and possibly sleeping, if your bed is in your rig). The Trasharoo is a solid addition, especially if you're in remote areas for more than a few days on end. The concept is a large, thick canvas bag that can be easily lined with a trash bag to keep it clean and make waste disposal easy. Removing it for cleaning is easy, too. These often mount to the bumper or spare tire, making it convenient and keeping the trash outside your vehicle.

Otherwise, a sealable container like a 5-gallon bucket is a good option for waste, as are ammo cans (though they've become absurdly expensive in recent times).

Remember to dispose of food scraps separately if you are in bear country!

Sleeping

If you're doing more than a day trip, you'll need some place to sleep. There are multiple options, including all the usual suspects: tents, hammocks, bivy bags. Increasingly common is the rooftop tent.

Rooftop Tents

When it comes to setup and takedown, the rooftop tent is hands-down the fastest way to go. They're comfortable, they keep you up off the ground, and with an anti-condensation mat, they can be both warm and reasonably dry. Since they mount to the roof, they're out of the way and don't take up extra ground space when hunting for a campsite. Most have an optional annex, which is a great way to include some private space to change, another room to sleep in, or a safe area for your pets.

The rooftop tent isn't without drawback, though. First, when it comes to putting it on and taking it off the vehicle, even a reasonably light tent weighs about one hundred twenty pounds, so unless you want to risk your paint or windows, it's a two-person job. The rooftop tent is a cinch and takes about five minutes to set up or tear down, depending on whether you need the rainfly, so it's a convenient way to go if you're going to be on a longer trip. Just don't anticipate it'll be fun or easy to mount or remove for an overnighter.

One of the biggest drawbacks of the rooftop tent is that once it's set up, you can't just drive off as you can with a normal ground tent or tent cot. You'll have to fold it up and zip the cover back on if you need to drive anywhere. This can get pretty annoying for short trips like weekend camping, but for longer trips into more remote areas, it easily justifies the drawbacks given that it's so quick and easy to set up and take down.

Pros

- Quick setup and tear down
- Frees up interior space
- Can store blankets while folded
- Comfortable and off the ground

Cons

- Costly, between $1000-$4000
- Requires sturdy roof rack
- Decreases fuel efficiency
- Requires teardown in order to move vehicle

The bottom line on rooftop tents: The rooftop tent is popular for a reason. Being fast to set up, comfortable, and out of the way, it's hard to argue that it's not the best in terms of ease of use and comfort. With the difficulty of putting it on, taking it off, and the costs associated, it's best suited for someone who spends a significant amount of time off-road or in remote camping areas. Without careful consideration of these points, you may find yourself selling one for cheap on Craigslist.

Tent Cots

Another option for off-road expeditions as well as temporary shelter if you're forced to leave your home is the tent cot. I was introduced to these while in the military, and they're an excellent, quick option for shelter. They're not particularly expensive, costing between $150 for a single-person cot and $275 for a two-person, and when it comes to size, they're not hard to pack, either.

These cots are about the size of a medium-sized folding table and should fit in the cargo space of most mid-sized trucks or SUVs without a whole lot of trouble. The double cot, at fifty-six inches, can make for a tight fit, so be aware of that going in. A truck should easily accommodate any size, but it may be hard to squeeze them into the cargo space in an SUV. Tent cots set up and tear down in about the same time as a rooftop tent, they keep you up off the ground, and they can be fitted with a rainfly, which makes them a really good option for short duration trips or overnight camping.

Pros

- Easy set up and tear down
- No mounting required
- Off the ground
- Water-resistant
- Can still leave camp without tearing down

Cons

- Narrow
- May not work for a large family
- Take up cargo space

The bottom line on tent cots: Tent cots are a sensible option for a small group, but if you start stacking four or five of them, they'll quickly take up most of your cargo space. For a couple or a small family, they may be ideal. For the cost, they're a great intermediate option, even if you hope to buy a rooftop tent further down the line. They are a cost effective, useful solution for shelter and can be quickly set up and taken down.

USE OF LIGHT

Imagine living three hundred years ago when darkness was an uncontrollable part of existence. Barring a lantern, a candle, or the light of the moon, once the sun set, so did your ability to see. Flash forward to present day. Light is a permanent part of most environments around the world. It can be made at the flip of a switch or press of a button. Ambient lighting lines our city streets, shops, and homes. A world that was once off limits to us has changed so drastically that we've coined a term for it: light pollution. It has utterly changed the lives of humans as well as animals and ecosystems. We care about this because we're used to being able to see. So, what happens when we can't?

Vision and Fighting

Vision is our primary sense as human beings. Exploiting our adversary's lack of ability to take in and process visual information is a major advantage in warfare. Night vision devices, thermal imaging, and the tactical use and depravation of light are all components of modern warfare that stack the deck in our favor. However, for citizens who may find themselves confronted with low-light emergencies in a more ambiguous sphere of violence, these advances mean almost nothing. Whereas military forces often have technological superiority—a network of support from close air support to casualty evacuation and intelligence—the citizen has skill and wit. Why, then, has the use of light doctrine from the military sphere of violence been carried over to civilian training?

Our visual field is broken into two types: foveal (forward looking) vision and peripheral (oblique) vision. Foveal vision allows us greater detail and focus. Peripheral vision allows us to sense movement from oblique angles. This makes the human eye very good at both detecting threats approaching from the sides and quickly adjusting our vision to give threats greater scrutiny.

How Natural Night Vision Works

The iris (the colored portion of the eye) is a muscle that can expand and contract the pupil, allowing light into the retina to be converted to visual information. The biochemistry behind this is a little more complicated, but here are the basics: The retina itself is lined with nerve cells called cones and rods. Cones relay information about the wavelength of light, giving our vision color, while rods allow gray-scale vision during twilight and low light.

Within the rods of the eye, a photosensitive protein called rhodopsin allows us to absorb photons and recombine opsin and retinol so that we see with less clarity and focus but perceive more light. Once rhodopsin comes in contact with photons, it splits into opsin and trans-retinol, giving us the ability to see detail and color.

Distance and Clarity

We need to account for how the distance of an object impacts visual clarity; the farther an object is from our eye, the less space it occupies, and therefore, the less information is available to our brain. That means in low light, more distant objects are even less discernible than they'd otherwise be. This is important because as we transition into how to fight in low-light environments, we want to know what's happening—both with our own ability to process information and with our enemies.

What we need to take from this is that there are several factors that are crucial to our ability to make good decisions under stress:

Our ability to see (the right amount of light)

Our focus (detect threats)

Our ability to deny vision and focus to potential adversaries
The role of distance and lighting on perception in high-stress situations

It takes about thirty minutes for opsin and retinol to reconfigure into rhodopsin, but we regain our foveal vision, color, and depth perception almost immediately when exposed to light.

Low-Light/No Light Environment: Stats and Mistakes

The first thing we need to discuss is this: Most training these days comes from police or military sources. Their experiences are incredibly valuable and have to be considered, but the citizen faces low-light environments in different spheres of violence, so we must consider context. Low-light situations are far from cut-and-dry for military and police, as well.

It's commonly known that the poorer the lighting, the greater the propensity for accidents, such as mistaken identity or intent, or a failure to recognize what may be in someone's hand—especially as it relates to the citizen and home defense. With that in mind, it's perfectly acceptable to verbally confront people you encounter or to take a defensive posture rather than trying to track them down. This solution is not only more prudent (especially for citizens), but it affords you a lower threat signature and the element of surprise if you do need to defend yourself. The confusion that occurs in low-light environments is often deadly.

In addition to verbal challenges, how often do you train to hold your fire at the end of a draw stroke? Said another way: Do you draw your pistol and make a decision to shoot, or do you just train to shoot? The reason for this question is that every year, dozens of innocent people are shot under conditions notable firearms instructor Claude Werner has dubbed "negative outcomes." A significant number of headlines pertaining to these negative outcomes read something like this: *Man shoots son returning home late from party*. The cause for this is a convergence of three major issues:

Lack of adequate identification

Training to shoot without making decisions before pulling the trigger

The belief that you should be able to shoot anyone who comes into your house.

Our primary goal is always to lose the least. As citizens, we'll never win if a gun goes off. So, please incorporate thinking into your training.

Low-Light Emergencies

Because a citizen could find himself in anything from an active shooter crisis against multiple assailants with rifles to a simple break-in at their home, as much of the thinking as possible should happen before the fight. This means training. Low-light doctrine is mostly about how to move and use light in an intelligent way. Done correctly, light does a few things:

Overwhelms the adversary's ability to see past the light, creating a wall (remember, vision comes back faster in light)

Provides visual information

Betrays our location to anyone looking

Resets the eye's "night vision"

For these reasons, using a momentary *on* to take information while moving allows us to see more clearly for identification and hazards while not remaining in one spot long enough to take fire. This is all good and well and should be trained on. However, in the civil world, light is often not so cut and dry. Before a raid, SWAT or SOF can disable a building's electrical infrastructure, leaving the occupants without control over the light within. We don't have that luxury.

So then, how do we deal with this? We need to use light to gather some primary information used to make decisions:

What parts of the room introduce transitional spaces (doorways, blind corners, etc.)?

What obstacles are in the room?

How can we use the layout to our advantage (cover, concealment, etc.)?

Can we simply turn the lights on?

The idea shouldn't be to clear a building the way a police officer or tactical team member would; we want to establish points that are difficult to pass through without being detected and from which our enemy will have a hard time passing without putting themselves at a disadvantage.

Transitional Light Environments

Notice the gradient in light after passing through a light room into a dark room:

Transitions in light are the very basis of the gradient, but they're also a distinct hazard that must be considered; whether you're moving from a lit room to an unlit room or from a daylight environment into a darkened room, you are moving across a gradient that puts you at a disadvantage. Conversely, if an unknown contact or hostile party is forced to cross these light thresholds, it is likely you will be able to see them before they see you. Good tactics, in this case, mean minimizing your exposure time in these transitional areas and putting unknown contacts in a position where they have to cross them to get to you.

This happens because of backlighting. Backlighting creates a silhouette, which is easy to identify if you're looking out from the dark and into the light environment. This often creates the additional disadvantage for the party moving from the lit environment because their eyes are subject to the recombination of retinol and opsin once again as they move into the dim/unlit environment. Understanding the environmental light gradient and how backlighting creates a silhouette is a critical point for further understanding of how to use light to our advantage.

So, where do we start if we are faced with this situation? Recall from earlier the concept of OODA by Col. Boyd: Observe, Orient, Decide, and Act. Once you enter the threshold, you are committed to your course of action. Therefore, when deciding on transitioning environments, you should:

Observe the entryway from a sharp, oblique angle that disallows those on the inside to look out. Be careful to avoid standing in front of windows; this is a sure way to silhouette yourself, as you're back-lit.

Orient yourself to the threshold itself. Is it a door? A hallway? Is there a handle or knob? If so, which way does it turn? Which way does the door open? Are you in a linear corridor? An open area? If you cannot get in through the proposed threshold, where is your next entry or egress point? These are all questions that can rob you of precious seconds in a tense situation, so learn to spot and analyze these features as you orient yourself.

Decide if passing through the threshold is in your best interest. Are you putting yourself at an unnecessary risk by doing so? Is there an urgent reason to enter? Are there alternative ways to enter? How about to exit? Is it likely that there will be people inside? If so, what is their disposition (hostile, neutral, friendly), and how will your entry impact them?

Act out your course of action. When you do, be committed, firm, and resolute that your decision is correct. If it is not, get yourself out of the situation before considering all the ways you could have done better or differently.

This component on environment cannot be overstated. Making good, efficient, and rapid decisions is going to be a time-saver in a tense situation, and time saved could very well be lives saved. The more you know about the area you intend to enter, the better. It could be the difference between entering, turning on the light switch and finding what you're after, or moving quickly across a threshold and continuing a very deliberate low-light search for safety.

Finally, consider that in many disasters in which power is out, we still have transitional light environments; it may be bright daylight outside, but as soon as you go indoors, the clock on your natural night vision resets if you don't have a torch handy. That can make navigating the post-disaster environment a challenge if you're not properly equipped.

Equipment and Usage

Plenty has been written on this topic. You can find opinions from professionals in any venue giving information to validate whatever decision you make, so let's discuss some of the lesser-known characteristics of light use, as well as provide a basic primer on terms. Our bottom line up front: We prefer medium output (350-500 lumens or so) lights with more splash than throw for utility lights. The simpler the light, the better. You don't need eight modes. You don't need different buttons. Under stress, you want simple, durable, and sufficient.

Focus on finding something that has simple operations, maybe a couple of outputs, and is either rechargeable or takes rechargeable batteries.

https://integratedskillsgroup.com/2021/06/low-light-tactics-for-th
regular-person/

Basic Terms

Lumens are a measure of how bright a torch is. It can apply to any light from a lantern to a weapon light and has the internet firmly divided into two camps: those who believe you need as many lumens as possible, and those who feel too much illumination is a disadvantage based on how it affects their own vision. Not all lumens are the same. There is emitted light and forward light. Lights with higher emitted light (even at the same lumens) will behave differently than those with more forward light or throw.

Throw is the forward light. This means that the illumination is tightly bound within a small, bright circle. Throw typically translates to better long-range illumination but at the cost of illuminating the general area. Indoors, a torch with high lumens and a focused throw can wash out the target and even make it difficult for you to see. Some people believe that this is a weapon of sorts and serves to blind your opponent. Our experience is that it's less important than people make it out to be, but you should test it for yourself.

Splash (or spill) is the opposite of throw. It's a broad circumference of light where the illumination is more spread out. This leads to a less powerfully focused beam, but it tends to reveal more information in general. Because it's less focused, there's less risk of a light with higher splash and less throw washing out important information about the target.

Types of Lights

One of the first questions asked is *what type of light should I get*? A lot of this depends on your intended use; is this a tactical light for a weapon? Is it for general purposes? We'll look at pros and cons of each.

Handheld: The handheld is the ubiquitous flashlight. It could be anything from the huge Maglite to a tiny, single CR123-powered LED light. Typically, the handheld flashlight is the most useful and least obtrusive tool. It's a common-use item handy in many day-to-day tasks. The primary drawback is that it requires a hand to use. If you have to employ a handgun, this means your accuracy will likely degrade.

Pros: Can be used independently from firearm. Allows for target illumination without pointing a weapon.

Cons: Degrades accuracy, occupies support-side hand (which can make other transitional tasks like opening doors or using a phone difficult).

Weapon-Mounted

The weapon-mounted light (WML) is far superior to the handheld in terms of maintaining accuracy under pressure. The problem is, if it's your only light, you'll find it looks pretty amateur to pull your pistol out to light something up. Additionally, there's mounting evidence that the sympathetic reflexes of the hands can bring about negligent discharges when trying to use WMLs under pressure. If you choose a WML, additional training under pressure should be a non-negotiable component.

Pros: Allows for greater accuracy while illuminating threats.

Cons: More difficult to operate under stress. Requires pointing a weapon at potentially non-hostile unknown contacts. May cause reliability issues.

Head-Mounted

The head-mounted light is a tremendous asset anytime you're away from the electrical grid. From camping to working on cars, this kind of light should have a place in your pack. How about responding to threats, though? While it can be used in a pinch, there are issues with this approach.

Pros: Allows for hands-free use of light that follows your natural foveal vision.

Cons: A light on your head could be a big target. It's hard to change modes or turn the light off and on when it's on your head.

Strobe

Strobing lights do two primary things for you as the wielder: they make your movement very hard to track and they disorient anyone looking for you. The feature can certainly be helpful if it's very dark, but as often as not, you won't be the only one with a light. This can affect the usefulness of strobing lights.

Pros: Disorients adversaries, makes user hard to track in very dark environments.

Cons: Often requires complicated switches or mode selections. (Stick with single button! Complicated lights are a recipe for disaster. You want to know exactly how your light will behave when you turn it on.)

Holds

In this section, we'll describe holds. However, this section benefits greatly from visual demonstrations. If you're able, the article "Low Light Tactics for the Regular Person" on integratedskillsgroup.com will be of use, as it gives visual aids for the descriptions in this section. Alternatively, you can use the QR code to be directly linked to the article.

Modified FBI

With the Modified FBI hold, the light is held away from the body at an arms length in an arc that ranges from shoulder level to head level, in the off hand. This hold became popular due to the notion that bullets follow lights, which is an assessment made for good guys by good guys. Not to say it isn't true, but with good light discipline, this hold becomes (in our opinion) obsolete, and while it still has a foothold, it's not very useful if you're not using it in conjunction with a firearm, and complicates simple tasks, such as passing through doorways.

Pros: Keeps light away from the body, and theoretically confuses aggressive action.

Cons: In practical usage, it's difficult to use this technique when going through doorways or in confined spaces. It tends to snag or hang up if there is a 540-degree debris field (as occurs in emergencies), and perhaps worst of all, it is harmful to your balance and compromises your postural dominance if attacked.

Surefire/Rogers Technique

The Surefire or Rogers hold was designed by the legendary gunfighter Pat Rogers, and allows the user to hold the flashlight between the index and middle finger of the offhand, using the tail cap with the palm or thumb. The support side hand could the be placed along side the pistol, for added stability.

Pros: The Rogers is a good technique that allows for a solid, effective grip on the light. Activation is done with large motor skills (a palm press rather than a finger press), which we find to be easier under stress. In addition, it's a bit more stable while using a firearm, and it points very naturally.

Cons: Requires a specific type of light to use—if it doesn't have a Surefire-type tailcap activation, the Rogers technique is going to be a bit clumsy. It also is a bit unnatural if you're not using it with a weapon, as other grips allow better control over the light.

Harries Technique

The Harries technique places the support side hand and light under the dominant hand, making a "plus" sign of the wrists. The notion is that this will help stabilize the firing hand.

Pros: The Harries hold keeps the light in an aggressive forward grip, at centerline, and makes it easy to transition between this position and the neck index. It also allows quick, effective strikes if one sets up their light as an impact tool. However, do not attempt to strike if you are using a firearm. This cannot be overstated. Don't put your hands in front of the muzzle for any reason. Shooting yourself would be a con.

Cons: Using in conjunction with a firearm offers little to no additional stability and creates poor balance by extending the support-side arm. Additionally, it requires wrist articulation for many, which is a weak point if you are attacked physically.

Neck Index

The Neck index places the flashlight at the jawline, with the thumb of the light hand resting on the clavicle. This hold has some great strengths, but it will also cause a lot of silhouetting if a handgun is presented.

Keeps hands well clear of your front, close to the body, and allows for an aggressive forward posture. Gives the same aggressive stance as the harries but keeps the support-side hand close in and secure close to the body. An unspoken benefit is that the hand and light actually block the highly vulnerable left carotid artery.

Cons: This technique tends to silhouette your firearm and create "shadows" in your visual field. Light near the body could be a hazard. It's also has the same disadvantage that the FBI technique attempts to circumvent—the light might draw assaults.

"Interview" Hold

This stance is my preference for use of light with or without a handgun. It's a cross between the FBI, Harries, and Neck postures. Often used by bouncers at nightclubs to ID people, it keeps the support-side hand high and on cue for a defensive posture (default position).

Pros: Keeps the aggressive posture of the Harries grip on the light and maintains the upright posture of the Neck Index but cants the light out away from the body eight to twelve inches. I like this because it allows me to keep a defensive arm up in situations that don't require the use of arms, but it may require use of force. It is also consistent, and the light is activated at eye level, meaning that your chances of using it as a method of distraction might help you save a second or so if things do go bad. The offset light may be enough to draw bullets away.

Cons: If held too aggressively, it can obstruct your peripheral vision, and if someone approaches from the support-side rear, the arm is not as secure as it would be in a Harries or in a Neck Index. As with the Neck Index, it casts a shadow.

Tactics

The tactical use of light depends on the circumstance, which goes beyond the scope of this section. What we can say is that there are a few useful concepts to understand:

Similar to shooting, you don't want to get pinned down after advertising your whereabouts. Lights, like gunfire, let people know where you are. After you use your light (assuming it's still dark), move!

Use short, brief sweeps of about a half second to scan. Hit the light and sweep it across the room. Look for possible areas from where you could be approached and look for debris or obstacles that you need to be cautious of. Then, move.

If your light is on, you should be moving. Strobe is helpful, both for disorienting your adversary and moving without giving away your exact location. Tracking someone who is moving by strobe can be difficult, and it's a feature worth looking at. If you do end up engaging, remember there are always potentially more aggressors, and you'll need to train to keep moving, keep using your light intelligently, and keep track of anyone who may have been wounded. This is an advanced topic, and scenario-based training should be done.

Don't expect low-light problems in the civilian world to look much like an entry team raiding a compound or executing a high-risk warrant raid. It'll likely be a slow, sketchy process of trying to make sure as much as possible of what's behind you is verified as "safe." Especially with in-the-home problems in low-light conditions, don't be afraid to hold your ground and use your knowledge of your home to your advantage. Remember, you can always move to avoid contact and issue verbal challenges, whether in your home or caught in a post-disaster situation with unknown contacts. If you find yourself dealing with an active shooter, be ready to identify and use terrain and structures to your advantage. Limit their vision, maximize your own, dominate the angles, and fight with all you've got.

PROTECTION AND FIREARMS

This is one of the more difficult subjects to write on for various reasons; everyone has a different idea of what they need. There is also the issue of their level of commitment, legal concerns, political predispositions, and so forth. It's easy to talk about firearms as a "topic" —you can comment on their particulars, weigh the advantages and disadvantages, and wax philosophical about what would be the best choice for a given situation—but that's not what this section is about.

This part of the book is to help navigate the process that starts once you've decided you'd like to purchase a firearm, and it leads to the ongoing process of establishing proficiency, maintaining safety, and building skill.

Opening Tones

The first and most important point to make is that guns are not *the* solution. They are *a* solution—and they are often not *the best* solution for a variety of reasons. This could range from scenarios where you're being physically attacked by someone larger and stronger (who could take a gun away from you and potentially shoot you with it) to ones where the threat doesn't justify lethal force. It's often hard to confront the fact that simply having a gun is a certain type of liability as well as an asset, but reality isn't always just the things we like.

As a person who is not your lawyer, I can't give you guidance on what constitutes justification for the use of firearms. Once you've decided that it is an option you want in reserve, you've accepted a tremendous responsibility that requires a significant investment in time, safekeeping, education, and upkeep. While I have no doubt that a person with very little training can be effective with a firearm, this book isn't about doing all we can to be average. It's about defending our lives with all the tools and resources available to modern humankind—which means being as good as possible without drawing unnecessary risk.

Understanding the Options

The goal when procuring a firearm is to fit the model you purchase to your own specific set of needs and capabilities. What works for one person may very well not work for another. For instance, what fulfills one person's requirements for needing a sidearm might be different than an on-duty police officer or a woman who cannot carry a pistol in a traditional holster.

Some folks lack grip strength and cannot retract the slide on an automatic. There are arguments that this is due to technique— sometimes yes, and often, no. For some, the "recommended" firearm may be too big to carry, which ideally everyone who reads this will commit themselves to doing, in addition to acquiring training. For this reason, we'll discuss a metric that will help you learn to make purchases based on solid logic, proven performance, and your projected needs.

A word of caution: There is no perfect solution. Any selection you make will be a compromise, but the key is to stick with your decision, learn, and become effective with whatever tool you find yourself using.

Firearm Lingo

At the most basic level, firearms come in three basic types: handguns, shotguns, and rifles. As we analyze the types of firearms, we'll break down and discuss some of the particulars within each subset since each type has its own unique qualities.

Before we do, it's important to define some terms. As with many topics, there is a lingo, and understanding it will help you better describe your needs to anyone you speak to about the issue.

Grip/Frame: The portion of the firearm that is grasped during firing.

Slide/Receiver: The portion of the firearm that houses the mechanism responsible for cycling the weapon.

Cylinder: The portion of a revolver that acts as a magazine for the cartridges and aligns them with the barrel.

Bore: The inside of the barrel.

Breech: The portion of the barrel where the bullet rests when it is chambered.

Lands and Grooves: The rifling that causes handgun and rifle bullets to spin as they pass through the bore.

Firepower/Capacity: The amount of ammunition held in a single firearm. High-capacity/firepower is generally considered greater than ten rounds, while less than ten rounds is considered low capacity. However, this is a very academic definition.

Stopping Power: The theoretical ability of a bullet to stop an aggressor. It is almost entirely speculative and based on opinion. The second someone brings up stopping power as criteria for their firearm selection, you should become wary about their advice.

Magazine: A magazine is a firm-bodied device from which the firearm feeds ammunition.

Clip: A metal strip that creates a horizontal line of cartridges which are fed through the top of the action of a rifle. Two types exist: internal and stripper. Internals are inserted and they eject when the last round is fired. Stripper clips require the user to press the rounds into an internal magazine.

Safety: A mechanical device which, if used properly and in functional condition, will prevent a firearm from firing.

Jam/Stoppage: An occurrence in which a firearm is prevented from extracting or loading a fresh cartridge but requires only remedial action.

Malfunction: A mechanical or component failure that causes the weapon to cease functioning properly until it is replaced.

Firearm Categories

Revolver (Handgun)

The Revolver is named for the revolving cylinder that rotates to align cartridges in the cylinder with the barrel at a point called the breech. Revolvers are the longest-serving type of handgun, dating back to1597 with the "revolving arquebus" —an archaic contraption that bears little resemblance to its modern cousins that use a very similar design to the 1836 Colt Revolver.

Revolvers are mechanically simple; they involve little in the way of moving parts and can be easy to carry and conceal since they range in size from something you could cover by making a fist to something most people wouldn't be comfortable shooting without a buttstock. Revolvers are chambered in common and widely recognized calibers, such as .38 Special, .357 Magnum and .44 Magnum.

Strengths: The barrel of a revolver is not (in most cases) in motion during firing. This gives greater consistency and accuracy during firing. The sights of a revolver sit right atop the barrel, resulting in a very low "height over bore" —meaning that the point at which you're aiming and the point that the bullet strikes will have very little deviation based on mechanics. Ballistics will be the primary influence. Accuracy is largely a measure of skill, but this is an inherent advantage of the revolver.

Weaknesses: Revolver cylinders are significantly limited in capacity—most major calibers (greater than .38spl) will only hold six rounds. While some models will carry eight to nine rounds, this comes at a significant increase in size.

Required Dexterity: Revolvers require a great deal more precision to load than autoloading (magazine fed) pistols. This coupled with the low capacity means that more time will be spent keeping the weapon in the fight than actual time spent fighting.

Mechanical Stoppages: Firearms in general are mechanical devices prone to failure. While revolvers cannot jam in the way an autoloader can (failure of the action to eject a spent cartridge), they can have mechanical stoppages that occur when dirt, debris, or fouling compromise the revolver's ability to cycle. This is a very serious situation that can often lead to the weapon being useless until it is cleared properly.

Bottom Line: While certainly better than nothing, the revolver continues to be popular among gun owners, but it has fallen out of favor with those who carry handguns professionally for the reasons highlighted above. Many persuasive articles have been written on the subject, but findings by end-users have shown that the limited capacity makes the revolver less suited to out-and-out gunfights. That said, for use in personal defense, many fine options exist. In addition, a .357 is an acceptable caliber for hunting deer in many states, and it can fire .38s. From a survival perspective, this makes the .357 a strong contender to have around—Being able to shoot two rounds through a robust platform that's capable of taking light game is solidly an asset.

Autoloader (Handgun)

The autoloader became popular with Colt's M1911, adopted by the US Army that year, and it found continued support through the Browning Hi-Power. The automatic pistol is characterized by an operation that uses gas pressure from the detonation of the cartridge to press the slide backward out of the battery, and at the same time eject the spent casing and load a fresh cartridge. This process occurs semi-automatically each time the trigger is pulled until the magazine is expended. Therefore, once the pistol is loaded (a full magazine inserted, slide pulled fully to the rear and released), the weapon is capable of firing until the magazine is empty.

Strengths: While generally more complex than revolvers, the automatic pistol can be operated more quickly; ejecting a magazine and inserting a "fresh" one can [practically] take around two seconds, whereas an average for a revolver would take around six seconds. In addition to this, magazines can be carried that secure a great number more cartridges than do speed-loaders for revolvers, and magazines require less fine motor skills, which is greatly important when stress is high. Because of their popularity, autoloaders have easily affordable and obtainable spare parts, replacement parts, accessories (such as magazines and holsters), and many more options in terms of accessories (such as flashlights and sights).

Weaknesses: One drawback is, due to the mechanism, empty shell casings can become "stuck" if the slide cycles too quickly or without enough force. This causes a stoppage that requires remedial action. The great variety and gradient with regards to autoloader makes, models, and quality require that the prospective owner more carefully investigates what they're buying. There are more parts that wear out, become stressed, and must be replaced. The more complicated design demands that the owner spend significantly more time learning to operate the pistol.

   Bottom Line: An autoloader is the most compelling choice among fighting handguns due to its ability to hold more ammunition, be reloaded quickly with a greater number of cartridges, and ease of operation. While not typically as powerful as revolver cartridges, the high capacity of the autoloader makes it a choice that allows the user to fight longer.

Shotgun

Shotguns are loosely categorized into three categories, much like handguns: Break Action, Pump, and Autoloader. Shotguns of all types suffer from a common inequity—a limited capacity. They also share several common assets, so instead of discussing the types at length, we're going to highlight the shotgun's strengths and uses rather than its mechanical operation.

Shotguns were the mechanical outflow from the blunderbuss—the firearm that Elmer Fudd used to hunt rabbits. The barrel opened like a trumpet to allow the shot to spread once fired. This differs from the single projectile which is stabilized by the lands and grooves of barreling as in handguns and rifles, so shotgun projectiles suffer from lower velocity, less accuracy, and a disperse shot pattern, which can be fairly inconsistent.

Strengths: It's common to hear gun people talking about all sorts of firearm mythos. Common among shotgun users is how you don't have to "aim" a shotgun, and a shot will knock someone back a dozen feet or the like. None of this is true, but as with all myths, there is an element of embedded reality.

> **Pattern:** Shotgun shells, with the exception of rifled slugs, create a pattern when fired. These patterns vary with the type of shot (lead or steel pellets used in shells) and gauge (diameter of the shell). Because there are many projectiles, shotgun blasts create jagged wounds, but because they lack velocity, they quickly become superficial beyond 25-50 yards, and in some cases, insufficient to stop an attacker.

However, this does make the shotgun more forgiving while giving multiple chances per shot to strike vital areas.

Energy transfer: Because shotguns create dramatic wounds and use a large powder charge, they produce quite a lot of velocity and energy up close, creating significant trauma.

Commonality/Familiarity: Shotguns are very common and familiar to many people. They are easy to reload and are forgiving with minor flaws in accuracy. They don't draw much attention from people, and they are considered "politically correct," if that enters into your thinking.

Weaknesses: The shotgun has various issues working against it for any purpose apart from hunting or very limited applications during home defense.

Slow to reload: limited capacity and slow reloads limit the shotgun's use outside the home. While they can be used for hunting large game, they lack the velocity and range of a rifle and the capacity of the handgun.

Limited range: Because of the smooth bore barrel of the shotgun, range is typically limited to approximately fifty yards and less. This may not seem to be a disadvantage—and in a home defense situation it is not—but if you select a shotgun as a "do all" weapon, you'll be handicapping yourself when it comes to other tasks.

Pattern: While an asset in some situations, it must be considered that in a situation where you're fighting for your life, such as a home invasion or if pressed to defend your community, a shotgun's patterning can lead to unintended injuries on hostages or friendly forces. Because of this, the same thing that is an advantage in certain situations can be a liability in others.

Ammunition Bulk: Twenty shot shells take up roughly the same amount of space as sixty rounds of 5.56 or forty rounds of .308. This consideration is not important outside of war, but it is something that should be calculated for "worst-case" scenarios.

Bottom Line: Shotguns have unique advantages and liabilities that should be considered. The shotgun bridges a very narrow gap between the pistol and rifle—it's more powerful than a pistol, but it has the concealing properties of a rifle (that is to say, it's not concealable). It has the range of a pistol (loosely), but within that range it will produce results comparable to a rifle. For this reason, I spend very little time with the shotgun as a weapon other than to familiarize myself in case I am forced to press one into service. On the other hand, it's extremely useful around a property or homestead, as it's good for killing snakes, taking game, and is a functional defensive tool.

There is one very important thing worth considering. If in a situation of resource scarcity, it's very likely that shot shells will be one of the most commonly available and reloadable types of ammunition. Because of their sturdiness, they will be more forgiving and longer lasting. In addition, the ammunition crunch that occurred in 2012 left plenty of shot shells on the shelves when most (if not all) other defensive calibers were sold out. Reloading shot shells is also pretty simple and forgiving, and for these reasons, a shotgun and the skills to use it effectively are of value.

Manual Rifle

Manual rifles are often found as bolt, lever action, or pump action. Unlike most autoloading rifles, they're chambered in "full-power" cartridges which are significantly more powerful than the cartridges found in rifles like the M4 or even AK rifles. They generally feature internal magazines which hold very few rounds (approximately five).

Strengths: Manual rifles have full-powered rounds, which are very powerful. They are excellent for hunting large game and have excellent range—most of these rifles are perfectly capable of producing hits out to six hundred meters with practice. They are mechanically simple and extremely reliable, robust, and durable.

Weaknesses: These rifles commonly weigh eight to ten pounds, making them a bit heavy compared to other firearms. They are slower to load and manipulate, and they have a low magazine capacity—this is a negative to some but may not be to you. However, since it is a "restrained" quality, it will be categorized as a limitation. They often use bizarre, exotic, or expensive cartridges which are produced in small quantities.

> **Note:** Similar to the shotgun, the full-powered cartridge can be an asset, but it can also be a terrible liability. In a home, the rifle round could easily travel through walls or cars and strike objects or people beyond them. This can be an asset, but it could also be very troublesome.

Bottom Line: The rifle is the best bang for the buck, so to speak. A good surplus rifle can be had for about $200 (as of this writing), will last a century, and will be useful for hunting and community defense. The rifle is to the community what the handgun is to the self, or the shotgun is to the home.

Autoloading Rifle

Autoloading rifles were born from WWII. After the war revealed the urban nature of warfare, the Russians perfected the autoloading rifle in the ubiquitous AK-47 and its variants. The West designed several excellent rifles of its own, including the FAL and M4 carbine. Sharing many of the advantages of the manual rifle with a drastically increased capacity and a medium-power round, the autoloading rifle is analogous to the autoloading pistol. It is mechanically more complex and carries with it a greater need for training and discipline to be used effectively, but it is superior to the slower firing, loading, and manipulating manual rifle cousins for engagements.

Strengths: The autoloading rifle fires medium-powered cartridges which are very effective from fifteen meters to three hundred meters with little to no trouble, and longer ranges are perfectly realistic. This firearm allows the user to fight longer, faster, and harder than any other firearm listed. Variants of the .30 caliber (M14, AK, etc.) can be used to hunt, legally. Autoloading rifles are rugged and durable—military-pattern rifles are made to withstand rigors that hunting rifles or commercial products are not. This battle-proven design will last for decades, if not a century or more.

Weaknesses: The stigma of owning a fighting rifle may attract unwanted attention or scorn. Depending on your location, owning one may even be illegal. These rifles are often very expensive, costing between $800-$2500 (at the time of writing). They may be overpowered for home defense, and a lack of training and discipline makes it easy to "spray and pray" rather than use the rifle effectively. These rifles require magazines and ancillary equipment, and many clones, knockoffs, or poorly made alternatives exist that will not be as durable or long lasting.

Bottom Line: Rifles are the best all-around choice when you look at the problem using the metric of accuracy, simplicity, and terminal ballistics. In the case of autoloading rifles, it continues this trend with capacity, and in the case of military-pattern rifles, durability as well. However, these aren't available to everyone, and they aren't practical to carry on your person. This is where we see the rise of the Survival Arsenal fallacy. Generally written by "gun people," this myth holds that you're not ready unless you have a pistol, a rifle, and a shotgun at your disposal. The reason this is wrong? Well…let's look at our criteria:

Criteria for Selecting a Firearm

We've defined the types of firearms available and looked at some of their strengths and weaknesses, but we haven't really talked much about what we need. Let's face it—we all have different needs. Does a couple in downtown Boston need a pistol, a rifle, and a shotgun? Playing the numbers, they'll have none of the above. So how do they start? What about a young guy or gal in rural Kentucky? Same needs? The answer is there are no *magic bullets* to determine what will suit you, but there are ways of minimizing the headache of selection, maintenance, and use of the tool you may have to stake your life on.

First, *buy quality, cry just once*, and you will end up ahead of the game. Trying to save money upfront often ends up costing more in the long run.

Second, don't waste your money on accessories until you've determined a need, not a want. Like the rest of America's industries, the firearms industry wants to sell you a lot of stuff you really don't need. There are important accessories (magazines, holsters, and such), but many are poorly made and don't overcome any deficiency you couldn't address on your own with more practice.

Third, take the salesman with a grain of salt. He'll tell you a lot of things that sound legit, but his job is to make money for his store. Do your homework and research your selection, and don't forget to apply the second point above.

Fourth, don't talk yourself into something just because you like it, saw it in a video game or movie, or it's the latest fad. Look for something tried and true, durable, common enough to keep running for years to come, and that fits your budget. High-priced, rare, and imported firearms might be of excellent quality, but finding spare parts will often be difficult or impossible. Think of how the tool will work in the worst-case scenario.

So, in a semi-prioritized fashion, here's what to look for:

Durability. In my opinion, having a weapon that is durable is more important than any other single influence. It simply has to work when you need it to. As a mechanical device, the quality of materials, craftsmanship, and engineering will all impact how long the tool will last. If, like me, you're buying this for the defense of your life, the most critical element is that it works under the worst conditions.

Reliability. While this may seem the same as durability, it is not. While durability vouches for the weapon's ability to take punishment, reliability is a measure of how well it will work under those circumstances, and of course, after. The mechanical operation of the weapon must run as unimpeded as possible. That means fewer parts break, fewer mechanical stoppages, and fewer full breakages. A reliable weapon that is durable will be handed down through the generations, while a weapon that has only one quality will be hung above a mantle.

Repair-ability. As a mechanical device, breakages are inevitable. When they happen, you want the tool you're using to be easy to fix with replacement parts readily available. This speaks to anything from the magazines getting lost, to breaking an internal component, to losing a spring or breaking the stock. It must be easy to replace or salvage parts to keep your firearm in operational condition.

Commonality. Commonality to me is a big one, and ultimately has helped me narrow down my selections to very specific tools. The areas I evaluate for commonality are:

Is it being used by police or military? If it is, ammunition, magazines, and parts will be produced en masse.

Is it in a caliber that is common? Again, I try to stick to calibers currently in use by the military. This ensures there will be ample ammunition produced, as well as brass and surplus for the long haul.

Is it something I can/would buy a second copy of? For obvious reasons, having a great variety of firearms is a liability to anyone other than the collector, and it's far more utilitarian to find one "pattern" and stick to it. This minimizes training, ammunition buying, magazine and spare parts selection, and familiarity concerns.

Capacity. Does it hold enough ammunition that you will not be continually reloading if your life depends on staying in the fight? When rounds are flying, exhausting your ammunition can be a serious liability to both you and anyone else you may be protecting or assisting. While this point has become contentious, it's important to remember that the enemy will not limit his options based on what he perceives as being socially acceptable. It's also entirely possible to own high-capacity magazines and not want to hurt anyone. Stunning, I know.

Once you've weighed your prospective purchase against these criteria, you will then have to assess whether the price is practical and fits your budget. While this is a critical turning point for most people, it should be noted that spending more and buying a quality tool will allow you a lifetime of service, while making a poor decision may leave you searching for a compromise at a desperate time. Buying on a layaway plan, purchasing used firearms, and saving up are all preferable to buying a less-expensive firearm that will not perform when it is needed the most.

Safety

Safety is an ongoing topic of concern for both pro- and anti-gun folks. I won't belabor the issue, but I firmly believe that safety is a byproduct of knowledge. You have to know what you're looking at, how it functions, and then how to apply the rules of gun safety.

As we develop our base of knowledge, we can begin to develop safe habits and apply safe handling principles. Be competent in these because, as a component of your training at a later time, safe "dry practice" will become a part of how you develop consistent trigger pull, reduce flinch, and practice malfunction drills and reloading procedures.

Let's look at the cardinal rules of firearms safety before we go any further:

Handle every gun as if it is loaded.

Know what's in front of your muzzle (barrel) at all times.

Keep your finger off the trigger until you're ready to fire.

Know your target and what's beyond it.

There are more complicated sets of rules out there, but the great thing about these basic rules is this: If you break one while following the other three, no harm will occur.

The first thing you should do anytime you receive a weapon is verify its status as "clear" —meaning there is no ammunition in the weapon unless you want there to be. Don't pretend to do this. If you don't know how to verify, don't just look at the firearm and pretend you know what's going on. This is like cheating on a test —you're only shorting yourself. Ask how to check it. Ask questions about how it works. Learn!

To verify that the weapon is empty, the following steps should be followed:

Remove the magazine or open the cylinder. If it's a manual rifle or shotgun, physically check to be sure the internal magazine has been emptied or no shells are in the magazine tube.

If the weapon is an autoloader, pull the bolt to the rear and visually inspect the chamber. *Triple check*. It never hurts to be extra safe, and this is a good habit to form before you learn to dry practice. Separate the magazine or ammunition and close the bolt, cylinder, or release the slide.

Firearm Training

Regardless of what you choose to do in terms of training, you are the one ultimately responsible for the safe and effective use of a firearm. While many levels of training exist (far superior training, in fact, to what most police or military members receive) to match your level of commitment, it's imperative that you at least understand the basic rules of safety and become familiar with the weapon you decide to purchase.

If you can't automatically identify several key features—barrel, trigger, safety or de-cocker cylinder/slide/bolt, chamber, magazine release, cylinder/slide release button or lever frame/lower receiver/ stock—then you need to devote more time to knowing your firearm. You should further be able to identify whether your weapon is single action, double action or SA/DA blowback, revolving, gas impingement, piston driven, pump, bolt or lever action or semi-automatic. Knowing this will help you understand the strengths and weaknesses inherent to the different designs so when you use your own metric for what fits best for you, you will be "armed" with knowledge.

Thoughts on Multi-Caliber Weapons

One of the most important things that can be said for guns is that they're useless without ammunition. Another thing to keep in mind is that ammunition is consumable, and most of the ammunition produced ends up in the hands of a very few people. This was punctuated by the ammunition scarcity in 2008 and 2012, and it gets a person thinking: If you can only own a couple guns, what caliber do you want them in? Something common? Something cheap? Something expensive? Something high-performance? There's a long list to choose from, and there is a set of compromises built into any decision you make. Another thing to consider is that regardless of what you choose, you never know if you'll be able to find ammunition for it in a shortage. With this in mind, the idea of a single pistol that can fire a variety of calibers gains major appeal as a choice for survival or EDC (everyday carry).

.40S&W caliber pistols can often, with a simple barrel change, be converted to shoot both 9mm and .357 SIG. This means if you carry a pistol, you can put a spare barrel and magazine(s) in your pack and quickly change between calibers. 9mm was extremely scarce in 2012-2013, but .40 and .357 SIG were more available. Similarly, the .357 Magnum can fire .38 Special, and .38+P cartridges. With autoloaders, you can go from a larger caliber to a smaller one in most modern makes, but you cannot go from a smaller to a larger caliber (9mm to .40, for example).

The frame size must also be considered. Large frame pistols such as the .45ACP cannot (at the time of this writing) be changed to smaller frame cartridges, such as the .40S&W, 9mm Para. and .357SIG. This concept has been tested over nearly sixteen thousand rounds with Smith & Wesson's M&P 40C—which has fired 9mm almost exclusively, is carried only with 9mm ammunition, and has been extremely accurate and reliable and has a current round count of upwards of 20,000 rounds. Many manufactures sell conversion barrels, and some are quite high quality. The M&PC made a compelling choice due to it being mechanically identical between calibers, with only barrel, magazine, and bore cuts on the slide being different. In addition, the pistol is concealable but carries a respectable amount of ammunition (12+1 in 9mm; 10+1 in .40S&W or .357SIG) and is a comfortable and reliable pistol to shoot. That said, you should also consider buying spare parts for your sidearm (which will wear out over time and can create light strikes, extraction issues, and mechanical stoppages).

One major consideration is that ammunition interchangeability comes with a very demanding drawback—you must absolutely use the utmost care when matching your ammo, magazines, and barrel. A mismatch can and probably will lead to a catastrophic failure that could injure you or someone near you. In order to prevent this, use different color paint or tape on the base of the magazine, and carve small notches and put a smidge of color on the barrel to match it to its proper magazines. This will go a long way to ensure that mistakes are not made, but it is still a personal responsibility that must be taken very seriously. In addition, the very act of scavenging for ammunition is very dangerous. The utmost caution must be exercised to ensure rounds are safe for use in your pistol.

Likewise, using ammunition in a pistol with a replacement barrel may void your firearms warranty. As with all topics in this book, *any and all liability for actions suggested in this text are solely the readers, and by reading this, you acknowledge that you accept responsibility for your actions.*

With that out of the way, it is worth considering a .40 caliber pistol with conversions and a .357 Magnum revolver as your choice in pistols. This gives you up to six calibers in two handheld firearms, should you choose to carry them. If you find yourself in a pinch and low on ammunition, this combination will make it very likely that you could use ammunition if you were to find it.

To date, no rifles have been shown to be multi-caliber and reliable in their functions, which makes it of the utmost importance to have a good multipurpose round for your rifle, should you choose to have one.

Understanding Ammunition

Ammunition can be a very intimidating subject for those who do not know much about firearms. Selecting ammunition for hunting or personal defense is a very important decision with strong implications for the performance and safety of your firearm. With a lot of opinions, misinformation, and geek-speak floating around on the topic, it can be overwhelming to the point of exasperation. The good news is, it's actually a really simple topic once you understand some of the basic terms.

Ammunition is generally expressed in a measurement. Most of the world uses a metric rating, while the commercial market in the United States uses a US standard measurement. This can create some confusion, but more on that later.

The measurements in metric are almost always a diameter-to-length ratio. For example, a bullet in the caliber 5.56x45mm is 5.56mm wide and 45mm long. A 9x19mm cartridge is 9mm wide and 19mm long. Shot shells are measured in gauge with a lower number being a larger diameter. Typical 12-gauge shells are 70mm long, which works out to be 2 1/2 inches, but they are offered in a 3-inch magnum as well.

Before we go on, it's important to note that a cartridge is made of four components:

Case (generally brass, nickel, or steel)

Primer (An ignition for the propellant; look for the round dimple on the base of the cartridge)

Powder/propellant (also known as gunpowder)

Projectile (also known as the bullet—technically, it's the only part of the cartridge that is a bullet.)

Types of Bullets

Bullets come in various types that are denoted as suffixed acronyms; these bullet types are generally the following:

SP (Soft Point): The tip of the bullet is left uncoated (exposed lead).

AP (Armor Piercing): This ammunition has an alloy core instead of lead.

BT (Boat Tail): The rear end of the cartridge is tapered to stabilize the projectile in flight.

BTHP (Boat Tail Hollow Point): A combination of the Boat Tail and Hollow Point Features.

Elements of Performance:

Now that we've had a quick look at the physical characteristics of these cartridges, let's talk briefly about some elements of performance. This topic is the subject of many books, articles, and internet posts and would take up a tremendous amount of space to fully explain in one section, but with an understanding of what these things mean, you can go forth and make decisions based on the knowledge you develop.

The word *ballistics* comes from the Greek word *ballein*, which means *to throw*. Just like a football or baseball, when a bullet is fired, it follows a trajectory and is assigned a velocity. These two things account for the lion's share of how a bullet performs. The bullet doesn't fly in a straight line; it is lifted by a 'tilt' in the barrel design and then begins to drop as it loses velocity. This gives the bullet two "zeroes." A zero is a distance at which the bullet itself has no drop or gain and the sights are perfectly aligned with the bullet's point of impact. So, the path of a bullet is not in a straight line, rather bullets follow an arc. This is often considered in how easy or difficult a particular caliber is to shoot—flatter shooting rounds (like the 5.56mm or 5.45mm) hit targets easily because they undergo very little change in elevation over the course of flight.

The bullet, upon impact, is assigned an "energy" rating which is usually expressed in pounds per square inch, and this value is calculated using the bullet's velocity and mass.

It's important at this point to discuss a very flaccid term: *stopping power*. This theoretical amount of energy is what people attempt to use when referring to the amount of energy transfer required to make a human being halt. This is such a dangerous misnomer because in order for a person to literally be *stopped* by the force of a bullet, the person firing that bullet would have to feel an equal or greater amount of recoil.

This means that when a person or animal is struck with a bullet, the impact is less than or equal to the recoil felt by the person firing the bullet, as per Newton's laws of motion, and that any observable reaction they display *is caused by the surprise of being impacted*—not from some indefinable power. So, from this we can assume that a person or animal reacts to the psychological pressures of the physical injury and the surprise rather than the actual force of the impact. In short, there is no numerical threshold that can be relied upon to produce stopping power.

Conceptual Checkpoint

The following is a table showing the muzzle velocity in meters per second, mass in grams, and energy in joules of some of the more common pistol and rifle projectiles. Apply some science and look critically for a substantial difference in energy.

For instance, a magazine of 7.62x39 provides 63,150 joules of energy continuously before reloading. A .308 with a 20-round magazine provides 65,920 joules of energy. The much-celebrated 1911, with eight rounds, provides 4,504 joules, while a full-framed 9mm with seventeen rounds provides 9,129 joules. However, energy alone doesn't tell the whole of the story. The ability to manage recoil, accuracy, and penetration, as well as the ability to manipulate the weapon and capacity all play into which choice is best for you.

A few takeaways from the most modern research into ballistics boil down into the following generalities:

All handgun calibers are roughly equal. The largest variance is in capacity, with frame size held equal: 9mm > .40S&W > .45ACP, in most cases.

Rifle cartridges are all superior to all handgun cartridges.

When your life is on the line, the difference between types of handguns or rifles is largely irrelevant. The person firing them is the decisive element and tactics are more important than equipment.

With that in mind, if you are still in the process of choosing a firearm, now is a good time to ask yourself what your purpose and needs are and which caliber best suits them.

Thoughts on Ammunition:

Ammunition (and caliber) is a hotly contested issue. The 5.56mm has been lauded as inefficient and underpowered, while the Afghans nicknamed the Soviet 5.45x39mm "the poison bullet" due to the smallest injuries resulting in death. There's less than 0.11mm difference between them, so why the disparity?

Truthfully, it doesn't exist, though design has a lot to do with it. The Russians designed the 5.45 with a hollow cavity in the rear of the bullet which causes its lighter rear end to turn immediately upon impact, sending it on a wildly erratic path once it enters tissue, a process called keyholing. The 5.56mm used by American forces, by comparison, is a simple, jacketed ball round, **not** meant to maim or cause excessive wounding. Bullet design has a lot to do with what the bullet is good at, and what it is not, and the ultimate factor in how a bullet performs is you.

Ball ammunition, for example, is notorious (in both handguns and rifles) for passing through the intended target (or drywall, OSB [plywood used for siding], vehicles, et cetera) and striking unintended targets. For this reason, most professionals and citizens use hollow point ammunition because upon striking a target, hollow points rapidly expand in diameter, creating drag and slowing the projectile, making it both larger and more likely to strike vital targets while decreasing the likelihood that it will pass through the target.

Another important note to make is that hollow points, though they sound terrible and nefarious, are actually far safer to use for defense than is ball (which sounds pretty unimpressive) because of this reason. Hollow points are not "armor piercing" rounds, and this means they are not regulated in any capacity (yet)—though some are restricted to military and law enforcement purchases. Armor piercing rounds, while we're on the subject, are often a misnomer.

The body armor worn by police officers (commonly referred to as IIIA, soft armor, or Kevlar) is penetrable by nearly every single commonly produced rifle round that's above .22 caliber. For this reason, all rifle rounds could be considered "armor piercing," unless we are discussing military-grade armor (commonly known as Level IV), which is made specifically to stop military rifle ammunition. Therefore, the only "armor piercing" ammunition that's made is made for rifles, and it only applies to military-grade SAPI (small arms protective insert) plates. This is an important academic point as the political rhetoric continues to boil over—as a ban on "armor piercing" ammunition could easily be taken to mean "pretty much all rifle calibers other than .22."

When you select ammunition for hunting or personal defense, it's important to learn:

- The ballistics of the cartridge you've selected (how high or low will the bullet be at a given distance?)
- How prone it will be to passing through walls, tissue, or vehicles (Very important for safety and liability reasons—it's incumbent on you to know where every round you fire goes).
- Is the type of ammunition you've selected appropriate to the task at hand? For example, there's no reason to buy hollow points to practice your marksmanship! They're more expensive and will perform better, but ball will serve just fine for this role.

Also, if you're very new to owning firearms, double check to be sure you've got the right cartridge. By now, you'll have noticed that there are very common cartridge diameters. The 7.62, for example, could refer to 7.62x25 Tokarov, 7.62x39 Soviet, 7.62x51 Winchester, 7.62x54 Russian, or 7.62x59 (commonly known as . 30-'06)! As well, 9mm could mean 9mm Kurz (.380ACP), 9x18 Makarov, 9x19 Para., or 9x21 Largo. While this might seem daunting, your firearm will have the correct designation stamped on it, and unless you've got a fairly uncommon firearm, it should be very easy to get the help you need.

Maintaining Your Firearm

Maintaining firearms is a simple task that adds another element of responsibility to firearms ownership. Similar to any mechanical device, firearms are prone to wear, breakages, and corrosion that accompanies any device that has moving metal on metal. Be it a rifle, pistol, shotgun, or anything in between, there are some very common things you can do to prolong the life of your firearm and ensure its proper and reliable function.

Before I press on with discussing the *how*, there are a few questions of *why* that need to be satisfied. No discussion of firearms is complete without some words of caution and safety. Cleaning your firearm carries the very real risk of negligent discharge, and as with all handling, you should physically verify that the weapon is empty.

When I clear my weapons to handle or clean them, I take the following sequential steps: Eject the magazine (if it exists), engage the safety (if it exists), and pull the slide of the weapon three times —rotate the weapon to the side of the ejection port to ensure that any shells or cartridges have to fight gravity as well as you. Once I've done this, I lock the slide to the rear. At this point, I visually inspect the firearm to ensure it is clear.

Many firearms-related accidents occur during routine handling, such as cleaning or when you're loading or unloading. Strict adherence to the three universal rules of firearms safety will help prevent accidents, and ensure that if they do occur, they don't hurt anyone. While there is some variation, please take the following three seriously:

Don't point a firearm (intentionally or otherwise) at anything you're not willing to destroy.

Keep your finger off the trigger and out of the trigger guard until you're ready to make a decision to fire.

Treat all firearms as if they're loaded.

It's absolutely imperative that you do not get in the habit of thinking that your habits apply to your friends—take this approach every time you pick up a weapon that you do not intend to fire— and save yourself, at a very minimum, an embarrassing and expensive mistake.

Minutia

Like many elements of gun culture, much of what leaks its way into popular culture stems from the military or from older times. The military's infatuation with spotless weapons, for example, can be traced back to the days of non-chrome-lined barrels, corrosive salts, and primitive bluing techniques at a time when leaving your weapon fouled could literally cause it to deteriorate into ineffectiveness. Today, with chrome-lined barrels, Parkerizing, and modern powders, some fouling on your firearm is not the end of the world. What we want to accomplish isn't stripping the finish off your rifle or pistol by over-cleaning it, but rather ensuring that no amount of buildup hardens on the surfaces, impedes function, or gums up small parts.

Subtle Lessons

Taking a weapon apart can be a confusing process until you're familiar with it. As often as not, you've got devices that are under spring tension (which can lead to some lost parts, or eye patches, depending on the firearm being cleaned) and parts that rely on a very specific order of assembly to work properly. It's a cliché to suggest that people just consult the manual, and often, if you're an enthusiast, you've probably decided that the manual can wait until you have a chance to disassemble your new tool and can't get it back together. Been there; lesson learned? Use the manual. Seriously. If your enthusiasm is so overwhelming that you can't wait, try to find a friend who knows the platform so that you're not in the dark about it.

The Process of Cleaning

Part 1: Prep work

What you'll need:

A solvent (I like using Hoppe's No. 9 solvent for regular cleaning. Rem oil works well, too.)

A bore brush and rod for the correct caliber

A cleaning cloth (old t-shirts work fine)

Cotton swabs or a toothbrush

After triple-checking that the firearm is clear, the next step is to lay out the cleaning supplies and clear a place to clean. As with all firearms-related activities, common sense must be used. Don't clean your firearm on the kitchen table while your wife or girlfriend looks at you like someone magically stole your forebrain. If you wouldn't clean a fish there, don't clean your guns there. Find a quiet spot, away from prying eyes, where you can keep all your pieces together.

Set out the appropriate bore brushes and cleaning rods. A good silicone cloth will help you take the fouling off without removing oils meant to help keep your metal components from wearing themselves down. If you're like me and like to grab a burger after time at the range, lay out some latex gloves. Nothing ruins a good meal like petrochemicals and powder fouling. Once you've got your tools lined up, it's time to get to it.

Part 2: Cleaning

Now that you're ready to start maintaining your firearm, begin by disassembling it. You don't need to take it down to the pins and springs—just look at the main components:

The barrel (bore)

The frame or stock

The slide or cylinder

The bolt and carrier (if present)

Magazine(s) (if applicable)

If you're unsure how to identify these components, please ask! There is absolutely nothing wrong with questions about nomenclature.

What to Look For

Barrel: The bore should be free of fouling, pitting, and rust. There should be no fouling hardening along the throat (where the bullet "sits" in the barrel) or feed ramp (the tapered portion that guides the cartridge into the barrel). The bore should appear polished. An unserviceable barrel will have pits where rust has changed the shape of the lands and grooves (also known as the rifling) in the barrel. Also, check the barrel links, which can be shorn from their bounds if you use overpressure loads. This is an uncommon problem, but also check around the links for stress fractures if your pistol has them.

Frame or stock: The frame should be looked over for any fissuring, chips, or excessive wear. This kind of damage is almost always the result of improperly hand-loaded cartridges that are too powerful for your firearm. Using factory ammunition will almost completely nullify the risk of a catastrophic failure. All the same, make sure you give it a look to minimize the risk. A rifle stock can split, as well, so be sure to inspect it for stress!

Slide/Cylinder: Checking to be sure they're free from obstructions and that it is not overly saturated with fouling are the main points of concern with the slide or cylinder

Bolt/Bolt Carrier: Again, look for stress fractures or wear marks, then lightly coat the exterior in oil, and wipe dry.

Now that you've inspected the weapon for wear marks, stress fractures, and bore serviceability, it's time to ensure function by cleaning and oiling your firearm. At this stage, you should have the items listed in part one (Prep Work): oil, a cloth, a bore brush, and a good rigid toothbrush.

If you're cleaning an autoloading rifle, lithium bearing grease is handy and will provide lubrication and viscosity for quite a high volume of shooting. The trick to this process is to knock the fouling off and coat any part where metal is touching metal. The military harps on polishing your rifle until there's not a speck of fouling, but this isn't beneficial. All it does is take the finish or Parkerizing off your rifle and leaves it bone dry while it sits. This contributes to mechanical stoppages in weapons that deposit fouling into the bolt, such as the M16/M4 series of rifle. Neither rifle nor pistol needs excessive oil. The important part here is that you pay attention to the following critical parts:

The bolt. It should have a light coat of oil (applied with a silicone cloth) to keep it healthy.

The bolt carrier (if applicable). The carrier should have a very light coat of oil and then be wiped clean. You do not want too much oil in here as it will snag particles that will gum up the function of the bolt. Clean and then wipe dry.

The bore. Pass swabs through the bore of the weapon until they come out clean. This is especially important in weapons without chrome lining. If you have a question as to whether or not your weapon is chrome-lined, consult the manual or ask! This is very important to know as it will drastically impact the weapon's service life.

Trigger mechanisms. Make sure these are wiped clean, they are cleared of debris, and have very little oil.

Moving parts. Apply a very light coat of oil anywhere you have metal riding on metal that move, and let it sit.

Once you've completed these steps, your weapon is ready to be stored, carried, or fired.

Carrying your Firearm

Once you've selected a handgun, you now have the latitude to pursue a concealed carry license and carry your firearm on your person. This is a highly personal decision, but there are some common terms that should be understood and some practices that should be avoided.

Concepts

There are a few methods of "traditional" carry, and these are what you're going to either have recommended or forced upon you via lack of options. In addition, there are two main holster types, so we will briefly examine each to get a working knowledge of what these terms mean. For this section, I'm only going to discuss concealed carry options, as tactical options are, by and large, extraneous and straightforward.

Carry Positions

Handguns are generally carried in three main places: around the waist, under the arm, or on the ankle. When carried about the waist, we generally refer to your waist as a clock, with your centerline being twelve o'clock. This makes directly behind you six o'clock, and depending on if your right- or left-handed, three or nine o'clock, respectively.

These positions are also referred to in different ways; six o'clock, for example, is referred to as "small of the back" (or SOB). Twelve o'clock (or thereabouts) is generally referred to as "appendix carry," while three or nine are commonly known as "strong side" carry. There are a few variations, but all in all, it's relatively straightforward. Ankle carry is referred to as such, but underarm carry is generally discussed as "vertical" or "horizontal," referring to the orientation of the pistol's barrel.

Holster Errata

This entire section could be summed up with one sentence: Cheap holsters aren't good, and good holsters aren't cheap. Like so many things, you get what you pay for. Before you get angry and lash out because a $15 Fobus or Uncle Mike's holster works just fine, honestly consider what you do with it. More often than not, you cannot buy "good" quality holsters in stores (with few exceptions).

Outside the waistband: An outside the waistband holster is simply a holster that is attached to the belt and sits outside your pants. In short, this holster will be visible unless covered with a garment, and these types of holsters are generally considered faster to access. However, they're also easier to detect, and thus, make concealment of a carry pistol more difficult.

Inside the waistband: Inside the waistband holsters are generally more discreet, but they sometimes require a tucked undershirt or sweat shield, and they sit closer to the body, making them uncomfortable for some users. They are, however, more discreet.

The Long and Short of Carry Positions

Strong Side: A strong side holster is generally worn on the hip in an inside or outside the waistband holster on the side of your dominant hand. It's almost always positioned at three to four o'clock, and it allows for a generally smooth draw.

Advantages: Common, many holsters available and in production.

Disadvantages: You can't see if your pistol becomes exposed. Drawing requires the shoulder rotation, which can cause imbalance during a fight, or drawing from nontraditional positions (while pinned, seated in a vehicle or at a table, et cetera)

Appendix: Appendix carry places the pistol in the front of the person, tucked into the waistband, in front of the appendix on a right-handed person, which is how it got its name. The appendix position used to be more common among criminals, and it was thought of as a generally poor choice for carrying due to severity of holstering accidents with this carry method. However, quality holsters and good practice make this carry method extremely quick, accessible, and safe.

Advantages: Accessible from nontraditional positions, discreet, and easy to protect in a physical altercation; easy to maintain control over during physical activity.

Disadvantages: Holsters generally require a special order, negligent discharge while holstering could be tremendously dangerous. Uncomfortable with larger pistols and very difficult (to impossible) to use with a light equipped pistol.

Small of Back: The small of the back holster sits at the five o'clock position on a right-handed shooter. It keeps the pistol entirely rear of the person carrying it, giving the sense that it is harder to detect when face-to-face with someone.

Advantages: Difficult to detect from the front.

Disadvantages: Awkward to access (especially in nontraditional positions), produces a significant signature with most pistols, and painful to fall on.

Underarm/Shoulder: Shoulder holsters were popularized by use by police detectives and military officers. These holsters come in two basic configurations: vertical (pistol barrel pointed toward the ground) and horizontal (barrel pointed behind the carrier). In both instances, the pistol sits opposite the dominant hand. If you're right-handed, the pistol sits under the left arm.

Advantages: Comfortable, accessible from nontraditional positions (especially sitting or in vehicles), and easy to retain during an altercation.

Disadvantages: Less discreet, requires a belt anchor (or the pistol is extremely hard to draw quickly).

Ankle: Ankle carry is generally thought of as a method for carrying a backup gun, or a method to carry a gun while wearing attire that's prohibitive (like a business suit).

Advantages: Very discreet with appropriate attire; convenient way to carry a weapon away from the belt.

Disadvantages: Restricts user to very small pistols/revolvers; makes running uncomfortable, and it is difficult to draw.

Off-Body: This refers to any method in which the weapon is not secured to your body via some sort of holster. Typically, purses or fanny packs are the mediums of off-body carry, but other packs such as Hill People Gear kit bags, camera bags, and messenger bags also constitute "off-body" options.

Advantages: Discreet with no visible signature on body.

Disadvantages: Difficult to access quickly, less secure, and often carried in a bag that is a target of theft. In some configurations, may require the pistol to be unloaded or the trigger could be exposed to lose items within bag that could snag on the trigger.

Nontraditional Carry Methods

In recent years, items like the Flashbang holster for women (attaches to bra, carries small revolver or autoloader) or Thunderwear have become popular as emerging groups of people purchase pistols and look for discreet methods of carry. These modalities are often dismissed by training venues as subpar. We disagree with this analysis and think nontraditional methods should be further explored and supported in training.

It's simply not practical for a field dominated by men to dictate that women emulate their practice. This further extends to older citizens and people with disabilities. Each of these nontraditional options carry unique advantages as well as disadvantages—as with all holsters. Just as it is with all other topics concerned with cheating the reaper, be adaptable and open to ideas that may not be consistent with existing doctrine.

One-Handed Shooting

There's a strange phenomenon among shooters: while we all know that one of the chief benefits of a handgun is the ability to fire it with one hand, it's difficult and no one likes doing it… mainly because it makes us look like we suck. There are plenty of reasons to shoot with both hands, but it's not always possible. So, when and why would we need to practice this skill?

Schools of Thought

It's pretty common to hear criticisms of one-handed shooting: why would you want to weaken control over the weapon and lose speed, efficiency, and time between follow-up shots? Ideally, you wouldn't, but if bullets are flying, then "ideally" has left the building. Just like we don't get to choose when a violent criminal altercation will occur, we don't get to pick the place, either. This means, like many things in the shooting world, context is very important.

The Four Major Situations

There are four major situations that require one-handed shooting skill. Once we identify these, we can rationalize why they're applicable and begin training in a way that's meaningful.

Transitional Tasks and Spaces: We define transitional spaces as those which force you to switch tasks and focus. Transitional spaces could require that you turn on a light or use a handheld flashlight, open a door, use a phone, or recover equipment from the environment. In short, anytime your focus narrows to a specific task, you can bet two things: your overall awareness diminishes, and you've opened a window for attack.

Entangled Fight with a Handgun: Being in a fight is complex, and it can turn on a dime. The presence of guns makes the fights even less predictable. Handgun access while at conversational range could be a full class in and of itself (and it is), but for our purposes here, let's say this: A traditional draw won't be happening.

Moving Around People: Whether these people are your responsibility or not, shootings happen in public spaces. This could be at a dinner table in a restaurant, in a shopping mall, or while you're holding your child. In all cases, it's important to be able to retain and fire your handgun while controlling the movement of nonhostile others. In fights, movement is a critical component of survivability.

Injury: Possibly the most important is the chance you'll be injured. The US Army's research on combat-related injuries shows that over half of their casualties had sustained injuries to the extremities. While warfare and gunfights aren't the same thing, it's important to consider.

Training Standard

Training for one-handed fights isn't as easy as you might think. Simple shooting with one hand requires a very solid set of fundamental skills, but to do it well and to do it quickly demands repetition. As well, we need to devote time to actually working around other people while we're shooting. To work your way up to safely doing that, however, spend some time working on the following:

Drawing from the holster, fire a one-handed headshot in under 2 seconds (3 meters from the target).

Using your support hand only (non-dominant hand), draw and fire one round to the body in under 3.5 seconds (3 meters from the target).

From low ready (weapon diverted from line of sight by 30 degrees, downward), using strong side only, fire two rounds to chest in under 1.8 seconds (3 and 7 meters from the target).

Drawing from the holster, using strong side only, fire two rounds to the chest and one round to the head in under 3 seconds (3 and 7 meters).

Drawing from the holster, using strong side only, fire two rounds to the chest, reload (using strong side only!), then fire two rounds to the chest in under 6 seconds (5 meters).

From low ready, using strong side only, fire five rounds to chest, and one round to the head in under 4 seconds (3 and/or 7 meters).

From low ready, using strong side only, fire two rounds to the chest in under 7 seconds (at 10 and/or 15 meters).

If you can, add a flashlight or cell phone to these drills. Working a flashlight under stress can be difficult, so this is a good opportunity to practice that, as well! Check yourself, time yourself, and record the results. This will give you a working baseline and some general ideas of where you need improvement.

Advanced Drills and Single-Handed Manipulations

Once you've become consistent on the above drills, it can be beneficial to work them with a partner. *We recommend doing these drills with an inert pistol to ensure safety.* During the drills, the shooter should point his weapon at the target, engage the threat, and bring the pistol into one of our discussed positions. Being careful not to unintentionally point your firearm (also known as "flagging") at your training partner, move around him and repeat. Try this as you get out of vehicles and negotiate objects like stairs. Keep in mind who is above and below you as you decide the best technique to match your clearing tactics. This will get you used to moving around people with a firearm in your hand.

Incorporate the use of light and after-action drills such as communicating with your partner to call for police, rendering medical aid, or acting as a lookout until the scene is safe. This is where training and experience really bake the cake. Without trying these techniques under pressure, it's difficult to truly understand how to apply them.

Before you settle into one particular method of carrying, line up some training. To start, a basic pistol course will show you the essentials. Once you've got those basics down, it's time to make yourself as uncomfortable as possible while you train. Shoot with one hand. Shoot with only your non-dominant hand. If you can, take more advanced courses to refine your technique and work on your ability to clear stoppages, reload your weapon quickly under stress, and react to violent situations. Learn to retain and defend your weapon from attacks in extreme close quarters.

Movement While Armed (especially around people)

This topic doesn't get enough play. If we're being honest—and at ISG we always are—any monkey can get good at shooting. It's rote 101-type stuff. Tactics aren't a whole lot different, but they do require the ability to think on your feet. Arguing high ready vs. low ready, for example, generally depends on whether you're getting trickle down from a SEAL or a Ranger. In their world, down means shooting the hull and up means shooting the rotors. What about for a citizen? Well, who's upstairs? Who's downstairs? Do you have people with you? Are you in a car, a house, or some other packed public space? For the citizen or police officer, the problems are as complex—if not more, so let's hit a pet peeve of mine first: Don't commit yourself to drawing your pistol.

If you're not being actively engaged, you can keep that weapon concealed, especially if you're entering territory with unknown levels of threats, hostiles, and unknown proximities. If that gun is out and an aggressor sees it, it's now a fight for the gun, not a gunfight. Don't think you're going to out-grapple a con who just got out and has been pushing your body weight on the weight bench for the last five years. You're not. This goes beyond the scope of this section, but if you're not doing some sort of fitness plan or martial arts and you're serious about self-protection, you're wrong. Don't waste another day.

Ready Positions (Pistol)

In this section, we'll discuss some of the common ready positions people use while moving with handguns. These are important to become familiar with, as handling a firearm responsibly requires that we not only carry it safely, but we understand how to hold it without pointing it at people unintentionally or creating unnecessary risk. If you'd like to see visual demonstrations, there are images on integratedskillsgroup.com, or follow the QR to be linked directly. https://integratedskillsgroup.com/2021/06/one-handed-shooting/

SUL (and modified SUL): Position Sul was devised to give a close-to-the-body position for a weapon that doesn't point it at others while stacking for entry. It gets its name from the Portuguese word for south. While Sul has its critics, it remains a viable solution for moving around people without sticking a gun in their face (which, yes, sometimes is necessary). Sul keeps the weapon close enough to the body to resist fends while it is pointed in a generally safe direction. It is often modified from its original form, but the core utility is to keep from pointing your pistol at people who don't need to have pistols pointed at them.

Of importance, the thumbs should be touching and the pistol should be braced against the support side hand. If you have to use the pistol or the hand for a transitional task, you can do so without the risk of putting your hand in front of the gun. Transitioning from Sul to pointed in is very fast and natural, and it facilitates shooting from a one- or two-handed position. It is often viewed as a novice technique or one taught to less-sophisticated militaries, and it's often done incorrectly in that in traditional Sul, the pistol should be pointed straight down, pointed away from the body at a very shallow 15-degree angle, and with the thumbs pressed together at the sternum creating a box between the thumbs and index fingers.

The Temple Index (for when there is no safe direction): If Sul has its critics, the temple index blows the roof off the internet; the temple index is made for some extremely specific situations, and mostly for use in and around vehicles, or in situations in which children are presented and we don't want a pistol pointed anywhere near the ground. The temple index is performed by placing the pistol bore up in front of the ear. Done right, the middle finger should point up along the temple so that the bore of the pistol sits just above the top of the head. Typically, it is held close, which also provides some defense from strikes to the head or neck.

While it has its weaknesses (it could occlude peripheral vision and puts the pistol right by your head), there are times when there is no *safer* direction, and the temple index gives a physiovisual reference of the pistol's presence. In short, it's better than flying a handgun out there like a flag. When dismounting a vehicle and moving to a protectee, the temple index can be a very useful technique. Incidentally, this is something citizens with children should consider as they are their family's protective detail. The temple index gives you positive control over your weapon while moving a vulnerable person. However, it can be awkward to assume a solid firing position.

Compression: Also called Isosceles Chest Point, this position allows for compression of the arms along the horizontal line of handgun presentation and is an extremely useful technique for movement in close confines when you need a pistol at the ready. While there is no visual reference of the sights by design, its use is such that you should be able to make consistent, reasonably accurate hits by point shooting at the ranges that may be required. It can also be quickly transitioned into other shooting positions and fends by either retracting further or extending fully. This position is a bit more advanced and requires subordinate skills to use properly, specifically the ability to use unsighted fire consistently and safely.

Compression can most simply be described as using the space the pistol normally travels during a draw stroke from when it's first collected in the support-side hand just at the chest to full extension. This line of travel can be "compressed" as we move through narrow passages or as we round corners to ensure we're not leading with our pistol (allowing the weapon to enter the room before we do, thus advertising our presence and the fact we're armed). When done correctly, the pistol will sit directly under the chin at its most compressed. The shoulders should be pinched together and tense, and the dominant-side wrist should be bent at about 90 degrees with the elbows high. The muzzle of the pistol will track with our chin, which allows the pistol to follow our foveal vision, and the torso and head will move together, similar to the turret on a tank.

This technique is often taught incorrectly or in ways that make little contextual sense, but as a part of clearing confined spaces properly, being able to compress and extend based on the environment is a useful skill that will allow you to move more cleanly when speed and discretion matter.

Fend Positions

Vertical Fend: Vertical Fend has two primary uses: defending the head and retaining the pistol, and it's easily adapted to off-hand light use (though it's less of a fend in that case). Note the key components: The pistol is pulled rearward, indexed along the body (thumb pectoral index), angled to consistently make hits and postured in a way that it's difficult for an attacker to get at.

In this position, the support-side arm shields the head from attack by placing the index finger on the occipital lobe, thumb down towards the base of the neck, and elbow protruding straight forward off the pectoral muscle. This guards the head and support side of the neck. The vertical fend is more or less an extension of a defensive movement that guards the head while the pistol is out. The contextual use here varies, and our goal is simply to familiarize you with.

Horizontal Fend: The horizontal fend is a retention position that works to accomplish a couple things. First, it makes a drawn handgun difficult to get to while giving the user the ability to fire consistent, unsighted shots. The way this is demonstrated is different from the way it's used. Under pressure, it'll still present a challenge for retention, but moving in this position is very easy. It is performed by placing the support hand with the thumb against the neck, so that the elbow protrudes like a triangle away from the body.

It is a very useful technique for moving through a crowd that's losing their cool as well as through close quarters such as narrow hallways. It is the only position discussed that allows the user to make shots without adjusting their gun hand, but it also requires extreme (and dangerous) proximity, and it doesn't keep the weapon in a safe direction while moving. Further, it's common for limbs to go flying in a fight, so it's important to remember that you must always know where that muzzle is pointing. Find an instructor and get a class under your belt before you feel like you know the horizontal fend. What it does on the range and what it does in a fight are two different things.

On the two above fending positions: PLEASE seek proper instruction. These are often mistaught or used mistakenly by instructors or YouTube experts in ways that will very likely result in injury or an incomplete understanding of how and why the techniques are used.

CYFG

So, you've decided to get a weapon. You've sunk hours into training and you're improving your fitness. The end of the discussion is close at hand, so I want to pass along this acronym: CYFG. *Carry Your Friggin' Gun.*

More and more, we're seeing people fighting back against active shooters, criminals, and violent offenders. While the gun isn't the only solution, it is much like a car's seat belt—when you need it, nothing else will do. So, commit yourself to your training and the inconvenience of carrying your gun on your person if you are so inclined. Don't be the type of person who thinks they hold some mystic power over the people around them when carrying a gun. Be the person who says you'll defend them as your own.

Additional Concerns

As mentioned, firearms are neither the only nor the best option. People commonly forget that most handguns employed by citizens are used in spaces that are confined, at ranges that are six yards or less. These statistics should help shape the way we train, but they should also clue us into another vital fact—those distances make it very easy for an attacker to turn a gunfight into a fight over a gun. In these instances, firearms are dropped, taken by physically stronger or technically more proficient fighters, and they inevitably experience mechanical stoppages (jamming). If you decide to carry a gun, knowing when to use it is absolutely critical. Please be responsible and plan your training around the situations that make you uncomfortable and compromise your view of your competency rather than validate your strengths. This will be the lynchpin that separates those who survive these kinds of altercations and those who become sad statistics.

Another thing to note is this: Firearms are a right, but they're also a responsibility. Politics and insurance have made it difficult to find decent places to shoot, but please don't take this to mean it's okay to run into the national forest and start shooting signs. Firearms are a part of the American cultural experience, and this culture has become less about self-sovereignty, individual empowerment, and the right to defend ourselves, our family, and our community against criminals and oppression, and more about the cowboy image or superficial emulation of the military and such. Whatever reasons you have for owning a firearm, don't let the encumbrance and responsibility slip from your mind. Be part of the silent majority who are responsible and cautious. Carrying your SKS into Starbucks to show off your rights just makes you look like the negative archetype that anti-gun lobbyists and politicians use to make gun owners look foolish.

FIGHTS AND TACTICS

There's a culture of martialism that has evolved in the decades since UFC crashed into the American mainstream. We've seen MMA and Jiu Jitsu come into their own as popular competitive sports, up there with weightlifting or soccer. It's given rise to endless debates between street fighters and martial artists about who's more effective, what happens "in the streets," and whose discipline is more practical, relevant, or beneficial. If you're new to this, there's a dizzying amount of information. If you've been around the block a time or two, the whole mess starts looking a little different.

If you've been familiar with ISG for any time, you know we don't tout credentials first; we present information that speaks for itself. Our guiding principle is to avoid talking on subjects that we don't have relevant, first-hand experience with, which means that if we take up a topic, then we've got something useful for you. In this section, we're going to take you through our experience dealing with everything from street-level, drug-based crime to competitive fighting. Bottom line up front: fighting isn't about guarantees promised by instructors or thug-life viciousness, and neither of these will "win" reliably. So, what is it about? Who wins when it comes down to it?

What Wins Fights

Once you enter a fight, there are two ways of looking at a "win."

Look from the outside of the fight in. If you wind up fighting it out, you have failed at all of your avoidance strategies. From this perspective, a fight is a zero-sum game in which you now have to lose as little as possible. That means no major injuries, no loss of conscious, and no court dates. In this view, there is no winning. Fights are to be avoided.

Look from the inside out. You now have to be as fierce and committed as possible to beat the other guy(s) into submission as fast as possible, so you avoid being hurt, maimed, or killed. From this view, winning means crippling the opponents' ability or will to fight before succumbing yourself.

So how do you "win"? If you asked one hundred experts, you'd get as many answers and we're no different—but the outcome largely depends on the type of fight. Are we talking some chest thumping at the bar, or a knock-down-drag-out domestic violence brawl? Is it shooting your way out of a carjacking in South Africa or fighting through an ambush in Afghanistan?

We asked this same question among our peer group, professional friends, and guys with some experience in brawling, and here's what we came up with: No matter what you want to call it, when all other things are equal, the fighter who wins is the one who is the most technical, fit, aggressive, and lucky.

Technical, Fit, Aggressive, Lucky

Whether we're talking fists, pistols, rifles, or hand grenades, technical, fit, aggressive, and lucky will win. There is, of course, the sad reality that "all other things" are never equal. Even worse, if you're not a professional fighter, winning doesn't mean you're taking home some massive jackpot while you convalesce for six months. It means not rotting in a cell, or not getting shot or stabbed or killed. It means you lost as little as possible under the circumstances. If you're a police officer or a grunt, it means you soaked up as little physical trauma as possible and prevented injury or death for your team.

If you think about it, this all makes fighting a zero-sum game. Even if you're the most fit, technical, and aggressive, winning comes at a cost. It might be sore spots and injuries later in life, or it could be debilitating PTSD. Furthermore, even the high-speed, dedicated, and professional practitioner isn't immune to bad luck. A friend of ISG who went to Infantry AIT with one of the ISG team and worked under another was killed in Afghanistan in 2014. By all accounts, he was a truly dedicated professional. He was killed by what amounted to a stray bullet while doing something he was exceptionally good at.

One of the reasons we practice extreme humility when it comes to our material is that bad luck can snatch your life right out from under you. It doesn't pay to get cocky about something you can't control, and those who showboat what they can control (skill at arms) are missing the bigger, worthier part of the picture—that there is a razor-thin line separating your existence as a sentient being from that of a rotting bag of meat, and we can't control it. So, let's level the playing field and talk about how to sharpen ourselves as much as we can and discuss how to control the playing field before it comes to blows.

Before a Fight
Pre-Attack Indicators & Body Language

Learning to recognize some of the asocial attack indicators can go a long way and spare you the trouble of getting bashed over the head and robbed or carjacked. It's easy to become lax because it's honestly not as big of a threat as it seems if you live a regular middle-class life, but as we discussed in Understanding Emergencies, sometimes circumstances make people act out in wildly irrational ways. Sometimes it's just being in the wrong place at the wrong time. Whatever the case, here are some of the pre-attack indicators we've seen over the years.

Distance: The distance a person allows you to maintain during a contact speaks loudly about the level of comfort you are extending to them and the level of safety you feel with them. Distance also shares a very important relationship with motor reaction. The farther a person is from you, the more time your brain has to observe and react to a threat. Conversely, the closer a person is, the shorter reactionary gap you have to make a move. This is the basis of initiative. When fighting, we always want to try to reframe the fight so that we're *acting*, not reacting. We do this through dominant positioning and angles.

Positioning and Weight Shifting: Where a person chooses to stand when verbally engaging can show either respect or disrespect. Staying too close or being in someone's personal space is typically seen as disrespectful and either an invitation or precursor to violence. Also, notice how a person stands. Most people tend to throw big hits hoping to knock the other guy out. As such, they often load their weight on a rearward leg before launching into their attack. Shifts in weight can indicate that a person is working up the nerve to throw a punch.

Verbal Clues and Challenges: The tone of a person's voice is closely related to their level of frustration. And the words they choose and/or the excessive repetition of the same words will give you a hint about their level of anger. Oftentimes, bystanders will be caught in these situations. Stay blank. Don't let them read you, but understand what it means if they are using obvious escalation tactics. Don't pretend it won't boil over just because you wouldn't do it. Don't respond to the challenge—be the challenge.

Hand Movements: Hand movements will show a subject's readiness to take action, kind of like a batter warming up in the on-deck circle. You'll see these take place when someone pulls up their pants or moves their hands into a jacket, hoodie, or pocket, or they start talking with their hands while slowly bringing them higher. This can be either defensive or offensive, but the objective is always to put themselves in a better position to throw a punch or make a grab.

Eye Focus: Where and how intently they are looking will give you insight into their level of focus. What their eyes focus on displays what they are thinking about doing. Glancing away from the target is another major cue that a person is about to strike.

Grooming: Movements about the head and face are called *grooming cues*. These can be stroking the jaw or hair, pinching or brushing the nose, or wiping the face in some other way. These are often used as an excuse to bring the hands to face level for a strike.

Movement: A person's movement can also give you clues as to what they're up to. These clues aren't hard and fast, but they can serve as a useful guide in tandem with our other elements of awareness.

Casual Pace: Walking at a steady but slow speed with no set time or urgency on their arrival, typically looking at what is in front of them, not caring too much about what is around them. If eye contact is made, there is usually no facial expression because you might be in their line of sight, but not in their mind's eye of purpose or view.

Strolling Pace: Walking in a slight pattern and direction, typically with no defined goal or purpose but with a destination or time in mind. This is an uneven pace, like three to five steps forward, casually looking at what is around their immediate area but careless of what is directly in front of them. Their steps are in spurts with no obvious purpose.

Targeting Pace: Walking with a direction and purpose in mind, paying very close attention to what is ten feet in front of them, very clueless as to what is going on around them. Their breathing is at a rhythm that matches their attention, but their eyes are focused on a specific location. This can also be referred to as tunnel vision. Their speed is much faster than a stroll and their eyes are focused directly on you as they walk, possibly bumping into others as they get closer, as if they do not see the other people. This could be a sign they are planning to attack you, or they could really need your attention.

Avoidance and Self-Awareness

It's easy to preach avoidance. It's another thing entirely to practice it. We're not angels at ISG. Our tempers and inability to just back down from a fight have earned us everything from free lodging in county to black eyes and busted lips. What we can tell you is this: The experience of having to call your significant other while she's at work and ask for bail money after spending a weekend in jail is far more embarrassing than just backing off the throttle when someone challenges you.

Almost all of what we call social interpersonal violence can be avoided (that means violence between two ruttin' bulls who wanna lock horns). You don't have to lock horns to prove you're a man. The truly dangerous animals don't waste their time on this sort of pageantry. Does the leopard go out and challenge the bull to a horn-locking competition? Nope. It's a stupid, unnecessary risk with no real payoff. The leopard is playing a different game than the bull. As such, don't overthink trying to look intimidating if it doesn't come naturally to you. Keep your capability like a predatory cat keeps its claws—tucked away until it's go time.

It might seem like common sense, but here are a few things you can do if you're serious about avoiding trouble:

Have situational awareness/locational avoidance.

Go easy on the hooch. Drinking is fine, but don't get drunk.

Quit flexin' and be cool. Being nice is both the easiest and the right way to treat people.

Getting Involved: When to Move and When to Walk

Our best intentions often blow up in our faces. From trying to step in and help a woman who was getting manhandled (and having her deliver a bottle to the head for the effort) to trying to calm tensions between people at a bar (got socked in the jaw for the trouble), getting involved is for Hollywood. That's because people who are escalating to violence aren't thinking straight. Whether it's because they're drunk or enraged, you can't expect them to reason.

Having dealt with everything from bloody marital disputes to severe psychological illness, we want to give you one rock solid takeaway: You can't understand what's going on in the mind of someone who's mentally ill. It doesn't matter if it's temporary (a jealous, drunken spouse beating his wife) or a schizophrenic woman with borderline personality disorder holding a kitchen knife. You can't think the way they do, and there's no reason to believe you'll be able to reason with them. In these situations, your best bet is honestly to sit them out. The best-case scenario is that you get thrown on the cold concrete to sit in handcuffs and think for a spell or get your hand slashed.

We live in a neurotic society. To some degree, you've almost have to have a mental disorder to accept reality as normal. Think for a second about how arbitrary it is to get mad at someone in traffic. It really shouldn't matter. We're probably less angry about that person than we are at the overall conditions that made the traffic, but we can't punch society in the face and give our anger a way to vent. So, when should we walk? That's easy. Any time we're not forced to fight.

Be judgmental, avoid problems, and don't end up bloody if you absolutely don't have to. And don't ever get involved in a fight between couples. I've been there a few times, and it never works well. Stepping across the spheres of violence, most police officers will say the same; one of the diciest calls you can get is domestic assault.

Forced to Fight

Sometimes you end up in a position where there's no choice but to throw down. The military has an adage they use for assaults: Speed, Simplicity, Violence of Action.

Not many of the military's sayings translate as cleanly to the civilian world, but in violence, these things are universal. Fancy stuff usually doesn't work. Striking isn't nearly as effective as you think. Pain compliance only works on people who aren't committed. Complicated moves don't work well, especially if it's two people (or more) against one. For example, an arm bar is excellent to use in martial competition. If you use it on a guy who digs out a blade or a gun, where are you then? How about if his buddy shows up and decides to start smashing your face with a bar glass or beer bottle?

Don't overthink this and don't use it as an excuse to avoid learning. Just be aware that limits apply to what translates from martial competition to street-level violence. Things get confusing fast, and our goal is to ensure we can maneuver, and that we don't get knocked unconscious. The fight will change as soon as it goes to the ground, so let's talk about some things that work and don't.

Defense: There are various instructors who teach various techniques for how to defend yourself against an attack. The best way to do it is to get some boxing gloves and have a friend try to sock ya for a while. Keeping your hands high using a technique like Geoff Thompson's fence concept makes reaction (and offense) much more efficient. The idea behind the fence is to keep one's hands high and compressed near the body, palms toward the aggressor. This loads the hands for defense or striking and gives a neutral tone that's non- threatening.

Just like criminal attacks have pre-assault indicators, we should have pre-assault tactics. Stepping offline, having a refined "fence" and loopholes to give the aggressors an option for a dignified out are all part of the discipline. Just like tactics, we want to be able to hit an adversary from an oblique angle rather than straight on. Work a discreet step into your conversational tactics.

Striking: Barring a solid, surprising punch to the mid-jaw, you're probably not going to knock someone out. The second your aggressor's jaw muscles clench, their body is in fight mode, and they're going to absorb a surprising amount of damage. Let's look at some of the strikes that are useful:

Headbutts: My affinity for the for the headbutt came from watching a fight in eighth grade. I saw one guy flatten a bully twice his size by headbutting him straight on. The kid dropped like a sack of rocks. After, I found myself in a couple fights where a good headbutt resulted in the other person being unable to fight. When well timed, a good headbutt will ruin a person's day. Obviously, it carries the risk of you getting hurt as well, and it typically works better if used against someone taller than you. Keep the headbutt in your back pocket. Most of the time, it's a bit of overkill; however, if a junkie is biting you while trying to stick you with a dirty needle full of air, a butt does the trick.

Jabs and Straight Kicks: You might not think about it, and in just about every fight I've been in guys throw big haymakers, but the jab and straight kick of opportunity do a lot to create and maintain distance. Guys will often lose their shit after being punched, and they'll throw some wild swings or try for a takedown, so use that distance to your advantage and watch how they move. Big punches are easy to deflect by keeping your hands up and staying light on your feet, and they often throw the attacker wildly off balance. This can open a window for a good straight kick to the knees or ankles, and, if timed well, often results in knocking them down. When someone does close in, use those knees and elbows!

Knees and elbows: Don't expect immediate results, but the sapping effects of a good knee to the floating rib or an elbow to the neck or head can't be overstated. Pushing a knee into that floating rib can really halt an advance. It's also effective and can open windows for clinches, throws, or escapes. In both fights mentioned earlier, I was able to use the window the knee created for a takedown or follow up attack.

The Non-telegraphic punch: It's stunning how many times you see the pre-fight indicators mentioned above right before someone attempts a strike. Being able to throw a decent cross without advertising it to the world can pay dividends in social violence, and it's gotten me out of a bind on a few occasions...mostly with drunks. Practice a solid, relaxed punch that doesn't require you to look all guilty before you throw it. Remember, strikes don't have to be haymakers. They're easy to see coming and rarely have the desired effect. Distance is a big part of the non-telegraphic punch, so get familiar with how long your arms are and where your "space bubble" really begins.

Clinching: We'll cover some very basic, simple, and effective techniques regarding clinching. Keep in mind, as with most things, you'll need some training and experience to make this information relevant. A good mixed-martial arts gym should cover most of the topics early in your training, so get out and build these into your repertoire.

Ties: Wrist, arm, and bicep ties form the basis of limb control during a fight. Being able to control a limb is more than just jockeying for position in competition; it's tremendously important in the weapons-based environment—specifically when edged weapons are present. Most of the ties have roots in Greco-Roman wrestling, which can be a tremendously useful discipline for street fighting.

Chokes: The rear naked choke is one of the main chokes you see used in fights. If you can take an opponent's back, it's one of the most effective and quickest ways to force an opponent into unconsciousness. When done correctly, the elbow will rest over the Adam's apple. Once you've set the arms in place, turning the palm of the choking arm toward the outside of the body (which is the opposite shoulder) activates the radius (the small bone of the forearm) and sharpens the occlusion of the carotid artery. Be careful using this choke. It can easily go from rolled back eyes and foamy mouth to morgue.

Takedowns and Throws: Takedowns and throw are honestly some of the most useful and under appreciated aspects of technical fighting. Not only are they useful for escaping from chokes or grabs, but when done right, they also allow you to maintain mobility while tossing the other guy into a heap of uncoordinated meat. That can certainly buy you time and options.

Judo is the crown jewel of under appreciated traditional martial arts, and if you can get into it, the throws and takedowns you'll learn will certainly make you a more formidable fighter for competition or for social violence. Traditional martial arts (TMA) aren't only for when you're fighting men in loose-fitting pajamas (which, stay away from married women and you should be okay), and a good deal of contemporary MMA draws from Judo, Aikido, and of course, Jiu Jitsu. Don't turn your nose up at learning from TMA.

Martial arts are the "technical" aspects of fighting, but they also improve your fitness. As such, they're a really worthwhile pursuit and can absolutely be applicable "in the street." However—and this is a big caveat—don't forget the following:

Martial arts are of greatest use in social/interpersonal violence. This is the one type of violence that we control to a large degree. Learn, get fit, understand the technical aspects, but keep in mind that beyond a certain point, you're over-training for situations you can control through awareness and avoidance. Living and breathing one specific discipline is fine if it's your thing, but there's time going in that just won't pay off.

Skill in martial arts is typically set to the backdrop of an even playing field. You start at the same time, fighting against the same (or similar) discipline, and there's usually only hurt or money on the line. While those things can be motivators, for the experienced martial artist, that mindset can work against you. Against someone

—or a group—who may be vicious, you'll need to tap your inner reserve of savage. On that note...

Use the Environment

Finally, if you are scrapping for keeps (against people who will kill you), don't be afraid to smash heads into walls or hit people with heavy objects. If you can bring someone off their balance (probably because they threw a huge haymaker or tried to kick or something silly like that), don't be afraid to grab them by the skull and bash their head into a brick wall. Stupid should hurt. It's amazing how disorienting blows to the head like this can be. Again, be cautious. This is something that shouldn't be done unless your life is seriously at risk, and if you don't like the idea of it, revisit the chapter on awareness and avoidance. There's no shame in that.

Likewise, loose brick or concrete can really turn the tides in a fight. During one altercation, three dudes were clubbing another guy mercilessly. One of our guys grabbed a broken chunk of concrete and threw it at one of the attacker's head, which caused a hard reset on their OODA loop. The amount of "holy shit" that came off their faces translated into *this guy is willing to turn the noise up loud, and I'm not sure this is fun anymore*. Don't underestimate the role of commitment to violence in serious fights. Most people don't have a lot of experience and are just there for the easy stuff. If it gets real, viciousness can break spirit quickly.

The Five-Oh

As we touched upon in Urban Fieldcraft, the law isn't going to hear your story and see you as the good guy. They're going to look skeptically at everything you say, and the person who contacts the police first does so with 90 percent of the truth. That means you have a couple choices: Get out of there before the police show up (in which case it's their word against yours), or call first (which is petty and stupid).

The days of a good ole, honest dustup between folks are gone, replaced with legions of people who chronically let their mouths write checks their asses can't cash because they know how to play the victim the way men in times past knew how to fight for what's right. So, as part of your acknowledging that fights can happen, also acknowledge that you need to control what you can control. Learn some technical aspects and work on your fitness. Avoid stupid people, places, and things, and be aware enough to spot them before they blindside you. Expect consequences, and above all else, don't think that you can force violence to conform to your expectations. You can't, and it won't.

Bring a Knife to a Gunfight

Everyone's heard the expression *You don't bring a knife to a gunfight*. It's one of those quips so often repeated that it's just accepted as true. What doesn't happen is a solid, unbiased look at why it's not only untrue, but it's a totally outdated way of thinking. Why? Well, there are different spheres of violence. If we accept that not all altercations are the same, we can extend that logic and say not all fights are the same. Advice like this oversimplifies the problem, and we're in the business of unpacking problems so we can really understand them.

Should you bring a knife to a rifle fight? How about a fistfight? In modern, urban warfare and close quarters battle (CQB), a rifle can be snatched, making the blade or handgun a handy tool to transition to. Should we say never bring a handgun to a rifle fight knowing the limitations of the handgun compared to the rifle? As with CQB, the conversational range altercation that turns into a lethal force encounter means that the handgun has to overcome some disadvantages. Let's get a list:

Handguns have mechanical stoppages.

They're not notorious for instantaneously stopping opponents.

Careless or negligent discharges while in a clinch-ranged gunfight can wound bystanders.

So why, given all these issues with firearms in close-range fights, do we recite the mantra that you should never bring a knife to a gunfight? Because gun culture is not thoughtful, experienced, or preoccupied with efficiency.

Knives, and a slice of reality

When we talk knives, we instantly open a can of worms that gets murky, dogmatic, and downright weird. Like all things treated as hobbies, knife guys just get lit debating what knife is the best and how to use it. Here's the thing: very, very few people have any practical experience with knives. On our content team, we've experienced a few knife cuts from fights and some full-tilt force-on-force. We're going to look at these, couple them with some research about how knives are employed in reality and knock some sacred cows between the horns so we can cook them up and eat them. So, borrowing from Mindset, let's first talk about some of the ridiculous stuff that goes around the blade work.

The Blade Dance

One of the first things you'll notice when you start talking knives is the technique they favor. You'll get discussions of earth and sky grip, Pekiti-Tirsia, retzev, bio-mechanical cutting, or the approach the Spetznaz uses in edged weapon sistema. Purge it all from your mind.

Here's the real deal: Knife fights between two equally motivated, equally armed dudes rarely happen. Fights don't follow a form, and they're not a martial competition. When we *do* see a street-level knife fight between two equally armed guys, it tends to be a "circle the wagon" effort until someone is caught slipping. Once that happens, it's not some clean technique that finishes the other guy off; it's an exchange of slashes and stabs in which both guys end up wounded and retreating, and sometimes one guy...well...I guess you'd say "wins."

More likely, what you will see is that a fight breaks out, a guy pulls a knife and uses a technique called *Monkey with a Screwdriver*. He swings and swings with the blade, and the other guy probably just thinks he's being punched until he collapses from blood loss or a punctured vital organ, or the fight ends.

If you dedicate all your time to blade dancing, you're not going to be well-prepared for an untrained, hyper-aggressive attacker. Focus your efforts on wrestling and limb control, then work in disarms and the ability to access your own weapons - but be cautious! If you've successfully subdued an attacker, it's possible they're no longer a lethal threat.

Some thoughts on Blade Geometry

The first thing to say on this topic is that most blades are gimmicky or boring. Choose boring. It's probably worked for a long time. If we study nature a little, we can turn this into a quick, high-level discussion on physiology, predation, and efficacy. Let's look at what are unarguably the two most efficient predatory creatures in the animal kingdom: large cats and raptors. As the saying goes, form follows function, so let's see how nature's most successful predators take down their prey.

Form and Function

Think about a talon: a curved, tapered edge that is broadest at the spine (posterior edge), narrowest (and therefore sharpest) at the anterior edge, terminating in a sharp point. This allows the claws to work in conjunction using a point-driven approach that does a few things from a physiological perspective:

They allow the predator to sink into tissue, while the curve increases the opportunity to snag a bone or sinew that will reduce the chances of prey getting away without causing further damage. They also work against the prey's biological impulse to pull away from the source of insertion—the talon. When prey pulls away, the talon's sharp, anterior edge further tears at the tissue, increasing the odds that the prey animal will suffer further bleeding, or a vital organ will be punctured. It allows the predator decent odds that the prey won't escape while they puncture vital areas with teeth.

Function, part one: Animals

With an understanding of the predatory claw and tooth, we can say that animals use piercing (stabbing) as their main medium of killing prey. It's cool to understand this, but we don't have two-clawed hands and teeth like a tiger, so we can't expect the same results by copying some of the moves of a predatory animal. What's important to understand is that the claw has some really effective functions:

It hooks into the tissue and allows the predator to move in closer using the stronger muscles of the limb.

It disallows the prey from pulling away from the predator without risking much worse tissue damage.

The predator is often able to kill prey much larger than itself.

We will return to this a little later.

Function, part two: Humans

Humans have developed point-driven methods as well—spears. The first hand-cutting instruments we devised weren't for killing prey, but for cleaning it and removing hide. Stemming from this, humans have two distinct categories of tools when it comes to pointy things: tools and weapons. Unlike our animal counterparts, the ability to use tools gives us a lot more flex when it comes to deciding what to use for any given task. We know that cutting is the domain of the tool and stabbing is the domain of the weapon because the subject has been studied exhaustively.

Cutting is largely effective when used in conjunction with piercing (sentry removal, for example) or when a very sharp instrument is used (such as a barber's razor). It also has a sapping effect—the more cuts there are, the less likely a person is to have the ability to properly defend himself. Without getting too into the weeds of technique, those who train for fighting with a knife typically recognize that there are two distinct, effective methods: The "sewing machine" (rapid short jabs to vital areas at clinch-range).

Pulling the adversary toward the blade while minimizing your own arm movement while driving the blade from the shoulders.

The bottom line: Blades that make use of point-driven methods and allow you to use your lats, triceps, and deltoids rather than your wrists and biceps work extremely well. We want to minimize articulation of the wrist and arms (which creates strength and disallows opportunities for grabs and disarms), so when you look at a blade design, think about how you'd employ it. That should be a useful guide when it comes to determining how much time is involved in reaching a passable level of skill.

We inevitably get questions asking which knife we recommend? There are four general designs that make sense physiologically, technically, practically:

- The Push (or punch) dagger
- The "stiletto"-type blade, such as the SOCP
- Reverse-edged blades such as the Clinch Pick
- the Spyderco P'Kal Tanto blades, like those offered from Benchmade

Mortality in the Weapons-Based Environment

There's an awful lot of statistical magic that goes into crime reporting, so it's difficult to make heads or tails of a lot of it. To date, the best study we've found seems to validate the *don't bring a knife to a gunfight* mantra. The study is from Perelman School of Medicine at the University of Pennsylvania,[8] and at present, it's the only decent study we've found that truly compares mortality for gunshots and edged weapons objectively.

Over the years, studies comparing the relative lethality between knives and guns have established some general facts. While the numbers vary somewhat from study to study and year to year, the reoccurring theme is that handguns result in death for about 1 in 3, and for knives, about 1 in 10 will perish.

A quick note on statistics:

Figures lie and liars figure. There are significant reasons that could play into why gunshot victims are more likely to die, and the study acknowledges that police response times when responding to a shooting are substantially longer due to the risk to the officer. This means that a person could be bleeding for much longer if there's a shooter on the loose, and police close in more quickly when they hear "suspect armed with a knife." We mention this for two reasons:

Don't plan for help.

Have medical equipment.

I've known two people who were stabbed, and one died from the wounds after eight hours in surgery; the other still has the blade of a kitchen knife lodged in his spine. Having been slashed myself, the psychological effects of having someone with a knife bearing down on you are difficult to understand if you haven't experienced it. If you can't easily overpower and disarm the person with the knife, don't shy away from the Nike defense and just run away. For a graphic and educational look at the types of edged and pointed weapons injuries, check out the work by Dr. William Cox titled "Sharp Edged and Pointed Instrument Injuries." Be warned—it's graphic.

So why, given the greater lethality of the gun, would you want a knife?

Why Would You Want a Knife?

There's a really common trope in the gun world. We hear it pretty much any time a guy justifies why he carries a knife. He'll say, "I use my knife to create space so I can get to my gun." I've put this to practice in training. It doesn't work.

You might have been wondering why we were talking about animals so much earlier. Well, here's where we connect the dots. The way predatory animals use their claws isn't to make space so they can get to their teeth. It's so they can *take* space so other animals can't get to theirs. Working with a knife is about dominant posture, and in the very close interval, a knife can do a few major things that give it an advantage over the gun:

Operate without malfunctioning

Inflict injury *while* taking dominant positioning

Take up space that disallows an adversary to introduce a handgun

A blade can be disorienting to manage and can force the adversary into focusing on damage control. This forces them into a reactive mindset rather than proactive, which means they are not setting the tone and pace of the encounter. As we discussed in Fights, this is pretty important.

Proximity and Efficacy

We often use clichés based on outdated logic as if they were true. For example, *a pistol is just to fight your way to the rifle you never should have left*, and *don't bring a knife to a gunfight*. Are they true? We say no. They are spoiled leftovers from Cooperean-era gun dogma. There are plenty of occasions where the handgun is not only sufficient, but ideal. Likewise, when we're discussing clinch-range lethal force altercations, a knife has some advantages. What people aren't expressing here is that there is a sort of band of efficiency based on distance and effectiveness.

First, let's define efficiency: Let's say simply that it is the metric of how fast you accurately hit your target, regardless of the weapon. Up close, at 0-3 meters, our position is that a knife is every bit as dangerous as a handgun. Once you get past 3-5 meters or so, the handgun starts to shine, as the person armed with a knife has to move more, which costs time and options.

At these same distances, rifles tend to have some minor drawbacks (over-penetration, height over bore) that make them a little less user friendly. By 25 meters, the handgun is at the end of its effective range for most shooters, and the rifle is coming into its own. At this range, the blade is functionally useless. The rifle remains the king from 50 to 150 meters or so and gradually becomes a bit more difficult to run after 200-250 meters. So, what does all this mean? It means pick the right tool for the right distance, and don't just accept clichés as gospel.

What the Blade Isn't

The blade isn't a less-lethal option. This bears saying because if you get rolling up and need to break the stalemate in a defensive encounter, you can't just draw a knife and justify it legally. While we can't tell you from the comfort of our computer desk what the point is in which you *need* to introduce a lethal force option, what we can say is that the aggressor needs to fit three criteria before you turn up the noise. If the following three criteria are *not* met, you don't have a lethal force encounter.

Motive to kill or maim

Capability to kill or maim

Opportunity to kill or maim

The worst part of this is, as we always say, the citizen has no legal tailwind to help. We have to constantly reassess where we are in a fight. What if a guy pulls a blade on you and then drops it? Is he still capable of killing you? Keep this in mind as you study fighting with a blade. If you keep sticking a guy after he gives up, you'll need to explain that. So, let's correct the quote above and say instead: *We use our knife to take up space so our enemy can't access a deadly weapon when we fear for our life.*

In extreme close range, in skilled hands, the blade is an effective tool. Like the handgun, it affords the user an option of elevating to match the threat if it becomes a lethal encounter, but it doesn't rely on mechanical operation to function properly, and it can be used to take space from the enemy. In doing so, we can create small windows for positional dominance. This means we can get to our feet and out of the situation as soon as possible.

Don't pull a knife on a guy with a gun across the room. Let's face it, that old "high noon" cliché stuff is dead and gone; it's the cup and saucer grip wisdom of by-gone eras, and the short blade absolutely has a place in the defensive profile of the modern-day soldier, officer, or citizen.

A final word on all this: Don't overlook hand-to-hand skills. Some wrestling, boxing, and Jiu Jitsu will go a long way in helping you control an enemy and denying them the chance to rob you of initiative in a fight. The blade is the logical intermediary between hand-to-hand and firearm skills, so devote some time to train on how to both effectively use and counter the blade...and don't forget to bring your knife to the gunfight.

Street Culture and Weapons

Contrary to pop culture, most homeless people usually aren't violent. While mental illness runs rampant in homeless populations (and indeed, may be considered a cause of homelessness), only a very small percentage of them are violent or addicted to drugs like meth or crack (which *are* associated with violence and risky behavior), but by and large, they're docile and drug addicted. While desperation may play into their decision-making, most are not bold, risk-taking criminals with big ambitions. They're meek, timid, drug-addled, and adrift. The idea of "hobo tactical," for example, is mind-numbing for the utter lack of forethought. When your list of priorities in life looks something like this:

Breathable oxygen

Dope

...Everything else

It doesn't leave a ton of space for calculating cold-blooded tactics, and you're crazy if you think hobos, who are largely drunks and opioid addicts, sit around in cardboard boxes improvising weapons all night.

Does that mean the homeless don't arm themselves? No. Of course not. They do. What it does mean is they're not sharpening ice picks or making blades from putty knives. The reason? They, like almost every other human on the planet, have access to real knives or better weapons. The streets aren't prison, and if a cop shakes you down and finds you with a sharpened ice pick, he's not going to say, "Oh, I guess this guy is just chipping ice; might as well turn him loose," because cops, unlike the tactical community, aren't motivated by what they see on Instagram. They know a weapon, be it improvised or not, so pretending your improvised tool is "low pro" is a laughably bad miscalculation.

Improvising Weapons

There's some strange space in the overlap of the tactical community's Venn diagram. Somewhere in between lock picking, shooting, survivalism, and martial arts, there's a gray space where the edgy kids gather to play the rebel. They claim to be using the secrets of tradecraft and the criminal underworld, and it has been making a significant impact.

Born from a desire to be able to improvise efficient tools anywhere, there are developers making low signature weapons that emulate those used in the seedy street culture of the homeless, the drug-addicted, and the criminal. We've got one problem with that, and it's a big one: It's all fake.

While there may be some tools like this used in prison or in extremely restrictive foreign nations, the lack of efficacy, durability, and utility means the trend of discreet improvised weapons is entirely fraudulent. When we say fake, we mean this from the perspective of having dealt with street people on a street-person level, and it's from that perspective that this section is being written.

When to Improvise

Improvisation does happen. One person we interviewed recalled an attack that happened with a regular pen. So, what do street people use as weapons? Whatever they can get ahold of. More often than not, what they can get a hold of falls into two loose categories: edged weapons and blunt weapons.

The ubiquitous pocketknife is lower profile than a sharpened ice pick. If you haven't seen them, vendors are now selling pointed pens that look like Crayola markers as low signature defensive tools. They're selling sharpened paring knives and box cutters. Real talk: What problem does that solve? *Any* adult who thinks these tools are going to slip notice is wildly out of touch with reality. As for claims of *if you know, you know*, roll your eyes. People who say that rarely know. Can you scramble someone's brain with an ice pick? Sure. That doesn't make it the best tool for a normal person (or even an assassin), and it sure as hell doesn't make it low key.

Almost any adult you come across would see an ice pick and think it's a weird thing for a grown man to be carrying around. This particularly bad idea has the added benefit of being a weapon that will attract children's attention. Brilliant work, guys. It is the same with a box cutter. If you're not opening boxes at Walmart, it's out of place. The entire purpose of being "gray" is to blend in and do things in such a way that if you *are* forced to resort to violence, everyone is completely caught off guard and thinks to themselves, *holy shit, I thought he was just a regular person.*

There are arguably no people more invisible than the homeless. They are society's untouchables. We shy away from them, avoid eye contact, get uncomfortable when they're around, and promptly forget them. They live without addresses, social security numbers, or checking accounts. There's a ton we can learn from them in terms of how to be resourceful in a worst-case scenario. Not included on that list is weapons selection.

So, just like on the street, if you're caught in a moment of unpredictable violence, you can improvise by grabbing a brick, a rock, a pen, or a purpose-built tool...but if you have access to better weapons, why not do exactly what they'd do and use the better weapon?

Blunt Weapons

One of the things we see most common among the homeless, in their squats or in their packs, is the blunt weapon. This could be an ax or a hammer, but the method of injury when they're used is blunt force trauma. Homeless people understand police can identify the difference between weapons (improvised or not) and tools. While some of this varies by location, it's legal to have a hammer nearly anywhere. So why do the homeless carry blunt weapons? For two main reasons: plausible deniability and utilitarian use.

If someone creates a weapon intentionally out of a normal object, they're showing that they've got violence on their mind. Backpackers carry hatchets. Hammers are ubiquitous and good for pounding heads or for setting up camps. They're easy to find, easy to steal, and don't raise huge red flags. They're not serialized and don't come in wide varieties, so it's hard to say, "Wait, that's MY hammer!" if it turns up in an evidence locker.

They're multipurpose items that are generally available, cheap, and not a high risk if caught with one. If someone confiscates one, oh well. Police are probably not going to arrest you unless the thing has blood and chunks of hair on it. It's just a hammer. When you carry your entire world in a cart or on your back, this is how you think. When you dig through social media trying to find what's cool this week, you buy pointy Crayola markers.

Efficacy and Interdisciplinary Fighting

Improvised weapons really aren't amazingly effective. Not only are they easy to break (metals are rated for a reason; think back to Bring a Knife to a Gunfight to recall how kitchen knives snap off in bone), but they're also hard to carry on your person. Whereas a simple pocketknife can fold up and go in a pocket, how do you carry an ice pick? How about a putty knife? While several of us have experienced fights where knives were present, we draw heavily on known research on edged weapons. Piercing weapons such as ice picks or screwdrivers can really be tremendously effective, but paring knives, pointy tipped pens, box cutters, and so forth typically only result in superficial slashes, which aren't immediately incapacitating. In skilled hands, just about anything can be effective...but if you don't know what you're doing, none of it matters.

Where talks on efficacy often stop is when the question of what happens in a mixed weapon environment arises. If you've got a marginally effective tool and you engage in a fight with someone who has a more developed fighter's triangle, you'll probably end up losing the positioning and posture needed to effectively use a contact weapon, be it improvised or not. If you're escaping from prison and you need to shank a guard, improvised tools and ambush might be the right recipe. But for the regular person, you're far better off with a well-rounded striking and grappling game and good awareness.

Improvising and Foreign Travel

What if you're outside the US and you can't find a good knife? Well, we have to stop seeing the weapon as the only solution. As we've discussed time and time again, awareness, judgment, and being fit enough to run or fight all work in the place of a poorly crafted impromptu weapon.

There are some legitimate risks associated with foreign travel, especially if you can't change the way you look to match the locals. Where reality collides with the fantasy, we have our basic tenets— be polite, stay low key, avoid criminals and criminal dealings, and be ready to move fast on short notice if you can't.

This shouldn't be construed as saying that you shouldn't be able to grab something and hurt someone badly with it. You should. Disorganized crime and petty thefts can escalate quickly in less-developed nations, and you need to have a plan for that. But the entire mentality of prioritizing an improvised weapon in a foreign country when you're at no real risk is straight up Walter Mitty nonsense. Think about it like this: Are you really going to kill someone over the thirty lira in your pocket and spend the next however many years in a foreign prison? Are you going to kick someone's ass into the dirt and get the shakedown by the local cops? What are they going to say about the table knife you stole and wrapped in newspaper (which, why wouldn't you just leave it in the bag with a receipt)? Sure, you can ditch that thing, but have you thought about actually using it and the consequences? Our advice to the people latching on to this phenomenon is simple: play it cool, killer. We've been overseas enough to know it's not that hard to stay out of trouble if you're not involved in drugs or drinking recklessly.

If you want to get serious about improvising weapons and fighting with edged weapons, spend time working against opponents who have training knives (or handguns, for that matter) to get used to how they're handled in an entanglement. You'll see it's still a game of physical chess, and even empty-handed, you have some advantages.

Who Causes Trouble?

Among street-level offenders, there are three demographics that are likely to use violence—drunks, gang members, and desperate junkies.

Drunks aren't really different in any sphere of violence. They're as unpredictable and dangerous to the police as they are to the citizen. Gang members, in this context, are usually in some position of the supply/distribution chain for illegal trade. Often, they organized enough to have some risk mitigation, and they're connected enough that if a desperate junkie tries to rob them, that junkie better catch a bus way the hell out of there because they'll probably end up dead.

As to the junkies...well, if you've ever seen a junkie in a state of dope sickness, it's a spectrum with flu-like symptoms on one end and some pretty hardcore delusions and erratic behavior on the other. They'll do just about anything to get "well," but let's face it, their ambition/desperation isn't really in lockstep with their ability. If you're worried about desperate junkies, keep in mind they're predominately thieves and aren't known for being determined fighters. This can have some variation between subcultures, but what does that mean to you as a regular person? It means if you aren't getting involved in drugs, your chances of dealing with any of this are pretty slim.

Also, worth keeping in mind is that regardless of alias or lack of address, street people know one another. If someone gets punched in the nose, well, that's just the dominance game. If someone ends up a chalk outline, it ups the ante, just like it would for an everyday citizen. This is the long way around making a *really* simple pair of points that almost shouldn't even need to be made:

Weapons can be improvised on the fly out of pretty much anything. If you can get a purpose-built tool for the job, that's always preferable.

Just like people fifteen years ago talking about using tampons to stop bleeding, we have people who've never been in a knife fight talking about fighting with fruit knives, improvising weapons, and determining efficacy by stabbing pig carcasses. Real life is a little more complex, so we'll say it again: Play it cool. If you absolutely have to improvise, actually improvise. Don't carry something around that's an obvious aforethought qualifier. You won't fool anyone, and foreign legal systems aren't as soft and fluffy as the West.

Tactics for the Regular Person

First and foremost, it's important to understand what "tactics" are, and how they contrast with strategy. Tactics, in our context, is the use of maneuver to achieve an aim in the face of opposition. This could apply to how we rehearse defending our children if someone breaks into our home, or how we react to an attempted contact on the streets by a criminal. By contrast, strategy is "a general plan to achieve one or more long-term or overall goals under conditions of uncertainty." We can say in general, our strategy is to be useful, productive citizens capable of assisting our families and communities during emergencies.

As you may be noticing, tactics and strategy are very similar to our Type 1 and Type 2 emergencies, and this is by design... and just as our Type I skills are used to address the uncertainty present in the Type II, we use tactics to achieve our strategic goals. While this may seem very "military" in nature, the functional aspects of thinking in this way are just a tool to better understand how we cultivate and implement the skills we identify as necessary. This works pretty well... and when we consider how conflict plays into our overall capability, very few other concepts translate as cleanly as tactics and strategy.

In this section, we will discuss some generalities as they apply to the citizen. It's incredibly important to acknowledge that good tactics, fitness, mindset, and the right tools help us engineer good outcomes - but they are NEVER a guarantee that things will work out in our favor. It's also important to say that this can mean life and death. Often, within the 'tactical' community, trainers soft peddle this to the citizens attending their training. It's very important that we enter into this portion clear-eyed, and without fantastic expectations of what conflict will look like. We need to state clearly that we're talking about the potential to both kill or be killed by humans, and that should not be taken lightly.

ISG's Tactical Philosophy

We should be clear about something: tactics need to be practiced under the guidance of someone who has significant experience using tactics—and not all tactics are created equally. In the citizen's context, what works for a Navy SEAL doesn't likely translate 1:1 to what you're doing, so seek out people who have experience working stateside in professions that require them to work alone or in small groups. Very often, these people work as undercover officers, special agents, or executive protection specialists, and in their fields, going to guns means they've failed. That brings their area of overlap pretty close to citizens. From a tactical perspective, the problems citizens face are the most difficult, and if mastered, they scale up fairly easily to involve more people and more advanced concepts, while the inverse is not true. Just because you've done years' worth of CQB with a SWAT team or conducted raids overseas doesn't mean those tactics will entirely apply. However, the unifying concepts of speed, simplicity, and violence of action generally apply, and the self-directed mentality of the types of people who find themselves in "high speed" career fields means they usually have some useful information. Let's move on and discuss tactics on the ground floor: for the citizen who has no support, no logistic supply chain, no airstrikes, and probably won't be planning a deliberate raid in which they can use intelligence and technology to tilt the situation in their favor.

Individual Movement Techniques

Individual movement techniques are somewhat a world unto themselves.

Once you add a second person, tactics function like a microcosm of larger scale squad or platoon tactics (on which plenty has been written and we'll cover very briefly). The individual tactician has far and away the hardest job, and the reason is responsibility. The more people you have, the more you can slice an environment into manageable areas of responsibility where a specific person is charged with keeping an eye on that sliver of world. When you're on your own, you absorb one hundred percent of the responsibility, and being forward-looking creatures, chances are you'll only ever be able to observe 30-40 percent of the world around you at a time, and that amount shrinks dramatically when you're pressed into a fight.

Key Points:

• All environments are composed of the 540° bubble— the 360° world in the horizontal plane, and the 180° overhead, vertical plane.

• The fewer people you have, the more of that bubble you are responsible for.

• The goal is to always use angles to give us as much information about that bubble as possible, while exposing ourselves to observation as little as possible.

Movement, Signature, and Initiative

As we move through a high threat environment, our main challenge is the unknown. Especially as citizens—and even more so as citizens who may have dependents who aren't combatants with them—we can't afford to be looking for trouble. If we've got rifles, we almost certainly need friends with rifles. Time for an unpopular opinion: You can clear buildings without having a weapon in your hand. We say this fully recognizing that most people are NOT trained to a high enough level that they're going to actively discriminate against people who may or may not be armed; even professionals tend to reflexively shoot when they're surprised by someone popping up in the environment in which they're working.

With that said, use some judgment. If there is no specific, active threat, don't feel like just because you have a gun on you that you need it in your hand. If we use good tactics, the observe, orient, and decide process will allow you to act intelligently when the time comes. Don't mistake what we're saying here: If you're up against a deadly threat in your own home or you've already identified a lethal threat—don't enter the fight at a disadvantage. Having the drop and turning up the violence first goes a long way in winning fights but recognize that different situations require different approaches and think about how simply having a gun in hand when you're alone in the 540° bubble would look from the 270° you can't observe.

Tactical Concepts for Responder Zero
Modulation and Angles

Just like in boxing or grappling, how you approach your adversary is crucially important. We don't want to face them head on, on equal footing. We're not talking about a Hollywood showdown, and in reality, there are no heroes. We need to do everything possible to put our adversaries in a position where they're unable to orient themselves when we press an attack. One of the main concepts to be considered when you're on your own is modulation of the pace you use to clear the unknown area around you. Humans are loud—even when we're trying to be sneaky. Especially in urban environments, most people are going to make noise by way of stepping on debris, using lights, banging into walls, talking, or creating odors that don't belong. For this reason, orienting yourself requires a slow, deliberate, and measured pace that's often far slower than you might initially think is necessary. When you're initially taking stock of an unknown area, move extremely slow and take in as much information as possible.

This generally means using angles to our advantage and putting ourselves in places where we have good observation while making anyone coming toward us bypass transitional areas that require them to use light, make noise, and task fixate. It could involve stairwells, locked doors, debris fields, or passing through well-lit areas, and if you find yourself in a situation that requires you to clear a structure you don't control, you're going to have to be able to quickly assess areas that present hazards to both yourself and anyone else moving through that space.As you approach potential danger areas, approach them in such a way that allows you to take in as much information as possible. This generally means approaching at a very shallow angle and gradually widening as you approach.

Slicing the Pie

Slicing the pie means using arcing, micro-steps and leaning the torso slightly to get a visual impression of the room before committing to entering. It is a fundamental technique for the individual. This process, sometimes referred to as "static" clearing, relies on very slow, quiet, and methodical movement that attempts to set up any engagement so that it's on "our" terms. Slicing the pie in a transitional area (such as a hallway, doorway, or stairwell) allows us to gather information quickly and quietly without drawing undue attention. This technique can be used when approaching corridors and rooms, but as you might guess, things get complex quickly in environments with long doorways with lots of doors. This is tough when you've got security and extra eyes, so expect that it'll be close to impossible to keep an eye on the flux that occurs as you clear and leave an area when you're by yourself. There might be other solutions, but the simplest answer is don't get comfortable. When working in teams, we have "clean" (cleared) areas and "dirty" areas that haven't been assessed yet. When you're on your own, every area is always dirty. Don't get comfortable, don't linger, and do everything to make your business in the unknown structure brief, or secure a spot you can hold down that gives you adequate warning of approach and avenues of escape.

T-Intersections

Often enough, corridors end in T-intersections where you've got a choice of going left or right. These pose a problem because it's extremely hard to cover your back while trying to assess two opposing directions. As you approach, use some discretion and knowledge of the layout (Which way is the front of the building? Which way do you need to travel? et cetera) and approach the intersection by slowly taking the wall opposite to it. Slice the pie as much as you can without exposing yourself to the other direction. This allows you to keep your back to the wall while assessing the corridor (though don't actually hug the wall; bullets travel along walls, and you're more likely to bump into it and make noise), and it gives you some peripheral vision for threats that might come from your rear. Once you're satisfied, cross the hall you're in without entering the T-intersection and reverse the process. At that point, you can move into the intersection and keep moving.

Stairwells

No matter who you are or what your job is, conflict around stairwells is a shit problem that has no clean solutions. Stairwells work well as ambush sites because they force an advancing party to work against gravity in a narrow confines where it's hard to use shoulder-fired weapons as intended. Stairwells are vulnerable to traps and hand grenades, and they usually have heavy doors that close automatically and make a lot of noise. The good news is, if your job isn't taking ground, you have some discretion in what positions you put yourself in. If there are signs that a stairwell might be controlled by an opposing force, you can try to dodge it altogether. That doesn't excuse us from training for them, and the way we take stairwells is essentially the same as how we take linear areas, except we do so vertically. We continue to take short micro-steps in an arc that allow us to take in information. As we traverse the stairs, we keep our back to the wall and arc (or hook) our way through landings, being careful not to neglect the areas we've passed through.

Weapons Handling in Uncertain Environments

As mentioned before, you don't always need to clear a building with a firearm. When clearing with a pistol in hand, it's important to fully understand how gun handling changes in extremely close quarters. Being able to compress the pistol and appropriately use retention positions for concealing yourself and preventing someone from grabbing for your gun are essential skills, and they require training with someone who understands the context. Along with positions to safely move around people you want to keep from danger, and a knowledge of weapons manipulation and marksmanship, this is the basis of our individual movement techniques, or IMTs, which will be discussed later.

Tactics for Home Defense

Far and away the most serious problem we face in the citizen's world is home invasion. The reason is simple: It requires at least some planning to execute. It could be as simple as someone saw you moving in a big screen TV or as complex as a psychopath who's been stalking you or your family for months, or anything that falls in between. The first thing we need to illuminate is that we often feel safe in our homes. It's where we relax, where we sit comfortably behind doors, and where we feel in control of our environment (unless you have kids, but that's for a different book). Stop feeling comfortable. It's an unpopular thing to say, and for the most part, most live and let live people just want to go about their lives without fear, but here's the thing: Life is inherently dangerous, and it doesn't have to be weird to take steps to safeguard it.

A good first step is to take the ISG home security audit, which can be found using the following QR code, or by visiting integratedskillsgroup.com

Home Security

Do you feel like you're responding to driving with irrational fear by having airbags and wearing a seatbelt? Is it paranoid to want to close the door on some of the most common mechanisms of injury? Most of the things we can do to prevent incursions into our home are pretty simple. You don't have to live like an armed encampment or have bars over every window. As we discussed before, we want to close the "ins" for opportunists.

https://integratedskillsgroup.com/2021/06/home-security-audit/

As for the tactics we use in our homes, some of this will be dictated by the layout of your home, but in general, here are some steps you want to accomplish:

• Disallow easy, discreet entry. Motion-activated lights and doors and windows with sound alarms that draw attention tend to steal the initiative from invaders and force them to react. That's a moment to seize.

• Create internal barriers that interfere with easy passage. Force an intruder to make noise via doorways (especially those that alert you when opened) or transitional spaces (such as stairwells).

• Keep family members close so they can be quickly accounted for, and have a chokepoint, such as a hallway or stairwell, that needs to be taken to access family sleeping quarters. This gives you a tactical advantage and reduces the complication of having to move through an unsecured environment against unknown adversaries.

Recall from Low-Light Tactics that light can create "walls," also referred to as "photonic barriers." Consider establishing such lights both inside your home and out. As well, consider how these lights would be powered in an emergency situation when you may not be able to rely on grid power.

If you do have to traverse your home to make sure your children are secure, have a way of communicating with your spouse or anyone else who lives with you. It may sound strange, but have your family rehearse this as if it were a fire drill. At the core, plans are just lists of responsibilities. Make sure your people know their responsibilities and are capable of acting them out. If the situation requires you to set up a safe, "no-pass" zone, have your spouse call 911 and relay the information and circumstances, or gather children in a safe location and create a second layer to your security plan.

In your Vehicle

As one of our five categories for skill development, mobility is a topic we cover exhaustively. Whether on foot, horseback, or in a vehicle, we view the ability to move as crucial to all things ISG. One of the biggest reoccurring sources of bad information is vehicle tactics, in which guys pull their pistols and blast out the windows of their vehicles in an attempt to demonstrate how dangerous they are behind the wheel. The problem here is that the type of tactics that are on display are almost always a dangerous concoction of out-of-context drills that don't really teach anything useful to the clients paying for the training and counter-ambush tactics taught to military or police that only apply in a very small set of circumstances and carry serious liability in the real world. There is also a lack of consequences for dangerously bad training—meaning you don't get shot for screwing up in training, and therefore the bad practice persists without question. Let's take a long look at exactly why our approach to vehicle-based problems needs to be reassessed for validity, as well as how to dodge some of the cringe-inspiring gun glam that, frankly, we think will get you killed or prosecuted. A vehicle's most vulnerable components are typically:

• The block, which houses the pistons but is generally built to withstand 100,000-plus miles of explosions. The block is situated under the head, making it hard to reach.

• The head and subsequent valves, camshafts, fuel injection systems, et cetera. These components synchronize and facilitate the engine, turning gas into movement. These are the most exposed vital areas, and in modern times, they are often aluminum rather than steel.

• The transmission, which allows the vehicle to change speeds by shifting gears. This is generally protected by the chassis.

• The driver. For obvious reasons.

Destroying any of these components will stop a vehicle pretty quickly. Less incapacitating, but still important are:

• The radiator and cooling system (including the fan). Loss of coolant will cause the vehicle to overheat and eventually fail.

• Tires. The vehicles tires allow it to gain and maintain traction. Without them, the vehicle is reduced to a slow, noisy, hard-to-control mess.

• Oil and fuel systems. Though not exposed, loss of oil will ultimately cause an engine to seize. Fuel is self-explanatory.

We've had some substantial riots as of the time of this writing in which police, security, and citizens were all caught up and stopped by mobs. While we should learn from the lessons of military or private security convoys and high-risk traffic stops, we shouldn't expect them to directly apply to the citizen or civil emergencies. Shooting it out probably isn't your best bet. It takes time to disable a vehicle, short of explosives or an IED/VBIED (which is why they're used), because the vitals of the vehicle are intentionally protected. So, if we're looking at drills to do so, let's do it in context. A big shootout in the streets using only rifles and pistols is pretty high on the totem of fantasy gun gods, and if you're going to get ambushed by a group, don't be surprised if they don't use guns at all, but rather firebombs or other mob tactics to disable the vehicle. Taken together, this means that vehicles have weak points and strong points, and we need to understand how those points influence our survivability, and we need to divorce ourselves from the weapon fixation that dominates training.

Most vehicle tactics courses presently being taught are recipes for disaster. Dudes are donning their plate carriers and grabbing their M4s, going hot immediately, before attempting to stay mobile. If you challenge them on the topic, they'll argue that they're practicing a "vehicle down" drill. Roger that, but is your mobility entirely reliant on your vehicle? Let's back up a bit. Vehicles are transitional spaces. They force us to interact with the environment before transitioning tasks or environments.

Think about it like this: if you're driving (or riding) in a vehicle, you can't, in most cases, transition to walking. You have to stop driving to start walking. This creates a transitional environment. If we stop to think about what a disabled vehicle is, it's a transitional event that says, "Okay, you're done being mobile." The ambush is a tactic designed to prey on that lack of mobility. When you hard reset to shooting instead of staying mobile, you're facilitating that ambush. If you can find a suitable range, try the following: use a shot timer to time yourself drawing and shooting a target from a seated position in your vehicle (if not, try to find an airsoft pistol to try the drill). Take that time, point in, and see how many rounds you can accurately place into a target in that same amount of time. Here's the point: Every second you spend trying to transition while you're stationary in an ambush is probably three to four rounds that a single person can put into your car. If you're fighting five or six cardboard dummies, solid man, rock out. If they're people who move and have AKs torching off, now we're talking twenty or so rounds coming in every second— and you can't move. You're giving the initiator exactly what he wants by having to change your focus, drop seconds accessing a weapon, fumble for target acquisition in a confined space, and then try to engage without full range of motion.

Our suggestion?

Everyone gets out of the vehicle as fast as possible from the side not taking fire. The first person out gets behind something solid and scans for threats. The second person out returns the favor after recovering anything important. This works whether or not your vehicle was intentionally targeted for an attack, and it gives you a solid plan that could help if you have to abandon your vehicle for any reason but can't risk cutting ballast entirely. We often say it's more important to not get shot than it is to shoot. Mobility is perhaps the ultimate expression of that. Deny an ambusher that hard reset by having a rehearsed ability to quickly and cleanly egress the vehicle and stay mobile. This might mean sacrificing cool guy points by initiating drills like this while you're still in your seatbelt. It doesn't seem like a cool skill to get out of your vehicle without snagging up on your belt until some knucklehead knocks out your window with a rock and grabs your throat. It might mean having to recover your rifle later in the game, or not at all. It might mean you have to sprint to a position away from the vehicle to draw the attack away (a point we'll revisit soon), and it might mean leaving down a dark alley after never having fired a shot while a mob flips and burns your car. Such is life, and if you don't like it, the other option—death—is yours to choose as well.

If the threats are from an oblique angle, taking a position closer to the front can be useful. If they're from the side (or present from the flank), you're better off from the opposite side. It's often said fights around vehicles are won from the rear. This is largely based on police altercations. For citizens, just assume that anyone you face will be armed and aggressive. While putting the vehicle between you and an aggressor means you've got more mass and distance they'll have to travel, it often requires getting out and maneuvering to the rear of the vehicle, whereas most officers are already on their feet and mobile. Having the diagonal approach from the rear of the vehicle allows you to keep from bunching up while staying behind semi-solid structures and having the majority of the surrounding environment available for assessment, but it could also put you at a disadvantage against multiple attackers approaching from different angles. Whether advancing or retreating, move while keeping yourself covered as best as you're able. Make it as close to a no win as possible. One of the unspoken outcomes of good tactics is often people will see that they're up against a situation in which they're severely disadvantaged, and they'll find elsewhere to be. This is the best outcome most of the time, once an altercation is on. Even aggressive people or "bad guys" aren't TV fall guys. Most of the time, most people of sound mind (including criminals) won't throw their lives away over something stupid. They'll throw yours away, but not their own. Use good tactics, and make it a no-win.

One more thing—if your vehicle isn't disabled, do not stop! But remember, the vehicle is a transitional space. Train to quickly get out of it without stepping into traffic, to sit in it while it catches fire (literally or lead), or get hung up, tripping, and falling flat on your face. It doesn't look cool, and similar to throwing a decent punch, everyone thinks they already know how. The social media crowd will be eerily silent about questioning what gun they saw, and you might suffer a boring lack of hearts and thumbs-up, but you'll actually have a useful skill.

If you have to counter an ambush, finish out the mobility mission first and prepare to fight while on the move to some place or thing that provides better cover than your vehicle. This is something that requires a cogent assessment of context and good instruction and rehearsal. Another subtle point we need to mention is that we drill on this *en extremis* because failing an absolute blowout or ambush, the protocols leading up to fighting around vehicles are generally useful for vehicle based emergencies, such as collisions or fires. A stepwise way of safely egressing, collecting valuables (or kids or loved ones!) are generally the same. So, we baseline our approach to vehicle problems this way because anything less should be manageable using the same 'tactical' template.

Vehicle-Based Ambushes

Let's go straight to the heart of this issue: Ambushes are complex (sometimes because they're amateur simple) and mobility is complex, too. The environments where they occur aren't always well-lit ranges (surprise, I know), and we can't count on the bad guys to hold still while exposing their vitals. We must account for variable lighting conditions, urban and rural environmental differences (burning trash and burning cars vs. deep mud and downed trees), and of course, the situation that has us moving in the first place. More often than not, if we're not deliberately operating in a conflict zone, we won't have rifles on our laps. If we're lucky, we've got more than one person armed with a handgun and competent in its use. If we're not lucky, we've got dependents who are utterly relying on us to keep them alive. This is why ISG drills on vehicle problems as much as we do; they're a massively complex series of tasks that test coordination, awareness, marksmanship, movement, and the ability to navigate transitional spaces.

Before going any further, let's make something clear: We are not saying all the established tactics on this are bad. We're saying there is a major gap when we translate these tactics to problems faced in common emergencies outside the military/ contractor or police sphere of violence. If you have a rifle or a mounted crew served weapon, and can send a wall of lead to break an ambush, do it. If you have armored vehicles that you can use as cover, do it. Those approaches just solve different problems. What we do have an issue with is trying to directly translate those protocols to the citizens for fun and profit because not much, if anything, makes sense if you do.

Fighting is different for citizens, military, contractors, and police. When we break down the differences, we can find the similarities and use them. This is good practice. Trying to force military counter-ambush tactics on a class for citizens is entertainment. Always anticipate that the problems faced in the citizen's sphere of violence will be more complicated, carry more severe penalties for failure, and demand a higher level of commitment than the others. These situations are endlessly complex, and no single tactic, technique, or procedure will solve them. Because of this, we can break our training from being contextual or scenario-based and make it a composite test of the subordinate skills. It's really unlikely you're going to be able to use the same tactics as the military with your EDC pistol and maybe a spare magazine. If you're dressing up to pretend that you can, take a hard look at whether that training is realistic. Even if you're a go-fast guy doing go-fast things, consider what we're saying for when you're at home with your family.

We can train on the subordinate tasks and combine them into longer, more complex drills that test our ability to integrate skills. Said simply, the skills we need to build for these situations won't give us a master key to the solutions lock, but training will give us the skills to handle the problems and the footing, so we don't fall flat on our face if something does go sideways. So, with this discussion, please understand when we say "ambush", we're discussing unwanted, aggressive contact from an unknown party. This could be someone trying to carjack you, someone road-raging, or being caught by a mob while in your vehicle. To state it plainly, a significant portion of our vehicle protocols are taken from experiences with these problems, and the threat of mobs has risen sharply as of late. As always, awareness and avoidance are the 'best case'.

Subordinate Tasks

Subordinate task, in this case, is really a fancy way of saying a skill we can improve by itself. Most of us don't do Brazilian Jiu Jitsu while carrying our pistol, for example, and the point of going to the range or training in MMA isn't so we can kill our training partners; it's so we get good at the specific skills that a fight might require from us. If we take these isolated skills, such as hand-to-hand fighting and pistol work, and we use a course that force us to fight other humans to test them together in a non-contextual environment, we can walk away knowing either that these things work, or we need to get back to the drawing board.

The scenario we use to test the integration of skills is less important than whether it sufficiently tests our ability to succeed in a complex task environment. Like any good training, which puts the student in a variety of roles requiring a variety of skills at random, we should structure our vehicle training similarly.

So, in this instance, what tasks should we consider?

• Can you get out of your vehicle quickly without falling on your face, or are you stumbling to get free of your seatbelt?

• Can you do so without letting your vehicle roll away and become a secondary hazard? • Can you keep your cool and defuse preventable violence?

• If a fight does break out, can you combine your vehicle-based skills with empty hand or weapon-based skills to minimize damage?

From the top, here's an at-a-glance idea of how to deal with the situation of a disabled vehicle and subsequent assault: Be physically fit enough to do the work. Be situationally aware of what's happening in your area. If you live in a city where there are riots going on, know where they're happening! It's not always possible to know exactly where they'll end up, but use some common sense, pay attention, and don't get caught with your pants down trying to drive through a known conflict area for no good reason. If rioting or protests come to you, don't stop. Keep moving at a steady fifteen miles per hour or so—not fast enough to threaten people, but make sure they realize you're not pulling over.

2020 handed us a wrecking ball of anecdotes regarding people driving through protests and riots, and quite a few of the stories ended up with vehicles being turned into area targets for gunfire and projectile debris. Don't expect that rioters won't be equally armed and that they won't outnumber you a thousand to one. If you're caught in a hostile crowd of ANTIFA or Proud Boys, just chant the party line and get out of there. That's not the place to make your political stand. Don't get aggressive, stay cool, and never underestimate your ability to start running people over. If you get choked in a transitional space, have the skills to get out of your vehicle quickly and safely. We use what we call the exit protocol, which is designed to work across the spectrum of situations—provided your vehicle isn't rolled over. Don't try to fight from inside the vehicle if it's not absolutely impossible to bail.

Think about the limitations of movement and weapon articulation. How many degrees can you move that carbine off zero? maybe sixty? What if it's a good ambush and they hit you from the rear and the side? Focusing on pouring fire out the back of your Explorer means you can't move to address threats from oblique angles. Escape the threat by driving away. If you cannot drive, then quickly assess for cover and concealment.

Know the hard and soft spots on your vehicle and stay alert when the conditions switch from a casual drive to a tense situation. There are some hard points on modern vehicles; the chassis, axles, and engine block provide some limited cover. Use them wisely; they probably won't last. Don't crowd your cover, either. Bullets tend to travel along flat surfaces, and when they strike hard surfaces, they tend to create spall, which can cause injury or distraction.

Also, training for popping up over cover is a bad idea. Popping up over thin-skinned concealment is a recipe for receiving a hot blast of lead. Remember, the panels on your vehicle are only cover if they're throwing spears. All calibers from modern firearms are going to punch right through it. That said, sometimes we've gotta do the best we can with what we have. Just remember those semi-hard points on the vehicle. Be able to make body shots on targets out to 50 yards with your handgun. Train with your people on contingencies: getting away by fire or recovering valuables by fire. Many of us practice individual movement techniques (IMT) or squad tactics, but small group movement—especially when some in that group might be family members—is mysteriously vacant.

If you have family and all you're training to do is blow the back window out with your AR15 from inside the vehicle to react to an ambush, congratulations! You now know you're wrong. Chances are you won't have the goon squad with you. If you do, getting a gun immediately in the fight while the others bail can make some sense. Train for that, too.

Don't assume firing positions that cripple your ability to move; keep one foot on the ground at all times. Don't throw yourself prone under your car (unless there's literally nothing else to hide behind within two hundred yards) and don't drop to both knees. Bullets skip along the ground and you're hampering your ability to move by dropping to both knees. Not only that, but you're off balance, can't lean as far, and can't get back to your feet as fast when you're on both knees. If you have to, find micro terrain—small differences in the landscape that are "better than nothing," such as curbs or craters—and do what you've gotta do. You might be better off prone behind a curb than kneeling behind concealment. Sometimes there's just no right answer.

Be able to get better weapons on-line, or transition to more capable weapons as opportunities arise. In this case, weapons might include things like smoke or pepper spray. A good ambush will probably have different directional and distance components. Can you get good hits from contact to three hundred yards with your carbine, or are you just smoking paper at fifteen yards? These are all skills you can practice in isolation. Paying attention to political unrest in your area, using good driving practices, staying aware while on the road, knowing how to move, shoot, and communicate, having functional handgun skills, and being fit enough enough to make this all count is well within anyone's capability. Make the effort, think critically, and shuck the pageant.

In All Reality

The final thought we want to leave you with is this: If you're in a situation like this and you're not in a military/paramilitary organization, chances are it's not with a bunch of jacked-up killers with carbines and war belts. You're probably going to be with one trusted partner, at best, who may or may not be your spouse, your kid, a friend, or just yourself, all on your own. What does common practice in vehicle tactics look like in those situations? Are you preparing for them by addressing this, or is training time an opportunity to dress up and play war with the boys? If you're the only one armed, do you want to lean out the window and start a gun-fight with an unknown number of mobile dudes who set you up?

All we ask is this: Please think through these situations. You can't plan for every possibility, in every environment, and for every vehicle. What we can do is have simple, effective protocols, train on them in isolation until we're pretty damn good, and then combine them to ensure we're not falling on our faces if the enemigos catch us with shields down.

So, a final list of things to do:

• Practice good situational awareness to head off problems before they happen. Stay low key, avoid trouble, and plan ahead if that's not an option.

• Work hard to be a good driver and have a solid exit protocol that doesn't turn your vehicle into a liability if you have to step out of it.

• Do some driver down drills. The fastest way to incapacitate a vehicle is to kill the operator.

• Get fit, stay fit, and practice some fighting from time to time. The situations you're likely to face often won't be of lethal threat, but it's a damn fine line, so...

Train to make center-of-mass hits with your handgun out to fifty yards and with your rifle out to three hundred.

Train with your partner(s) on methods of movement by fire that don't include shouting out everything you're doing. Doing that when everyone else speaks Pashto or Arabic, here as always, is more complicated.

• Know your vehicle, stage your kit consistently as if you're dealing with a Type II or III emergency, and be ready to grab what you need and hoof it, whether to or from a fight. Have a medical kit on your person (1st line/Type I), in your bag or kit (2nd Line/Type II) and stashed in your car. Know how to use it. Don't just get a tourniquet and expect you'll figure it out. Be ready for reality. You might love those you fought alongside like a brother or sister, but you'll never love them like your children. This is high stakes, and there's no room for error. The reality is, if you get involved in gun play, people get killed. It doesn't matter who's at fault; it happens, and if you're not willing to accept that outcome, then you have two choices: stay back or get as competent as possible. Spend a few minutes considering your priorities. Are you more likely to be immobilized in an ambush or deal with road rage? How about dealing with road rage versus witness-ing a devastating collision? Focus on the high-risk, high-likelihood events first, and then slowly work your way out to the less common or the outright rare.

In Public

The previous two sections discussed tactics for the home and vehicle. Those are usually thought of as our own space, but random violence in the public space has always been an annoyingly consistent earmark of modern life in the West. Whether attacks at concerts using small arms, marathons using explosives, driving down a sidewalk in a panel van, or shooting up a school, there are countless examples of the way violence unfolds in the public space.

To give credit where it's due, Greg Ellifritz has canonized this topic better than anyone we've seen to date. His website, activeresponsetraining.com, should be a stop for anyone who's interested in a no-nonsense account of how active shooters and violent actors carry out their plans. For our purposes, we're not going to go deep into the history or study of the events themselves, but rather the way we respond to them.

Circling back around, these types of situations are all Type I emergencies. They're direct threats to our lives, and we will very likely have to address them with only what we have on us at the time they happen. Here are some points for while we're out and about that keep us a step ahead:

• Head up, Phone Down. In almost all cases of violent attacks in public spaces, there are pre-attack indicators that, if noticed, can be used to your advantage.

• Consider that obvious exits and paths are often used for secondary attacks or explosive devices. Avoid lingering near glass or other substances that fragment in explosions or around gunfire.

• Keep an eye out for things like AEDs/medical kits, fire escapes, and rooms without exits. When panic hits, it can be easy to get swept up without a plan. Be looking for hardened areas that allow you some options, some security, and don't block you off from further egress.

• Be aware that with mass attacks, explosions and gunfire are often used to drive people into a kill zone where secondary explosions or more attackers are staged. Don't just stampede to an exit.

• Be fully aware that once this kind of situation has started, mercy and parlay are out. It's for keeps, and you better play the game accordingly.

• Don't stop to help until the threat is gone. It's no different than putting on your oxygen mask first—you can't help any-one if you're dead.

COMMUNICATIONS

Communications systems have never been more ingrained in our lives than they are now. In the age of digital communication, cell phones, and social media, news travels faster than the truth. While that has its own pitfalls, what's more important to us is that in emergencies, we should have no expectation that our communications infrastructure will be intact. It may be a temporary issue due to call volume, or it could be a broader situation, such as a Digital Denial of Service attack (DDoS) or a natural disaster that impacts cell infrastructure.

Whatever the case, communications are vitally important on a fundamental level; without good information and communication, we get stuck in the observe phase of our OODA loop, and we can't get around to orienting ourselves so we can decide and act. This lack of information can be crippling, and from time immemorial, methods of getting information into the right hands have morphed from runners to satellite phones. So, if you found yourself in an emergency that affected the communications networks we rely on, what would you do?

Basic Communication

Most often when you see this information presented, it's complete with alphanumeric alphabets and radio protocols. There's nothing wrong with that, per se, but it's less important to us that you can pass an efficient message using an encrypted military radio, and more important that you're able to communicate in a timely manner with people in your neighborhood. And while it's not unusual for households to have simple handheld radios, the broader problem here is organizing in the age of social distancing. That phrase has come into its own as of 2020, but let's face it, we've been doing that for a decade. Very few people have good relationships with their neighbors, so the most basic place to start with communication is here: talking to people. We've alluded to it throughout, but the truth is, good ole interpersonal skills are tremendously valuable, and conversation, persuasion, and discussion are often the default during periods of disaster—especially if you're out there trying to work.

If talking isn't your thing, take a class. It might seem silly to suggest, but there are classes on public speaking, rhetoric/debate, even improv comedy or organizations like Toastmasters. All of these can help you become more comfortable thinking on your feet and reading your audience. Most people don't like being the orator, but the bottom line is that we're here to do the difficult things.

Digital Communications and Tools

As we advance beyond the basics of HAM radio, the next step is Software Defined Radio (SDR) and using HAM frequencies for digital communications. At this level, we're reaching specialized knowledge, and just as we would recommend for any of the other skills, it becomes necessary to seek out competent instruction if you intend to pursue this level of proficiency in communications. When we start on this path, we can find ourselves with some very interesting projects. SDR, in conjunction with decoding software can capture and display satellite images from weather satellites. Tools like the LoRa (long-range) from TTGo are capable of creating small networks which can pass text messages (or receive sensor information) using networks that can reach quite far while being energy efficient. These devices use Meshtastic nets that can be had on your cell phone and used independently of cell service, with the download of an app.

Another device that can help during emergencies is the RTL-SDR. Not only is it capable of scanning a wide range of radio frequency channels (from AM/FM to some HAM bands), but it can also be used to collect and interpret data broadcast by aircraft and satellites. RTL-SDR.com has instructions on how to set up a device to collect data from weather satellites independent of the grid. With some basic field meteorology, this is a powerful tool in emergencies, specifically those such as fires and flooding, which may require ongoing information that could make a substantial difference in your planning! Perhaps best of all, the RTL-SDRs are very inexpensive, costing under $30 at the time of this writing.

An understanding of signal theory and knowledge of what signals are used for what devices can streamline the integration of security practices (as well as audit them) in your own home. Devices like the Flipper Zero are capable of exposing vulnerabilities of infrared, sub-Ghz signals, among other interesting features, and can communicate with a broad range of devices, from vehicle key FOBs to RFID gates and NFC (near field communication) bank cards.

Book 4: The Final Steps

WHAT CAN I DO?

During the course of preparation, you may be asking yourself, *What should I do?* But underlying it all is a subtle question that often remains unasked: *What CAN I Do?*

This is a question of pivotal importance. If you're reading this, you're at least aware you're not capable of doing everything yourself. As humans, we have two choices: We continually audit our readiness in terms of supplies, wealth, ability, and skills to provide for ourselves...or, we reach a point where we feel comfortable, and we devote time to things that are more enjoyable or less taxing. But we rarely stop and do a practical and comprehensive audit of what we can do should necessity call upon our most basic abilities. So, with that, let's learn how to audit our abilities to provide the items we need for ourselves.

Framework

There is a longstanding tradition among survivalists and self-styled preppers that gives a curt nod to the Heinlein man (or woman) who is, in short, a jack-of-all-trades and a master of none. This approach is admirable and definitely something that we should strive for, not only for the useful skills it provides, but also for the self-satisfaction that comes from being capable of taking on difficult tasks and prevailing. Being exposed to many different concepts and skills can help build upon others and enhance the ones you are more proficient at.

Even so, the concept is out of date and out of step with ten thousand years of post- agricultural revolution of humankind. The specialization that modern society has afforded us is, however, a byproduct of societies that are not in "need." Because of this, we believe that one of the most important skills is the ability to foster community and establish connections to other skilled people. As you continue on your path of honestly evaluating your skills, improving your capabilities, and making and maintaining contacts with others who are skilled, you'll find multifactorial benefits:

It affords us injuries or illness without removing the only member of a group who is *in the know* on a specific subject.

It grants us the opportunity to develop our skills under the supervision of those more capable than us.

It gives us the chance to solidify our knowledge base by teaching those who wish to learn.

Truly, in every instance, sharing skill development is the epitome of community and the root of commerce.

Meaningful Measurement?

One of the most difficult aspects of self-evaluation is that we often have no meaningful way of measuring our skills or our progress. We may assume or expect that we are making strides and improving, but without a way of measuring, it can be very difficult to parlay one's practical ability into a measure of overall skill. I don't believe that a simple "strongly agree, agree, disagree, or strongly disagree" is the best method for the individual to use to determine skills. It's a great diagnostic tool for others to get a view of you, but as an individual, you can afford yourself much more detail and honesty than these categories provide.

While it's not possible to say what constitutes proficiency in all the areas of knowledge that we think should be pursued, we can set points on a continuum that should allow us a rough gauge of where we are at, starting with the very most basic skill level and working toward mastery. In each of the topics presented, consider your level of proficiency and how you would handle said situation. Make note of your level of confidence, and if you're unsure in any way, ask and discuss with others who know more! Once you've developed an honest, cogent assessment of where you're at, we can begin to share the necessary information to improve.

So, we can identify some skills and weigh our own sense of priority with our level of proficiency with the task. A high-necessity skill with no proficiency is an oversight in one's training and should be fixed, whereas a low necessity skill that you're already proficient in is something that you can teach others as you advance other knowledge bases.

It should be noted that this process is not supposed to be easy —it's supposed to be an honest audit of what you know and what you need to learn. It should be uncomfortable (like any form of change) and should make you feel vulnerable. Find the time, write out the following questions, and then answer them. Use the results to make an actionable plan to enhance your preparedness.

With that in mind, we would like to provide the following as an audit of your individual skills. Please keep in mind it is not all-encompassing, but rather focuses on some select skills that we've seen effectively employed by both disaster management and citizens while weathering various types of emergencies.

ISG SKILLS AUDIT

Welcome to the Integrated Skills Group Skills Audit. Before we go any further, above all else, be honest. This self-assessment is designed for users to honestly assess their level of competence and readiness on a very wide variety of tasks and situations using a multiple-choice format that best describes their familiarity with a topic. Each question will have a rating between 1 and 5, with 1 being Unfamiliar and 5 being Mastery. In general, we'll assume mastery of a task requires that a person has devoted a decade or more to it. Let's break down the rating system and what it will be used for:

Unfamiliar Entirely. You may know this task exists, but you have no idea how to successfully complete it.

Basic Awareness. You know the task requires some special knowledge and experience, and you are aware that you do not possess either.

Limited Experience. You've performed the task and have some limited experience doing it, either with help or supervision, but you wouldn't feel absolutely comfortable performing the task alone.

Substantial Experience. You've performed the task routinely and feel comfortable completing it without supervision—except in unusual cases.

Mastery. You've performed this task routinely for a period of time long enough to establish yourself as a demonstrable subject matter expert, and you can demonstrate competency consistently, on command.

It's important that if you do not meet the criteria for the next highest skill *in any way*, you accept the rating below it. The idea here isn't to score the highest number—it's to ensure you have a template from which to work as you go on to build greater skill. We can't all master every skill, and that's normal.

The reason we're using this rating system is to demonstrate that there is an absolutely staggering array of skills we can develop. This test will be long, and it will take a while to complete, but if you're honest, the results will give you feedback that will show you the tasks you've trained on to competency and those that you could stand to firm up. In the end, the skill categories we use will allow you to look at both the big picture and the individual skills.

We hope that you find this diagnostic tool to be a useful and valuable addition to the ISG culture, and if you have suggestions for improvements (keeping in mind we ourselves haven't mastered all these skills), please feel free to contact us at integratedskillsgroup@gmail.com. As well, if you'd like to take this audit digitally, you can follow the QR code or URL here:

https://www.flexiquiz.com/SC/N/Skill-audit

Which of the following best describes your relationship with the neighbors within the nearest homes to yours?

1. I don't speak to them or know anything relevant about them.
2. I've spoken to them in passing, and I know obvious details (their vehicle, basic facts about their ethnicity, gender, et cetera).
3. I am on cordial terms with at least half my neighbors, and I know them well enough to be comfortable inviting them over infrequently.
4. I know my neighbors well enough to discuss their religious or political beliefs, their occupations, and voluntarily socialize with most (75%) of them.
5. My neighbors are all close, personal friends or family with whom I've spent years cultivating relationships.

Which statement best describes the area nearest your home?

1. There are no open green spaces, dense housing, or parking lots.
2. There are other homes with small (.25 acre or less) lots within a subdivision, or I'm isolated without infrastructure which allows me to travel freely.
3. There are homes with reasonably large lots, green spaces, and access points that are clearly defined.
4. My home is a functioning ranch with livestock and/or gardening spaces, and I have close friends or family who live within yelling distance.

My home is a well-established, functioning ranch with trusted neighbors and a supply of clean water.

Regarding your supply of water, which best describes your situation?

1. My water comes from municipal sources and requires infrastructure for me to access.
2. My water comes primarily from municipal sources, but I have some stored water on hand in water bottles (or similar) that could last a week.
3. My water comes from municipal sources, I have stored water, and I have some form of water catchment system.
4. My water comes from a well for which I'm responsible for the treatment and potability.
5. My water comes from a combination of well and catchment, and I have access to a source of fresh water on my property.

Regarding your community's access to food, which best describes your situation?

1. Food in my community mainly comes from fast-food restaurants or convenience stores.
2. My community has access to grocery stores which are resupplied by shipments on a regular basis.
3. My community has grocery stores and also has farmers' markets that bring food from local farms.
4. My community is an exporter of food, and production of crops and livestock is tended using industrial equipment.
5. The food in my community is grown across a diffuse community that produces livestock, eggs, milk, and fruits and vegetables largely independent of industrial equipment.

With regards to my knowledge of winching and recovery, the following best describes my level of skill and experience:

1. I have never seen nor used a winch for vehicle recovery or to remove an obstruction from a trail.
2. I have been present for an effort to use a winch in recovery or obstruction removal, but I have not used one on my own.
3. I have used a winch for simple tasks, such as removing a vehicle from deep mud or snow or pulling an obstacle off a trail.
4. I have a winch that I use frequently while off-road, and I can solve most problems associated with off-road travel using a combination of a winch, soft shackles, and a snatch block.
5. I use winches frequently to solve complex recoveries requiring knowledge angles and placement of multiple snatch blocks and single and double line pulls.

Where I live, the following statement best describes our average rainfall (this information can be found using National Weather Service databases):
1. I live in a polar region.
2. My climate typically sees < 10" of rainfall per year (arid).
3. My climate sees between 10-20" of rainfall per year (semi-arid).
4. My climate receives between 100-200" of rain per year (tropical).
5. My climate receives 20-40" of rain per year (temperate).

With regards to your ability to clean and purify water, which of the following best describes your situation:
1. I have some pots and pans I could use to boil.
2. I have a water filter that I have little experience with or that could serve as a temporary solution if I didn't have access to clean water.

3. I have a water filter that I've used substantially and could be used to provide water for my family as long as water was available.

4. I have a home-based filtration system that's independent of the grid and that provides substantial purification of high volumes of water.

5. I have a combination of home-based water purification and distilling that could provide adults and infants a fresh, drinkable supply of water for as long as water was available.

Regarding my home's heating/cooling system, the following statement best represents my situation...

1. I use electric heat and fans that are dependent on grid electricity to operate.

2. I have an electric A/C unit or pellet stove that requires supplies of pellets made in a factory and bought from a store to heat my home.

3. I have a combination of the above and another, high efficiency heating/cooling solution such as radiant heating/cooling, but it's still largely based on grid electricity to function.

4. I have high-efficiency grid-tie AC/heating solutions that are augmented or supplemented by renewable energy.

5. My home's heating and A/C are entirely independent of grid support by way of wood heat and alternative energies.

If I were to lose electricity, which best describes my ability to prepare food?

1. I would eat cold food or have to find a "rock or something."

2. I have a limited ability to cook without electricity, such as a Coleman camp stove or Jetboil.

3. I have an ability to cook without electricity and a supply of fuel that could last me four weeks, such as propane or natural gas stoves, pellet stoves, or wood stoves.

4. I have a method of cooking that relies on wood heating or gas that would last me three months or less.

5. My method of cooking utilizes a combination of renewable resources (such as wood) and natural gas that could keep me supplied for 6 months or greater.

Regarding your home security...

1. I rarely lock my doors.

2. I lock my doors and have a Wi-Fi security or camera system.

3. I lock my doors and have reinforced doors and windows, but no security system.

4. I have a combination of security practices that include good habits (doors and windows), a hard-wired security system, and alerts for doors and windows being opened.

5. In addition to point 4 above, I live in a gated neighborhood with on-site security.

You smell smoke...the fire alarm goes off! Which best describes your most likely course of action?

1. I run from the house and call the fire department while cursing the fact I don't have fire insurance.

2. I grab the fire extinguisher that came with the house that I've never checked, and I look for the fire.

3. I grab the fire extinguisher I selected for weight and rating and work toward extinguishing the fire.

Regarding the home you now live in, which statement best describes your ability to produce your own food?

1. I could probably grow some herbs in a hanging basket.
2. I have limited space, but enough for a small garden that could grow some simple vegetables with shallow roots (such as tomatoes and lettuce) and/or herbs.
3. I have a small yard that is set up intelligently which I could use to offset some of my grocery consumption by growing herbs and simple seasonal vegetables.
4. My yard is substantial enough that, if well managed, I could seasonally offset 25% of my food consumption.
5. I live on a property that could offset 80% of my family's food consumption, such as a farm or ranch.

Describe your current situation with stored food. Go to your pantry and select the option that best fits your situation.

1. I have a few days' worth of food and could probably boil a boot or two.
2. There's enough food for my family to eat for a week, but we might have to start getting creative.
3. There's food enough for three weeks, but it's largely staple foods without other necessary macronutrients (such as animal fats and proteins or vitamins found in fresh fruits and vegetables).
4. My family could meet our minimum caloric needs for three months without a major resupply.
5. My family could meet our caloric needs indefinitely based on domestic food production and storage.

Which best describes your ability to hunt and clean game?

1. Ew. No.
2. I've never hunted, but I would be open to learning.

3. I've hunted before and dressed an animal with help before taking it to be processed.
4. I've taken large game periodically throughout my life, dressed it, and could process it with the right tools and space.
5. I've consistently taken game for a decade or more, I can clean and process the animal, and I have adequate ways of keeping it from rotting (salting, smoking, canning, deep freeze).

When it comes to fishing, which best describes your knowledge?

1. I know where to look for fish, for the most part (Hint: in water).
2. I've fished before, but mostly for recreation. I don't kill or clean the fish, and I'll probably end up with a tangled line.
3. I've fished a bit and feel comfortable killing and filleting a fish. I can rig my own fishing pole and tie leaders from store-bought equipment.
4. Fishing is a consistent part of my life, and I am very comfortable cleaning and preparing fish. I can make my own lures and leaders, provided I've got some line.
5. Fishing is something I have done for a decade or more, and I am comfortable with every aspect of fishing from equipment maintenance to preparation or preservation of the fish I catch.

When it comes to trapping animals...

1. The idea is appalling to me.
2. I understand in principle that animals and fish can be trapped, but I'm not really sure how to do it.
3. I've built some rudimentary traps for fish or small game, but I have little experience harvesting meat from them.

4. I've successfully trapped animals for meat before, and with the proper equipment I could either improvise or set and bait a trap.
5. I've trapped animals routinely for years and am well-acquainted with the types of traps, snares, or corrals for game and fish. I could improvise them in a pinch, and I wouldn't need much in the way of purchased equipment.

Regarding your knowledge of foraging...
1. Are you sure that won't make us sick?
2. I've scavenged very common seasonal berries or mushrooms a couple of times while with friends.
3. I know what grows in my area and when, and with some guidance I could probably prepare it to offset some calories.
4. I forage seasonally for wild edibles in my area that I'm well-acquainted with, and I could do so without help.
5. I've been foraging for years and know not only what types of vegetables, roots, berries, and fungi are indigenous to my area, but I can also identify edibles from surrounding regions, as well.

Regarding caring for livestock, which best describes your experience?
1. I've never had an animal that wasn't just a pet.
2. I've been around or assisted with other people who have chickens, rabbits, or other small, coup-kept animals, like game hens.
3. I've had coup-kept, small animals that didn't require slaughter, such as chickens or game hens, or goats for milk.

4. I have a combination of animals that are pen-kept and those which are slaughtered for meat, and as long as I can get feed and grain from the store, I could continue.

5. I have extensive experience starting with programs like 4-H that I've kept up, and I now have a combination of poultry and livestock that produce eggs and meat, and I have either sufficient stores of feed or domestic production that could keep my animals well-fed for six months or more.

If you found yourself outside your home tonight in a rural environment, describe your ability to create shelter, assuming you have no additional supplies apart from those you carry every day.

1. Huddle up against a tree or something and hope for the best.

2. I could build a basic shelter out of natural materials, I think.

3. I've built shelters in the past using only natural materials, but it would be a cold, restless night.

4. I've built shelters and insulated them using natural materials before, and in an environment I'm familiar with, I could do it again.

5. Building shelters is a normal part of the outdoors experience for me, and I'm comfortable in my ability to construct, insulate, and waterproof a shelter in a safe area with the equipment in my sustainment pack.

You're cut off in an unfamiliar city without access to money or a hotel - which statement best describes your ability to find shelter in harsh weather?

1. Find a wall and huddle up, hoping for the best.

2. Find a bridge seat or other out-of-the-elements location and hope for the best.

3. I could make use of improvised material to stay out of the elements and out of spaces commonly used by other transients.
4. I'm confident I could find shelter based on my history of using interpersonal skills or rapport-building to get off of the streets.
5. I've consistently had to find shelter in the urban environment based on past homelessness, and I know well the areas that transients frequent and how to avoid or use them to my advantage, and I'm familiar with shelters and safe places to hole up out of the weather.

Which of the following best describes your ability to start a fire?

1. Give me dry material, lighter fluid, and a lighter and I could probably figure it out.
2. I've started some fires before using a lighter and dry materials in controlled conditions.
3. I start fires as often as not when I go camping, often with just matches and dry material.
4. I've started fires in wet weather using flint and steel, I know how to find dry tinder in wet environments, and I know how to make a respectable tinder ball.
5. I've started fires using primitive methods in various environments for years, and I am confident that I could start a fire without any technology.

Oh no, the water is out and there's sewage backing up...I'd:

1. Desperately call a plumber and hope for the best.
2. Roll up my sleeves and plunge, trying to set aside water to flush after manually filling the tank.

3. I have an alternative method of sanitation, such as an RV, a camp toilet, or other collection tank that would last a short period of time before it needs to be emptied.

4. I've got space enough to safely build a latrine that could be managed without posing a health risk to family or neighbors.

5. I have a composting toilet and/or outhouse that poses no real risk of backing up.

If trash collection stopped tonight, what response best describes your situation?

1. Set aside an area for trash collection and hope normal services return promptly.

2. Collect refuse and burn or bury it if it's not possible to reuse it.

3. Compost or feed food scraps to animals that will turn those scraps into protein and dispose of waste in a designated area that is sustainably managed.

Oh, for pity's sake...The power is out, the water isn't flowing or treated, and on top of all that, a family member in your home has come down with a terrible illness. He/she is vomiting and experiencing diarrhea. Which best describes a solution you're currently capable of implementing?

1. Pitch the soiled clothes over the balcony and keep away from them.

2. Do my best to keep them hydrated and clean while isolating the soiled clothing and waste.

3. Remove the soiled clothing from the home and disinfect them outside while providing additional water while your supplies hold out.

4. Isolate the patient in a clean space and the clothing in containers that isolate the pathogens. Use gloves and clean, treated water to keep the person clean and hydrated.

5. I am a doctor or have a doctor in my immediate family who's capable of treating this patient in a professional capacity.

An emergency has shut down trash service in your area, and vermin and varmints are showing up. How do you keep them away?

1. Try to isolate any waste outside your space or yard.
2. Rely on pets to keep rodents or scavengers away.
3. Improvise traps for bugs or vermin, shoot varmints.

Which of the following best describes your ability to bypass locks without destroying them?

1. Find another way or leave.
2. I can bypass simple locks (such as filing cabinets or cheap locks) using improvised tools.
3. I have a set of lockpicks that I use infrequently, and I have opened a few padlocks. I am aware of false set and counter-rotation, but with difficulty. I can pick low-security locks under pressure.
4. I have used lockpicks frequently or as a part of a job, and I can pick most pin tumbler locks to include medium-security padlocks (American), doorknobs, and deadbolts. I can feel false set and counter-rotation and can select the correct probe or rake based on keyway size and torsion tools based on cylinder recess and keyway access. I can pick medium-security locks under pressure.

5. I have picked locks as a profession for years, and in addition to point 4, I'm capable of picking advanced and high-security locks (Abus, et cetera) with consistency, under stress.

Choose the statement that best defines your ability to navigate using a map and compass.

1. Why would you need a map and compass when there's GPS?
2. I've had some training on navigation in the military or Boy Scouts but haven't read a map in years.
3. I can read a map, identify features on a topographic map, pace count, and understand azimuth, but it'd be best if someone double checked my work.
4. I know my pace count for various conditions. I can navigate day or night, relate terrain on a map to physical features, and have navigated professionally or as a part of my job for years.
5. In addition to knowing my pace count for various conditions, I can navigate effectively during day or night, and I have navigated professionally or as a part of my job for years. I can assess magnetic declination and use various types and systems of maps and coordinate systems, as wells as instruct others efficiently on the topic of orienteering.

When it comes to fixing automobiles, which statement best describes your level of proficiency?

1. I know enough to take it to a mechanic when the dash lights come on.
2. I can change my own fluids and make basic replacements of consumable items, such as headlamps and turn signals.
3. I have installed or replaced components, such as alternators or radiators, that didn't require significant internal repairs.

4. I've performed significant restorations of the mechanical components of a vehicle with some guidance.

5. I've routinely performed advanced repairs on vehicles, which includes dismantling the engine and repairing or replacing them in a variety of vehicles, and I've done so professionally for five years or more.

Which best describes your driving history and habits?

1. I frequently drive in a way that puts me at higher risk for injury or death (no seat belt, driving under influence, texting while driving).

2. I wear my seat belt most of the time, rarely drive after having a drink, and text while driving with regard for the driving conditions.

3. I wear my seat belt every time I get in the vehicle, I don't drive if I've had a drink, and I don't use my phone while driving.

Which of the following best describes your primary vehicle as it sits right now?

1. I have unexplained noises and check engine/warning lights on. It has less than half a tank of fuel in it.

2. I have some small issues that I'm aware of and haven't had a chance to have them looked at, but none of them are serious mechanical issues.

3. My maintenance is up to date, and I have more than a half tank of fuel in my vehicle.

4. My vehicle is well maintained, and it has all the factory-recommended tools and a maintenance schedule inside that is up to date.

5. High-wear items have been replaced preventatively; my vehicle rarely gets below a half tank of fuel, and I have a fire

extinguisher and medical kit accessible. I keep a log detailing repairs or modifications as well as a maintenance schedule and a kit for repairs.

Regarding your level of medical training...

1. I have no formal training, or I completed a course in the past but have not kept up on certification or licensing.
2. I've completed a first aid/CPR course.
3. I've completed an EMT course or equivalent experiences combined with first aid/ CPR/AED course and attended Bleeding Control/TCCC courses which I keep up to date.
4. I am a licensed medical professional working as a nurse or EMT, and/or I served in the military as a medic.
5. I have medical training as a physician, physician's assistant, or nurse practitioner.

Which of the following best represents your ability to perform a deadlift?

1. I can lift 50% or less of my body weight.
2. I can deadlift between 50% and 100% of my body weight.
3. I can deadlift between 125% and 150% of my body weight.
4. I can deadlift between 150% and 175% of my body weight.
5. I can lift 200% of my body weight or more.

Which of the following best describes your ability to perform a weighted squat?

1. I can squat between 25% and 50% of my body weight.
2. I can squat between 50% and 100% of my body weight.
3. I can squat between 100% and 150% of my body weight.
4. I can squat between 150% and 200% of my body weight.
5. I can squat more than 200% of my body weight.

Regarding your ability to perform a weighted bench press, which best defines your ability?

1. I can bench press 50% of my body weight or less.
2. I can bench press between 50% and 75% of my body weight.
3. I can bench press 100% of my body weight.
4. I can bench press 125% to 150% of my body weight.
5. I can bench press more than 150% of my body weight.

Which of the following best describes your ability to do a dead hang pull-up (palms facing away from you, arms fully extended, body raised until chin is above the bar, return to dead hanging position):

1. I cannot perform a pull-up.
2. I can perform between 1 and 6 pull-ups.
3. I can perform between 6 and 12 pull-ups.
4. I can perform between 12 and 18 pull-ups, or more than 6 pull-ups with 20% of my body weight in pounds (or more).
5. I can perform more than 18 pull-ups, or more than 10 pull-ups with 35 pounds (or more) weighted.

Which of the following best describes your ability to run 400 meters?

1. I cannot run 400 meters.
2. I can run 400 meters in more than 1 minute and 30 seconds.
3. I can run 400 meters in between 1 minute 15 seconds and 1 minute 30 seconds.
4. I can run 400 meters in between 1 minute to 1 minute 15 seconds.
5. I can run 400 meters in less than 60 seconds.

Regarding your ability to ruck (move on foot with a backpack), which best describes your level of experience/ conditioning?

1. I've never rucked before.
2. I've backpacked with 20 pounds or less on day hikes on occasion, but it's not something I'm used to doing or do for training/recreation.
3. I consistently hike between 3-5 miles for recreation while carrying a load of 20% of my body weight.
4. I have rucked professionally or extensively for recreation up to distances of 12 miles while under a load of 20% of my body weight or more. These kinds of trips required me to set up camp out of my backpack, and I have done this between 5 and 25 times. I can still perform this on demand.
5. I have rucked extensively for distances over 12 miles under pressure, during which I was responsible for keeping a strict pace, setting up camp and/or food planning, while making objectives. I can still perform this on demand.

Which of the following best describes your experience with violence?

1. I have never experienced violence outside of the media.
2. I've been in a few schoolyard fights or taken martial arts, but I no longer practice.
3. I work in a profession in which physical confrontation happens; I have some training and experience with fighting, but not on my own without backup.
4. I've been a part of asocial/institutional violence such as war or military contracting in which people were killed for political reasons.

5. My life has been significantly marred by social/interpersonal violence in which people were seriously injured or killed for personal reasons.

Regarding cell phone use while driving, which best describes your habits?

1. I watch movies while I'm driving.
2. I infrequently check my phone while driving.
3. I wait until I'm stopped to check messages or make calls.

With regards to my driving history...

1. I frequently get tickets for moving violations.
2. I haven't had a ticket in years, but I've periodically been given citations for moving violations.
3. I haven't had a ticket in 5 years or more.

With regards to violence around vehicles, which best describes your experiences?

1. I frequently become enraged when driving and often engage someone who angers me on the road by doing things like tailgating, following, stopping and/or physically confronting the other driver.
2. I get angry from time to time but don't usually look to escalate the problem.
3. I remain cool when people get crazy on the road.
4. I keep my cool, but I've been in situations on a few occasions where I've had to use defensive tactics or physically fight my way out of a situation based around vehicles.
5. I stay calm in traffic, but as a reoccurring part of my life, I have fought in and around vehicles and utilized both driving tactics

and physical defensive tactics to deal with enraged or criminal drivers.

On the topic of off-road driving, which best describes your level of proficiency?

1. Do dirt or gravel roads count?
2. I've driven off-road on very simple terrain with a clear path that didn't require special skill or equipment beyond ground clearance.
3. I have driven off-road in 4-low through terrain such as mud or sand that required some caution but no special skills, such as going mudding on trails with friends or up to the mountains for a day trip.
4. I've driven off-road in a vehicle specifically suited to off-road travel, and in addition to using locking differentials, I've used recovery equipment (winch, tow straps, et cetera) to recover other vehicles from situations where no other rescue was possible. I've done this for extended periods of time without support from anyone outside my traveling group.
5. I've driven off-road extensively for more than five days on end in situations that were substantially challenging and required special equipment and vehicles, and I've used recovery equipment extensively. I can perform these tasks on demand, without assistance, as well as teach skills such as winching and recovery, off-road driving techniques, line selection/spotting, and field repairs safely and competently. I've participated in a significant off-road event, such as the Dakar Rally or Camel Trophy.

With regards to your experience level fighting with a knife, which best describes you?

1. The idea of fighting with a knife is hard for me to consider.
2. I carry a knife as a tool, but I don't view it as a weapon, outside of an emergency.
3. I carry and train with a knife as a defensive tool during full-contact sparring by using a training knife.
4. I've attended a course in interdisciplinary knife fighting in a weapons-based environment or have military experience in skills such as sentry disposal, and I use training knives to routinely pressure test my skill.
5. I have a combination of training and experience in fighting with knives that led to serious injury or death.

Regarding your ability to fight with a pistol, which best describes your experience level?

1. I have no experience with a pistol.
2. I've attended training or classes for concealed carry and occasionally carry a firearm. I shoot less than six times per year (once per two months) and don't typically do progressive, structured training.
3. My level of training is such that I have taken classes above and beyond basic pistol work, and I maintain my level of proficiency by training at the range using structured drills more than six times per year, though I've never had to draw my firearm in response to a threat to life or limb. I carry my firearm most of the time when I'm able, but not daily.
4. I have a combination of skills and experience that include advanced-level handgun classes that incorporate force-on-force, and I've been involved in situations that required me to draw my firearm in response to a threat to life or limb. I carry my firearm daily.

5. I have been required to draw my firearm frequently in response to lethal threats, and I shoot competitively, attend training three or more times per year, and have taken high-level pistol skill courses that incorporate force-on-force in addition to progressive skill training. I carry my firearm daily.

Regarding my level of experience with rifles, choose the statement that most closely represents your level of skill and experience.

1. I've never fired a rifle.
2. I've fired rifles infrequently as a part of recreational activities without any structured training.
3. I've fired rifles for training, either as a civilian or military member, and can zero a rifle, identify its basic components, and accurately hit targets out to 300 yards with some consistency.
4. I have used rifles extensively as a part of my job or lifestyle, have experience using them out to 300 yards while under stress or fire, and can perform reload, malfunction, and stoppage drills consistently in four seconds or less.
5. As a part of my life, I've carried rifles for long durations under stress or in combat, engaged targets out to 600 yards, can perform reload, malfunction, and stoppage drills in under three seconds, and have done so repeatedly (eight or more instances of deployments six months or longer, or a combination of experience equal to four years).

With regards to your experience using verbal de-escalation or persuasion, which best characterizes your experience?

1. I am not a persuasive talker, or I avoid situations that require me to confront others about uncomfortable topics.

2. I occasionally try to persuade people to see things my way, but I'm not exceptionally comfortable doing it, and I'd prefer someone else take the responsibility.

3. If no one else is available, I will try to talk to people in an attempt to get them to see my point of view. It's worked on occasion.

4. I've consistently used my ability to appeal to people's interests, ego, or emotion to redirect their attention in a way that's benefits me. It might not always work, but typically I can avoid a bad outcome or influence a positive one.

5. My ability to persuade people has consistently provided me a way of escaping trouble or persecution, has significantly reversed my fortunes, or influenced others to assist me against their best interest. I can demonstrate this on demand.

Regarding your knowledge of construction and home repair, choose the answer that best defines your level of experience/knowledge.

1. I have never done construction or home repairs of any sort.

2. I've done light home repairs requiring materials sourced from a store that required no technical expertise (repair a cabinet, et cetera)

3. I've worked to build a structure using framing techniques, specific tools for cutting and mitering angles, and used brackets specifically for structural integrity, but I did so under supervision and wouldn't feel comfortable doing it again.

4. I have worked in a field of construction that required me to consistently perform tasks related to framing with little to no supervision. I could perform most of the common tasks to working in construction and have done so for several years.

5. Construction is my profession and I've worked to construct structures with various types of materials, and I am able to demonstrate my abilities on demand, given the appropriate tools and equipment.

Regarding my knowledge of plumbing...

1. I have no knowledge of plumbing.
2. I've tried to fix minor items around my house, such as leaky sinks or broken toilet linkage, but I'd require some instruction before tackling them again.
3. I've successfully made repairs such as wax seals on toilets or plumbing a sink from an existing fixture installed by a professional.
4. I have worked as a professional to install plumbing as a part of home construction, and I've done so frequently for three years or so.
5. I've worked in plumbing as a professional for more than a decade and am entirely comfortable with new construction plumbing installation, industrial plumbing, and remedial tasks and service such as broken pipes, septic service, et cetera.

When it comes to my knowledge as an electrician...

1. Electricity makes my hair stand on end.
2. I can perform basic tasks such as changing simple fixtures or swapping fuses in appliances, but I have no knowledge of home electrical systems.
3. I've worked around my home enough to know how to turn my breakers off for simple fixes such as installing fixtures and doing basic wiring from a junction box.
4. I've worked as an electrician and have wired homes and buildings from the main. Given the appropriate tools, I can,

with some assistance, troubleshoot electrical problems, detect and repair hazards, and wire a home with electricity.

5. Not only have I worked as an electrician and mastered the tasks in point 4, but I also can use my knowledge to engineer alternative forms of energy to augment or replace existing systems.

My knowledge of tactics can best be described as...

1. Steven Seagal is my spirit animal.

2. I understand some basic ideas, such as cover and concealment, but I have never given it much thought or had to apply tactics in reality.

3. I've had some training in tactics in the profession of arms and can define cover and concealment, traveling/overwatch/ bounding, and some basic principles of communication in tactical situations.

4. I've had enough training and experience to understand MOUT/ CQB, room clearing, and the dangers of these approaches in various environmental weather and lighting conditions. My experience with tactics has been as a part of an overt activity and was reinforced consistently on a timeline of four years or less.

5. In addition to point 4 above, I have experience serving in environments where an imminent risk of being captured or killed upon discovery existed. I have used a combination of skills, interpersonal communication, planning, and asset management to engineer solutions that saved lives. This could be experience in the clandestine services, undercover work, having grown up in street culture, or experience in prison. My experience with this type of situation occurred on a timeline of more than four years.

Regarding my drinking habits...

1. I drink nightly in excess of three drinks per night, and have had problems with the law, my family, friends, and relationships due to my alcohol usage.
2. I drink significant amounts on weekends and occasionally get out of control, leading to fights or problems at home, but nothing serious.
3. I drink when I feel like it, but I don't feel like I have to. This usually means a few drinks a few times a week, but nothing excessive.
4. I drink infrequently and avoid being inebriated in public.
5. I don't drink alcohol, or I drink extremely rarely.

Regarding my smoking habits...

1. I chain-smoke cigarettes or cigars and have for years.
2. I smoke regularly, at a rate of about a pack per day.
3. I smoke socially, but otherwise wouldn't smoke (5-10 times per year).
4. I smoke only on very rare occasions (3-4 times per year).
5. I don't smoke.

Regarding my drug use...

1. I use drugs that impair my mental clarity and performance daily, and I am dependent on them to prevent withdrawal.
2. I use drugs recreationally a few times a week and have had problems with drug use in the past.
3. I use drugs socially and set limits for myself that keep me from having problems with the law or disrupting my ability to function in society.
4. I rarely take drugs to manage excessive pain or stress.

5. I don't take drugs with exception of doctor-prescribed medications for specific circumstances.

Grab your spouse and ask him or her the following question: How would you rate our family life? Which statement most closely matches theirs? If you're not married/ involved with someone, choose the answer that best describes your contentedness.

1. Very poor. There are significant challenges financially, emotionally, and in terms of compatibility. It is an abusive or volatile relationship.
2. Poor. Stresses are caused predominately by circumstances that are beyond your immediate control (how you treat one another). You may love, trust, or respect your spouse, but not all three. There is neither love, trust, nor respect in the relationship.
3. Normal. The stresses and problems you're experiencing as a couple are normal, and apart from normal arguments and problems, you find yourself functioning fine most of the time. You love, trust, and respect your spouse.
4. Good. Your relationship is strong in terms of stability, trust, love, respect, and intimacy. Apart from irregular frustrations, you have no major issues.
5. Excellent. Your ability to communicate and tend to one another is exceptional. Fights are an extreme outlier, and you continually feel love, trust, and respect for your partner who is meeting your needs in all ways.

Regarding your ability to perform Basic CPR, which best describes your level of skill and experience.

1. I'm not trained in CPR.

2. I've been trained in CPR/first aid, but I haven't kept current.

3. I've been involved in an emergency where CPR was administered and have had some training.

4. I've administered CPR and am currently certified through the AHA or the Red Cross.

5. I've administered CPR numerous occasions and am certified through the AHA or the Red Cross.

Regarding your ability to control bleeding, which describes your level of experience?

1. I have no experience or training in controlling bleeding.

2. I've treated very minor, capillary bleeding using common methods, such as direct pressure and bandages.

3. I've infrequently treated basic bleeds, as well as more significant venous bleeding, using pressure, elevation, and dressing/bandages.

4. I've successfully managed complex bleeding problems with multiple injuries, bleeding types, and accompanying tissue damage on several occasions.

5. I have routinely dealt with bleeding caused by trauma which included venous and arterial blood loss requiring immediate intervention to prevent loss of life.

Regarding the things you carry on a daily basis, which answer best describes your practice? NOTE: If you're military or police, consider only when you're off duty.

1. Keys, wallet, idiosyncratic items (sunglasses, clothing, et cetera).

2. Keys, wallet, folding knife.

3. Keys, wallet, folding knife, multi-tool, flashlight, lighter.

4. Keys, wallet, folding knife, multi-tool, flashlight, lights, defensive tool(s).
5. Point 4, plus medical equipment laid out in a way that the items most immediately necessary are accessible to your dominant-side hand.

If you were left in a situation where you had no access to clean drinking water, what best describes your approach? Assume you have whatever equipment you normally have while in remote or primitive environments. If it's not in your backpack or kit right now, default to the lower tier answer.

1. Drink unsafe water.
2. Attempt to treat the unsafe water using a method that can't guarantee purity.
3. Construct an improvised filter or use a temporary solution filter such as a LifeStraw.
4. Use a purpose-built water filter.
5. Use a combination of purpose-built water filter and container that can be used to boil the water.

Given the tools you carry when in the woods, what is your most likely approach to building a shelter if you became stranded?

1. Find a place to huddle for warmth.
2. Collect natural materials that you suspect might insulate your clothing and body from the elements.
3. Collect natural materials that you've used in the past to insulate yourself from the elements. If you can't name three in your current area right now, default to two.
4. Use a combination of natural materials and impromptu materials carried on your person to establish a shelter that is

both waterproof and heat-retaining. If those items aren't in your pack or on your person now, default to point 3.

5. Use a purpose-build shelter that you carry on you any time you're in the woods.

Describe your practical knowledge of weather forecasting while afield...

1. I frequently get caught unprepared and under-equipped and only occasionally watch the news report on the weather.
2. I watch the news weather reports and generally am aware of what they're predicting.
3. I am able to identify the difference between altostratus and cumulus and define their role in frontal passage.
4. I can observe changes in wind field, observe wind direction at various elevations by observing clouds, and assess cloud types in order to make accurate predictions of the weather that's likely to occur.
5. I've used weather forecasts and field weather data to plan and conduct activities reliably and with acceptable accuracy under pressure to prevent damaged property or loss of life.

Regarding your ability to apply situational awareness, which best describes you?

1. I'm usually on my phone in public spaces.
2. I occasionally use my phone in public spaces but try to minimize having my back to large groups of unknown people.
3. I rarely use my phone in public, keep an eye on exits, and generally keep my attention focused on the world around me.
4. I intentionally limit my phone use and can describe key facts about the crime rate in my city, the likely threats faced, and what neighborhoods/areas they're likely to occur in.

5. I understand and apply situational awareness continually and can demonstrate awareness by both observing key facts about people in my surroundings as well as recall them on demand. Additionally, I can be relied upon to identify "marks" of certain behaviors or professions such as modes of dress, carry of concealed weapons, and behavioral traits of people while occupying public spaces.

If you found yourself in an unfamiliar city without a method of communication (no phone, no computer), which of the following best describes your solution?

1. I'm not certain how I would communicate my situation or get in contact with someone without my phone.
2. I've memorized the phone numbers of a few key people in my life and feel confident I could find either a pay phone or borrow someone's phone (if you don't carry cash, return to point 1).
3. In addition to point 2, I have a method of using public infrastructure (active library card, government credentials that would grant you access to public buildings) which I could use to log on and send an email to someone or request the use of a phone.

You wake up to news that the banks have closed and are on an indefinite holiday. Which of the following describes your situation?

1. I have little to no cash to see me through, and I've never bartered for goods.
2. I have some cash on hand, but less than $100.
3. I have between $100 and $1000 accessible.

4. I have a combination of cash and precious metals available with a value of up to $10,000 on hand and accessible without accessing the bank.

5. I have access to more than $10,000 in cash and alternative currencies at your immediate disposal.

Regarding your level of experience with street culture...
Note: This question scores negative experiences more highly. In the context of resilience, those who've faced these problems are intrinsically more able to negotiate these problems, which makes them valuable experiences, even if they're commonly thought of as "bad."

1. I've lived my life in "polite society."

2. I've traveled enough to have seen some of the difficulties faced by the urban poor, but I haven't experienced them.

3. I've lived among impoverished populations, have had family or friends arrested, seen frequent drug use, and have been victimized by those circumstances.

4. Living in severely impoverished cultures has led to drug use, jail time, and social/interpersonal violence that's caused me to learn to be aware of the threats and problems of living in such conditions.

5. I have been intimately impacted by deep poverty resulting in major problems from incarceration, interpersonal violence, drug addiction among immediate family, and having faced the criminal justice system.

NOTE: For this question, do not look up any terms until you've selected an answer.
While in a remote area, you find yourself treating an injury with significant, but non-life-threatening blood loss. After your

efforts to stop the blood loss succeed, the injured person looks diaphoretic and pale with mild cyanosis and altered mental status.

- Place the patient in the lateral recumbent position and assess for trauma.
- Administer an intravenous 0.9% lactated ringers solution at 0mL/kg until the patient's condition improves.
- Encourage the patient to drink water and reposition them in the Fowler's position.
- Quickly look for injuries you may have missed and cover the injured patient to retain some body heat.
- Cover the patient in heat reflecting material, elevate their legs and recheck for injuries and the patient's status frequently.

Regarding your experience in post-disaster environments, which best describes your experience?

1. I have no experience with post-disaster environments.
2. I've observed and studied the effects of disasters on urban centers but have never experienced one firsthand.
3. I've infrequently experienced minor disasters firsthand or have experience in exploring urban environments in which environmental hazards exist.
4. I've experienced a significant disaster firsthand and/or have spent significant time in badly damaged urban environments in which environmental hazards exist (name five hazards you've experienced or default to point 3).
5. I've been a part of major disasters on more than three occasions in which I assisted in a relief capacity by providing goods, security, or transportation to at-risk locals, and/or I have experience in destroyed urban environments in search-and-rescue or with relief work. I'm well-acquainted with the

hazards of the post-disaster environment. (If you can't name eight, default to point 4).

Regarding your ability to scale an 8-foot wall with your EDC and sustainment kit, which best defines your ability?

1. I have not attempted to scale an 8-foot wall under load.
2. I have scaled a wall under my equipment on occasion, but it's been a while since I performed this task.

Scaling walls and barriers is a routine part of my physical fitness training, and I'm confident in my ability to perform this task on demand.

With regards to your ability to reload ammunition, which best describes your level of skill and experience?

1. I do not reload my own ammunition and do not know how.
2. I have tools and dies for reloading, but rarely, if ever, do it.
3. I reload a significant portion of my ammo for training and practical use.

With regards to archery, which best represents your level of skill?

1. I have never used a bow.
2. I've use bows recreationally on occasion but wouldn't be able to consistently hit a target at 25 yards.
3. I have my own bow, shoot regularly (once per month or more), and can consistently hit targets at 25 yards.
4. I use my bow for hunting and/or competition and am confident in my ability to hit targets out to 50 yards with consistency.
5. I have been shooting archery regularly as a hunter or competitive archer for more than five years and have taken

animals/awards consistently for my performance. I coach or instruct others on how to effectively use various types of bows.

The power has been out for a week and your personal devices (flashlights, phones, computers) are starting to run low. Which best describes your ability to recharge them? Assume only what you have immediately on hand.

1. I have no ability to recharge my devices or batteries.
2. I have no way of recharging my batteries, but I do have supplemental sources of power such as spare batteries and power packs that I keep charged.
3. I have a combination of supplemental power sources and renewable energies capable of trickle-charging small devices (such as a folding solar panel or small generator).
4. My home has a grid-tied auxiliary power and/or a generator (with sufficient fuel) that can provide power for 4 weeks or more.
5. My home has the ability to produce energy independent of fossil fuels, on a renewable basis, or has a supply of natural gas, propane, or other.

Regarding your debt, which statement most closely matches your situation?

1. My debt-to-income ratio is 10:1 or higher (example: I make $50k per year, and owe $500,000 or more).
2. My debt-to-income ratio is between 5:1 and 9:1.
3. My debt-to-income ratio falls between 5:1 and 9:1, but of that debt, at least 50% is self-liquidating (property that's rented out, property that has oil reserves, et cetera).
4. My debt-to-income ratio is less than 5:1, and 50% or more of my debt is self-liquidating.

5. I am debt free and have properties or ventures that create passive income.

Regarding rappelling, the following statement best describes my level of experience...

1. I have not rappelled and do not know how to safely set up a rappel.
2. I have rappelled in controlled conditions such as a rappelling tower or climbing gym, but I haven't set up my own rappel.
3. I have set up a rappel and rappelled with the help of a trainer on a few occasions.
4. I have set up and rappelled using my own equipment in various environments without supervision.
5. I have rappelled and set up rappels in various, highly technical environments for a period of time measured in years. I've been involved in rope rescue and instruction.

Regarding my ability to operate a motorboat...

1. I have no experience operating a motorboat.
2. I've been on motorboats under someone else's control or assisted with launching or recovering the vessel but have limited experience.
3. I've used motorboats before under supervision, but have maneuvered them to and from docks, understand throttle control, and how to fuel and launch a boat.
4. I have significant experience with boats to include maneuvering while in the water, launching and recovery, operating on plane, and understand how to operate the controls related to piloting as well as the bilge and drain plugs. I've operated motorboats in a small group for several years.

5. I have the experience in point 4 above and have operated motorboats independently for five years or more.

Regarding your knowledge of radio communications

1. I have no experience with radio communications.
2. I've used handheld radios casually on public channels (FRS, CB, et cetera) on occasion.
3. I have passed the Ham radio technician licensing process and can program and use my Ham radio for basic communications. I could wire a radio into my vehicle in a pinch.
4. I have experience setting up radio communications networks, programming handheld, vehicle, and base stations, and I am technically proficient at the technician level of licensure.
5. I have significant experience setting up and programming radio networks, and instruct on the topic, in addition to being able to demonstrate the skills to arrange and set up radio base stations on demand, and I've done this for a period of 10 years or more and have my general or plus Ham radio license (or OCONUS equivalent).

With regards to your ability to ski, choose the answer that most closely defines your experience.

1. I have never skied before.
2. I've skied a few times recreationally but would not be confident selecting my own equipment or routes.
3. Skiing is a regular pastime for me, and I am comfortable selecting and configuring my equipment and skiing on developed slopes or trails without help.
4. I ski both cross-country and downhill with a high degree of proficiency and am capable of skiing difficult routes up to

black diamond, and/or I'm capable of cross-country skiing in the backcountry and have experience of three years or more.

5. I ski at a competitive level and am considered a subject matter expert.

Regarding your ability to fly small aircraft...

1. I've never flown in a small aircraft.
2. I've been in a small aircraft as a passenger.
3. I've received the minimum 40 hours of flight time in order to be considered a private pilot and fly occasionally to maintain my license or I've held a license but allowed it to lapse.
4. I have experience as a professional pilot, or mountain/backcountry/bush flying, and I have ≤ 2500 hours of flight time.
5. I have extensive experience as a private or professional pilot, and/or backcountry/bush piloting and have 2500+ hours of flight time, and am considered a subject matter expert on flying private aircraft.

Regarding your ability to ride horses and use pack animals...

1. I have no experience with riding horseback.
2. I've ridden horses in controlled environments under supervision, and may have assisted in pack and saddling, but have never done it alone.
3. I have ridden horses on reasonably even ground and understand the basics of packing, saddling, and using tack to move across short distances, with assistance.
4. I can saddle a horse and have used pack animals to frequently on trips that spanned days and am generally considered an accomplished rider.

5. I've planned extensive horseback trips into the back country for five or more days and have done so frequently for more than five years.

The worst has happened, and your partner has passed away... Do you know the value of their possessions?

1. No, I'm uninterested in my significant other's hobbies and pursuits and wouldn't know where to find information on the value of their possessions.
2. I've seen the charges and heard the excuses over the years, but I would need to consult someone more knowledgeable to determine how and where to sell valuables.
3. I'm capable of making informed decisions based on my own research and selling and sales security are things I've given thought to or done infrequently in the past.
4. My significant other has prepared me with honest estimates of the value of their possessions and I feel comfortable that personal contacts could help ensure my appraisals are correct and current.
5. I know my significant other's possessions and their values as well as my own, have appraised, listed, and sold in the past, and/or have personal contacts whom I trust implicitly with the handling of such transactions.

Circumstances have gone completely out of control, and you've lost your home. Which best describes your approach to homelessness?

1. I have no plan for this situation, and I lack the ability to store or liquidate possessions which I may have to leave behind, and/or I have dependents who I couldn't take care of if I were forced to leave my home.

2. I could store some of my possessions and live in my car for a few days before the stink of dirty laundry and fast-food wrappers overwhelmed me. I have dependents who would be significantly impacted by homelessness and have nowhere for them to go.

3. I could live out of my car for a week and have enough liquid cash to be able to do laundry, enough knowledge of rest areas and truck stops that I could find resources for hygiene, and enough fuel to get to a loved one for an unscheduled visit. However, I would not be able to secure most of my valuables for transit.

4. My vehicle is set up in such a way that it could support me and my family for a couple weeks without hygienic problems, and with time to pack, my family could secure some of our valuables for transit.

5. I have the ability to store or liquidate most of my valuables and a vehicle that I could live out of comfortably, providing food, clean water, shelter, sanitation concerns, and storage for my entire family for a period of a month or more, as well as loved ones who've I've discussed this or similar situations with.

Regarding your ability to swim...

1. I do not know how to swim, and am scared or uncomfortable with swimming.

2. I only dog paddle.

3. I've spent significant time swimming recreationally, but have no specialized knowledge or skill beyond basics, such as lifeguard training.

4. I have specialized training in swimming, such as swift water, rescue swimming, or competitive swimming at a junior level. I

am confident in my ability to swim and am able to 500 meters uninterrupted without fins.

5. I am a professional swimmer, who has competed in collegiate or greater level swimming, have completed military dive school, or served as a rescue swimmer on a search and rescue team for more than 4 years, and I could swim a mile or more without fins.

A crucial piece of electronic equipment requires soldering. Which best describes your situation?

1. I would start by asking someone else to do it.
2. I have soldering equipment, but can't tell you if it's for electronics or plumbing, and I'm not sure what the mesh or sponge are for.
3. I can solder larger items that don't require special stabilization or magnification, such as wires or jewelry.
4. I can describe the correct gauge and alloy to use on various boards, and possess the correct equipment to solder fine circuits such as those found on chip boards.
5. In addition to point 4, I've been performing this task professionally or as a pursuit for 5+ years.

A pipe just burst under your sink! You...

6. Panic, because you don't know where the water main shutoff is.
7. Have the appropriate tools and knowledge to turn off the water main so repairs can be made.

Regarding your digital security...

1. I use the same passwords for everything, change them only when prompted, and often forget them.

2. I use complicated passwords that vary between application/ website, and I change them if there are data or privacy breaches.

3. I use a digital password manager that creates encrypted passwords at random and stores them in a password protected database that only I can access.

Regarding your level of community involvement...
For the purposes of this question, include ONLY involvement that creates no victims, and is apolitical in nature.

1. I have no interested in helping my community.

2. I will occasionally volunteer with an effort that directly benefits me if asked, (school fundraisers, fire protection benefits, etc) but don't go out of my way to get involved.

3. I volunteer with community or faith based services as I'm able, once or twice a month.

4. I'm regularly involved with organizations that chiefly benefit others (boy scouts, cub scouts, mission work, faith community outreach, etc), though not more than 2 weeks per year is dedicated to this.

5. A substantial part of my free time is dedicated to community services that are for the explicit benefit of others, such as in point 4 above, but I'm able to contribute more than a month per year to these efforts. Additionally, I serve in leadership positions in these organizations, am considered a subject matter expert, and have been for more than 4 years.

Regarding you ability to speak a non-primary language...

(Non-primary means NOT the main language spoken in your home as a child)

1. "No fumare Espanol."-J.A.
2. I took a couple years of foreign languages in school, but beyond some basic vocabulary, I can't communicate with native speakers of that language.
3. I speak a foreign language at a basic level, but it's not useful in my region, as it's not often spoken, or, I'm able to speak at a basic level, understand when it's written, but lack intricate knowledge of grammar and speaking conventions.
4. I have passible language skills in a language that's regionally relevant to me (such as speaking Spanish in the border region of the US), but I would not be confused for a native speaker of that language, though I'm able to read and write and generally communicate unassisted.
5. I am fluent in a regionally relevant language to such a degree that I could pass for, or am, considered a native speaker, understand and can accommodate regional dialects of that language, and can read and write it fluently.

Regarding those in your home...

1. I have, in my home, at least two people who are entirely dependent on me for full time care, such as an infant or ailing elder.
2. In my home, I am responsible for minors or elders who can accomplish basic tasks, but generally require the presence of another adult for their health and well-being, or, I live with roomates with whom I have personality conflicts or who may bring others whose presence my cause conflicts.
3. I have no dependents in my home, or I live with roommates to whom I have no deep attachments.

4. I have adult or adolescent dependents who help with basic tasks, and who can be trusted to help with basic home tasks, such as cooking, waste disposal, and cleaning.

5. Within my home, I have no children who depend on me for full time care, and all members of my household are trusted members of my family who can relied upon for common tasks, security, and who bring useful skills to the table (logistics, security, communication, engineering, sanitation, medical, etc).

Ending Notes

Costs and Practicality

This list may seem long and costly, and it is. The skill sets presented throughout this book are meant to be the foundation that, if practiced properly, will ensure your basic needs are met. It is incumbent upon you to develop those skills. Turning these words into practical, useful skills will require an investment in time, energy, and patience. It will cost money, pride, and comfort, but as you invest in yourself and build confidence in the things you can accomplish, you'll see the investment return all of what it has taken. The self-development journey is very long and lonely, and at times it will have you questioning your motives, intent, and possible outcomes. It should be harsh, painful, rewarding, and humbling. The training you complete is an investment in your most integral asset: yourself. Budget for it as you would any other expense and continually view it as a way to weather yourself against the unexpected challenges.

Some of the simplest things you can do are:

Take martial arts.

Take good care of yourself physically.

Find two courses per year that you've never taken before; budget for and attend them.

Consider equipment only after you've identified need. Continually reassess yourself based on your observations. The skill audit can be taken online, for free, as many times as you'd like, and the hard copy in this book can be scored and recorded on a separate paper.

Skillset, mindset, and tactics. This is a point I return to over and over again because I want to clearly emphasize—especially after talking about gear—that owning equipment but never training speaks to a misallocation of time, money, and priorities. Many people do not like to train because it compromises their self-image. To be hurt physically by someone who trained harder than you or to be challenged mentally by being forced into an austere situation such as urban escape and evasion or a woodland survival class is not comfortable.

It is also important to recognize that some skills are based on knowledge and experience, and others are more physically intensive, demanding more repetition. At this point, you should have a good understanding of what possible emergencies exist. We have presented situations not to fear them, but to understand them. The clarion call of this particular addition is this: You've been exposed to some fundamental skills, you've been exposed to some of the calculus behind preparation, and we've loosely defined sets of emergencies that could impact us—so it is now time to act. While it is important to assess yourself for strengths, weaknesses, and abilities, it is of far more value to test yourself and to know how to handle emergencies.

With these things in mind, it's critical to set realistic priorities that focus on what is practical, realistic, and uncomfortable. Don't fall into the routine of taking classes over and over again. If you find yourself comfortable with the material, you're not being challenged. Think of how ridiculous it would be to take Writing 101 over and over again. You could turn in the same work, modify it to the teacher's expectations, and correct yourself ad infinitum. But will it improve your ability to write? In this same way, martialism, physical fitness, primitive survival skills, and experience in dealing with adversity must be continually nurtured and pressed beyond what you know.

"The true science of martial arts means practicing them in such a way that they will be useful at any time, and to teach them in such a way that they will be useful in all things." ~ Miyamoto Musashi

Thank you for Reading "Carry the Fire"!
Communications with the author can be made by emailing integratedskillsgroup@gmail.com, or by visiting our website at www.integratedskillsgroup.com

References

[1] US-RSOG, "Six ways in, Twelve ways out." 2007. https://usrsog.org/manu.htm

[2] RICH MORIN, et al. "Behind the Badge." Pew Research, 11 Jan. 2017 www.pewsocialtrends.org

[3] Gary Kleck, Marc Gertz, Armed Resistance to Crime: The Prevalence and Nature of Self-Defense with a
Gun, 86 J. Crim. L. & Criminology 150 (1995-1996)

[4] USGS. The 100-Year Flood, United States Geological Survey, www.usgs.gov/special-topic/water-
science-school/science/100-year-flood?qt-science_center_objects=0#qt-science_center_objects.

[5] Roth, Rachel. "Here there is no why", 2nd edition. 13 September 2013. Createspace independent publishing platform.

[6] P. Tjaden and N. Thoennes, Full Report of the Prevalence, Incidence, and Consequences of Violence
Against Women, Nov-2000. [Online]. Available: https://www.ncjrs.gov/pdffiles1/nij/183781.pdf

[7] https://www.fbi.gov/services/cjis/ucr and https://www.usgs.gov/faq/natural-hazards

[8] https://www.pennmedicine.org/news/news-releases/2014/january/survival-rates-similar-for-gun

www.ingramcontent.com/pod-product-compliance
Lightning Source LLC
Chambersburg PA
CBHW071132130626
46553CB00004B/1345